Dog Ear Café:

How the Mt Theo Program beat the curse of petrol sniffing

Andrew Stojanovski had a turbulent youth; running away and camping became his escape from the city. His parents bribed him to stay at school by sending him on a geography excursion to Central Australia. There he witnessed the material simplicity and self-reliance of the Aboriginal lifestyle. It was a trip that changed his life. When he finished school he hitchhiked back to the desert 'for a gap year' where he lived with Aborigines in the dry Todd River of Alice Springs.

After studying a degree in Anthropology, Stojanovski took a job as School Liaison Officer in Yuendumu, a Warlpiri community 300 kilometres west of Alice. Petrol sniffing was the biggest issue facing the school and the Warlpiri were determined to confront it. Like others in the community, Stojanovski committed his life to the cause.

In 2007, together with tribal elders Johnny Hooker Creek and Peggy Brown, Stojanovski was awarded the Medal of the Order of Australia for work on the Mt Theo Petrol Sniffing Program.

He currently lives in by a river in the forests of south-east Australia with his wife Vesna and daughters Jessie and Deua. 'I'm trying to be a good dad.' He dreams of one day returning to the desert.

Warning

This book contains images, names and stories of deceased persons which may be distressing or taboo for members of Aboriginal communities.

DOG EAR CAFE

Andrew Stojanovski

HYBRID
PUBLISHERS

Published by Hybrid Publishers

Melbourne Victoria Australia

First published 2010

National Library of Australia Cataloguing-in-Publication data:
Author: Stojanovski, Andrew.
Title: Dog Ear Café : how the Mt Theo program beat the curse of petrol sniffing / Andrew Stojanovski

ISBN: 9781921665066 (pbk.)

Subjects: Aboriginal Australians – Health and hygiene.
Petrol sniffing.
Inhalant abuse.
Substance abuse – Australia.

Dewey Number: 613.8

Cover design: © Gittus Graphics

Painting on front cover © Liddy Napanangka Walker
Warlukurlangu Artists Aboriginal Corporation
Photo on back cover © Frances Mocnik
Printed in Singapore by KHL Printing Co Pte Ltd

Author royalties from the sale of *Dog Ear Café* will go to the Mt Theo Program.

Foreword

This is a personal memoir with a difference. The author, Andrew Stojanovski, was in a unique position to write this book because he was a protagonist in – and largely the sustainer of – the Mt Theo petrol sniffing program of which he writes. He tells the story of what has become a well-known 'outstation'-based program, which succeeded in curbing the practice of petrol sniffing among young Aboriginal people at the Central Australian community of Yuendumu. There are some profound insights here that demonstrate how a frontline worker can actually make a difference to petrol sniffing – which has to be one of Australia's most intractable and challenging drug issues.

The Mt Theo program is quite a triumph, but the program met with many trials and tribulations along the way. His description of these tribulations is full of humour and is disarmingly honest (qualities that clearly must have helped him to thrive and survive as a bush youth worker). But the book is also a narrative telling of the author's personal journey, how he found his way to Yuendumu in the first place, and his internal (at times almost spiritual) struggles to fulfil responsibilities to both his Aboriginal friends and kin as well as to his partner and later his family.

The author manages to thread another theme through this account. As someone who studied anthropology and who also had first-hand experience with government bureaucracies, Stojanovski is in a position to provide interesting interpretations of the social worlds of Yuendumu and of the departmental staffers who either impede or assist the program. He does this in a remarkably unpretentious way by using real incidents or conversations to explicate complex traditions of kinship and avoidance, and of joking and flirting relationships. He writes of his role as having 'diplomatic immunity' from kinship obligations, and illustrates how important such neutrality can be. These concepts and examples of the social norms and expectations of daily life are at the very core of an anthropological world view, but instead of weighing the reader down with academic theory, he brings this 'anthropology' to life. It becomes real.

There is also solid policy advice in these pages for those who care to read between the lines. Personal relationships are paramount, both on the ground, and between the grassroots and the bureaucracy. Valuable programs can be threatened by petty officials. Stojanovski describes many incidents, developments and improvised solutions to problems that seem to run counter to accepted ideological or bureaucratic wisdom. For example, he questions the widespread assumption that petrol sniffers are 'addicted', when he knows from experience that kids who sniff in one place will refrain from doing so at another place where sniffing is not the 'done thing'.

He shows how offering and sharing tobacco is a way of building rapport and managing crises. His accounts of how he dealt calmly with threatening behaviour from time to time are masterful pieces of advice on defusing aggression and avoiding violence.

I found this a compelling read. As the author has stated, by writing it he is fulfilling a cultural responsibility to pass on his knowledge, and there will be many who want to learn from the experiences documented here. Many ordinary Australians, as well as those more directly involved with Indigenous policy or service provision, have heard about Mt Theo, despite its isolation and size. I believe the book will find an audience among both groups, as well as it being of great interest to those involved in youth work, juvenile justice and drug and alcohol prevention. Stojanovski's account will also make an excellent primer for new frontline workers and for young anthropologists entering the field.

Maggie Brady PhD
ARC QEII Fellow
Centre for Aboriginal Economic Policy Research, ANU
March 2010

To my beautiful and much loved daughters
Jessie and Deua

Contents

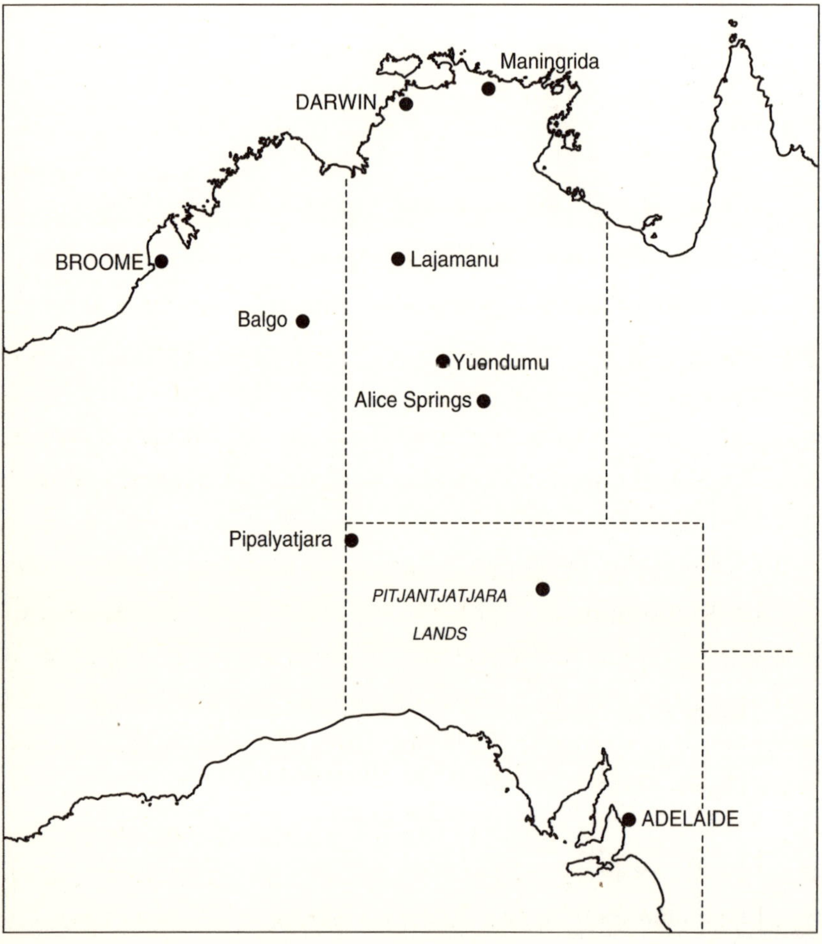
Maningrida
DARWIN
BROOME
Lajamanu
Balgo
Yuendumu
Alice Springs
Pipalyatjara
PITJANTJATJARA
LANDS
ADELAIDE

Preface

The whole of the Yuendumu community pulled together to make the Mt Theo Program work. If I were to write a list of all the people who helped, there would be more than one thousand names. Some people may have only helped out once or twice. But sometimes that one occasion was critical, like the time when one young fella tackled a sniffer who was trying to stab me with a screwdriver outside the Council building, putting his own life at risk and in the process saving mine. On that occasion my body was weak from hepatitis and I could not defend myself or run away.

So many Yapa (Aboriginal people) and so many Kardiya (whitefellas) helped us. It might be Sam at the Mining Store letting me buy rations after hours, when she was already exhausted after a long day's work, or Freddy Williams helping us track sniffers at Willowra. To list every event and every person in this book would make it so big that it would be too hard to read and then no one would learn our story.

There is so much love in this Mt Theo Program, and it connects us all. If you read these words and you get a feeling, then you know who you are and that I am talking to you now. Even my 'adopted' Warlpiri mother, Judith Napangardi, was surprised to find that her name was not in the book. She was my mother and had fed me and raised me in the Warlpiri way; she had done more than one hundred Mt Theo trips with me.

In the process of creating this book many stories, both

humorous and sad, have been edited out, simply due to the constraints of space and readability. So if you don't see your name in this book, don't be sad – it does not mean that we don't remember you, or that your help was not valued. What makes the Mt Theo Program so powerful is that we all helped, we all helped do something that was bigger than just ourselves as individuals: we helped save young people's lives. So be proud, look at this book and remember that you were part of this too, you helped make this great thing possible, this story of hope.

Andrew 'Yakajirri' Stojanovski

Author's notes

Petrol sniffing is a substance use pattern that permeates marginalised indigenous communities throughout the world. Petrol is a hallucinogen that causes the neurological pathways in the brain to short-circuit, producing a high. Sniffers feel euphoric, aggressive, paranoid and powerful.

Petrol is sniffed by young people on American Indian reservations, in remote Australian Aboriginal communities, in the ghettos of Malaysia and in the Inuit communities of the Arctic.

It wreaks havoc. Sniffing-related violence and fires can kill instantly. In the long term, petrol sniffing can cause brain damage that leads to permanent disability and death. It is often described as an unsolvable problem. In places throughout Australia it has been quietly eroding generations of indigenous youth for the past 40 years.

A note about names

In some stories personal names and details have been changed to protect privacy. Likewise the details and names of some communities have been changed.

I'm going to kill you

I am having a crazy and upset weekend. It is a pretty hard time for me. In fact just for today I feel that I have 'popped a gasket'.

I have been working with petrol sniffers. Three weeks ago one of them, Farris, went off his brain and tried to kill me. We were sitting in the Council room together. Farris was next to me. He brandished his fist and said, 'I'm going to kill you.' He then started to hit me and grab at me. The councillors pulled him off me and the meeting was adjourned. I rang my wife Vesna to warn her of what was coming.

Farris and the other sniffers then went around to my house and pelted my car with rocks and smashed a nulla nulla against the mesh windows of my house. Vesna and our Warlpiri neighbour, Tanya, were hiding inside the house. Vesna hid under the kitchen table, terrified, while Farris and the sniffers wrought their vengeance.

I was waiting outside the Council office talking with the elders when Farris came at me again, armed with a boomerang, a nulla nulla and a star picket. First he threw the boomerang at me. Someone moved in to restrain him. I ran into the building seeking refuge. Farris must have wrested free because he came after me swinging a nulla nulla. I ran down the corridor, hoping to escape through the door at the end. The door was locked. I had no escape. Farris charged at me. My vision was filled with this youth with bulging, bloodshot eyes and anger fuming out of him. With his nulla nulla swinging he aimed at my skull. I had no way out and no weapon to block the blows of that fire-hardened mulga.

1: Sniffing Business

The first thing you notice is the fumes: it's overwhelming. In the darkness I can make out a dozen figures, mostly teenagers, some huddled beneath blankets, every head bent over, shoulders hunched, a soft drink can held close to the face. The lids of the cans have been cut off to make sniffing easier. Every can holds petrol.

'Hey Andrew, give us a smoke,' yells a voice. I take it as an invitation to approach the group.

The building is a derelict two-room shed called a 'donkey house'. There are five other donkey houses in this row, and another row behind them. This one has got holes smashed in its besser brick walls, no glass in any window or door on any hinge. Half the roof is missing.

In Yuendumu it's sniffing central.

I had been following a group of kids after disco. I was meant to give them a ride home in the school 'night patrol' bus, but the kids walked away, preferring to go to the sniffers after-party.

Running the disco and driving the bus for the elders on night patrol were jobs I volunteered for. As school employees we had all been asked do something. Other teachers like Morgan and Cowen put on football and basketball to try and distract the kids from sniffing. At night, School Council elders armed with boomerangs would patrol the streets and order kids to go home and not sniff.

The 'donkey houses' had been built as part of the assimilation era of the 1950s and '60s. Officially called 'transitional houses', they looked like a cross between a humpy and a real house. They were designed to encourage hunter-gatherers to make the transition to urban living.

In traditional Warlpiri culture when a person dies their humpy is burnt and their camp is abandoned. And that's exactly what happened. After forty years of 'assimilation' followed by 'self-determination' policies, there were rows of abandoned burnt-out transitional houses in Yuendumu. These houses became the sniffing ghettos.

Petrol sniffing provided a secluded social scene for young people. The sniffer houses were the outback equivalent to the punk and hippy squats of cities: those derelict warehouses where spontaneous 'raves' are held. There was a similar vibe.

Music blared from the ghetto blaster, people used drugs (petrol) and partied, mattresses were thrown on the floor. My friend Solomon was there. He always welcomed me. A tall, muscular bloke, he was really popular with the girls. A piece of graffiti on the wall read: 'Solomon – you black Elvis'. If you were a 'cool' teenager in Yuendumu, it was the place to be. This was where the action was. This was where you could pick up chicks.

Solomon, Farris, Brando and Rudy were like kings of the place. There were about six young men who lived there and would sniff constantly. At night, there would be easily 30 or more people at the parties, sniffing petrol from old soft drink cans, partying hard. Not everyone sniffed every moment of every day. Most young people tended to be 'recreational' as opposed to chronic sniffers. I kept a list of everyone I met who was sniffing. There were over 60 names, more than half the teenage population of Yuendumu.

As well as being 'cool fun' there was peer-group pressure to sniff. Sometimes the sniffer kings would set up during the day in the roof of an abandoned house next to the school. Then they would walk around outside the classrooms trying to encourage the teenage students to come and sniff with them. In the mornings as I drove the school bus on its rounds I would come across groups of kids as young as six hanging out at the sniffing ghetto. They weren't sniffing; they were just hanging out.

I had arrived in Yuendumu four months earlier, a refugee from urban Australia. Living in the desert on an Aboriginal community had been a long-term dream of mine. I'd studied a degree in Anthropology and was jealous of my lecturers who went on field trips to the desert. I wanted to be there, too. But when I arrived in Yuendumu, this community of 800 people, 300 kilometres out of Alice, it felt like I'd arrived in another world. I knew nothing.

Yuendumu itself looked like the scene of a cultural collision. Like two cars having a head-on, white culture and Aboriginal culture. Scattered remnants of both cultures were left at the scene. Broken boomerangs and mangy half-breed dogs fighting over kangaroo carcases next to smashed-up houses and the rusted wreckage of broken-down cars. My professor at uni, Nic Peterson, had said that Yuendumu looked 'like a bomb had hit it'.

There was rubbish everywhere. It seemed as though people still practised the hunter-gatherer values of throwing away what was not needed. Pre-contact, such a practice might have been fine … what is a broken boomerang other than a stick? But introduce the waste of industrial consumer culture and you get packaging, cans, plastic bottles, disposable nappies, all blown about by the wind and scrounged through by the hundreds of roaming dogs that live in the community.

People lived in houses and humpies, with some houses containing as many as thirty residents. Toilets overflowed and blocked up with such overuse. There was still something endearing here: despite having houses, people mostly cooked on campfires, and often slept under the stars or on the veranda. Houses seemed to be more like storage places, rather than living places. Humpies were even more intriguing – small camps were set out in a traditional way yet made use of the remnants of industrial culture: corrugated iron water tanks cut down the centre to form mini Nissen huts; old car bonnets combined with sheets of roofing iron and eucalypt branches to form weatherproof shelters. They symbolised a sense of self-reliance and resourcefulness that urban Australians seem to have lost. The kids played around and the adults sat and talked or went out hunting and collecting bush tucker.

East Camp, Yuendumu (photo by Frances Mocnik)

Apart from the smell of smoke and dust that filled your nostrils, and the ever-bright blue sky, the sounds were different; even the human sounds, wailing from sorry camps, yelping and barking of too many dogs, and the language. For the first time in my life I was surrounded by a town full of people who spoke another language, an Australian language that I didn't understand.

To the north and west of the community was open country, spinifex and mulga plains that stretched on to distant mountain ranges; places you could look at and feel total solitude. I got culture shock pretty badly. I felt so naked. I had no skills in Warlpiri culture. I couldn't even walk around the community without making mistakes: stumbling into a sorry camp, or going on an afternoon bushwalk and entering the forbidden zone of the business camp (where secret sacred ceremonies took place). Once when out collecting firewood I even stumbled upon an old grave. I apologised for that one, but I was warned by old Jangala, the mentor the school had assigned to me, not to roam the country without permission.

Compared to my life down south, I knew nothing. I didn't know where the waterholes were or where the sacred and taboo places were. I didn't know how to survive in the desert.

I tried to make friends but, while Yapa (Aboriginal people) were friendly, I felt a lack of real connection. There was a gulf between us. My life felt lost.

One thing I did know how to do was run a holiday program. In my pre-Yuendumu life I had worked as an urban youth worker running holiday programs to support myself through university. At least that was something I could offer. Everyone said that kids sniffed more during the holidays because they were bored.

My relationship with the king sniffers and their mates was weird. On the one hand, I was an authority figure because I ran the disco and I worked with the elders on night patrol, driving the bus while the old people would track down sniffers and order them home. On the other hand, I was the same generation as Solomon. We were both in our twenties and we were friends.

I tried to balance the negative relationship I had with the sniffers at night by being friendly during the day. One morning, I took a stack of pancakes and billy tea over to the sniffer house to share breakfast with them. Most sniffers are clear headed in the mornings, although, that morning, fourteen-year-old Brando Brown had been sniffing all night. When I woke him he was lying face down on a mattress with a can of petrol wedged under his nose.

White people don't have feelings

One hot afternoon I drove the bus around after school and picked up groups of kids to take them swimming. This was part of the 'give them something else to do other than sniffing' strategy. We drove out to Big Dam: it is only about a ten-minute walk away from Yuendumu but the idea of driving the bus was to get a fun group vibe going, so the young people would want to join in. We drove around the community with the bus's stereo blasting, and filled it up with young people and kids. As we drove around, obviously having a good time, kids would call out to us, 'Where are you mob going?'

'We're going riding,' the group would reply. 'We're going out swimming to Big Dam.'

Inevitably the bus would stop and more kids would pile in, adding to the congestion, laughter and fun.

We had been swimming at Big Dam for about ten minutes, when fourteen-year-old Trent, a sniffer, approached me.

'Take me back to Yuendumu,' he demanded.

'Trent, we'll all go back when everyone's finished swimming,' I replied.

I wouldn't leave the group of kids swimming unsupervised as I was responsible for them.

'No, don't worry for that mob, take me back now.'

'No Trent, I can't, I have to stay here until the whole group comes back.'

'Take me back now, or I'll smash this fucking bus!' yelled Trent, picking up a large rock.

'No Trent, I can't. I've got to be here while the kids are swimming, just in case one of them drowns. If I go back now the whole group has to come back.'

'I want to go to fucking Yuendumu now!' Trent moved towards

me with the rock in his hand making out that he was going to smash me, not the bus.

Shania and some of the other girls saw the argument and came over to find out what it was about. I explained to them that I could not take Trent back and leave the rest of the kids swimming unsupervised. Trent was so insistent about wanting to go back that the girls called the other kids out of the dam, telling them we were going back to Yuendumu.

Trent, Carson, Shania, Chelsea, Rina and Polly Anne were all young people who sniffed. They were all aged about fourteen and they were my friends. They were the kids I made a special effort to reach out to. They were the ones I hung out with at night when they were sniffing and they were the ones I invited home for lunch and videos, as an alternative to sniffing during the day. I knew that if I dropped them back in Yuendumu that afternoon they would go to the sniffer houses and sniff petrol, so I invited them home for afternoon tea and to watch TV.

I was very upset. Trent was my friend and yet he had treated me like crap: I felt used. As we sat around the table drinking tea, Shania and the other girls noticed that I looked like I was about to cry. They asked me why I was so sad and I explained to them that I was upset at the way Trent had treated me. Trent was sitting outside on the veranda having a smoke. The girls went outside and chastised him: 'You've really upset Andrew. He's nearly crying, wiyarrpa (poor thing).'

Trent appeared shocked that he was being chastised for yelling at a whitefella. His reply was crystal clear, questioning that he had done anything wrong: 'Kardiya don't have feelings,' he replied.

He expressed this in a way that indicated that he really believed that statement and it made me stop and think. Compared to Warlpiri, whitefellas often appear emotionless. In our professional facade of dealing with Yapa community members we try to appear rational and unemotional. We keep a stiff upper lip. We attempt to manage resources rationally and often refuse requests for personal favours or loans (humbug); in doing so, we act as though we have no feeling or compassion for the other person. It was possible that Trent treated me differently to Yapa because he genuinely believed that as a whitefella, I had 'no feelings'.

Firebrand

One morning after the sniffers broken into the Mining Company Store, a big community meeting was held on the basketball courts. The social security office was closed and everyone was told to go to the meeting before the cheques were handed out. Lots of different Yapa talked at the meeting.

People had tried everything. Enormous energy had gone into stopping sniffing, with Yapa and Kardiya working together: putting on activities like discos, basketball, football, swimming to entertain the kids and doing night patrol. It seemed to be working as we only had seven chronic sniffers left.

The parents of these chronic sniffers often seemed frustrated and defeated. Many times when I would report to parents that their child was sniffing and they would say to me, 'I don't know what to do about that kid.' Occasionally the parents followed my report with swift action like sending their kid away to another community, or gave the kid a flogging with a boomerang.

At this meeting, Jakamarra, an old man, said the sniffers should be given a flogging. Sniffers had been flogged at a previous community meeting. Family members had hit them with boomerangs and told them to stop sniffing in front of everyone. More than half the kids who were flogged sniffed again that very afternoon.

Jakamarra did his bit though. The sniffer houses were near his camp. He often hunted the sniffers away with spears. Although he was an old man and his muscles were weakened with age, the sniffers were frightened of him. He had power. He could 'sing' people; even the adults were intimidated by that.

Everyone who wanted to take action against sniffing had a sense of urgency: we had to do something right away. People reminded each other that Yuendumu had got rid of petrol sniffing once before. In the 1980s, a substance abuse program, HALT (Healthy Aboriginal Life Team), started in Yuendumu and went on to work in other desert communities. They felt they could do it again.

Lloyd Jungarrayi Spencer was a firebrand of a man: articulate, full of energy, he spoke at a million miles an hour when he had an idea. He coached the football team and it seemed as if he was coaching me. He was frustrated at the lack of any action coming out of that meeting.

The next morning he called out to me, 'Come on, *bunji* [brother-in-law]. My aunty's got an outstation for petrol sniffers at Hermannsburg. You and me are going to take those sniffers there. My aunty will fix them.'

We borrowed the school Toyota ute. Back then it was still legal to carry passengers in the back of utes in the Northern Territory, so lots of vehicles in Yuendumu were utes where you could throw in people, swags, dogs and firewood.

We drove around to the sniffer house where Lloyd yelled at the sniffers.

'All right, all you sniffers, get on that Toyota. I really mean business, you gotta get on that Toyota.'

Fifteen sniffers sullenly walked out of the sniffing ghetto and climbed aboard. Lloyd ordered me to sit in the back to guard them. Maybe it was Lloyd's power as a football coach that gave him such authority over those sniffers. Maybe they were used to following his orders on the football field. Maybe he had some special ceremonial standing, something from *Jukurrpa* (Dreaming). I have never seen anyone exercise such command over sniffers before or since. It was Lloyd's moment.

Once we had the sniffers in the ute, we drove around the community to ask permission from the sniffers' families to take them away to the aunty's outstation. The families of the girl sniffers didn't want their daughters taken away and publicly beat them instead. The boys' families gave permission.

After stopping at the Mining Store to buy pies and cool drinks, we drove south on the sand-dune road to Papunya. It's a beautiful road that skirts around a big wedge-shaped mountain which is full of hidden sacred sites, and then proceeds through a forest of desert oaks, before coming to the sand dunes which give it a real desert feel. I sat in the back of the ute with the other young men, munched on pies, drank Coke and listened to music from a ghetto blaster.

After four hours of bumping along desert roads, the ute ride had lost its romantic appeal. We all hid under blankets in the back to keep the windblown sand off our faces and wished it was over.

Lloyd's aunty didn't welcome us in the way he said she would. Her outstation ran a proper rehabilitation program. Clients had to have a psychological assessment before being admitted. There were procedures to go through. You could not just turn up unannounced with a truckload of sniffers.

Brando suggested we leave him and the others with his uncle at Papunya. Lloyd told me that the boys would not sniff in Papunya. I did not know that Papunya had more sniffing problems than Yuendumu. So we drove back to Papunya, another two-hour drive. There, Brando's uncle said he would look after the young blokes and stop them from sniffing.

The next morning in Yuendumu, Long River was angry. 'You and that Lloyd been take my two sons to Papunya. You never ask me. You been do wrong thing. You gotta ask me first.'

He was right, there were only women and uncles present when we had talked with his family.

'You gotta go back Papunya and bring my sons back. Today, not tomorrow, today!' he demanded.

I asked him for a senior man from the family to come with me on the trip. Long River would not come himself, as he was confined to a wheelchair. No other men volunteered. Patience Napaljarri, Long River's wife, and his daughter Brooke agreed to come.

The families of the other sniffers told me not to bring their sons back to Yuendumu. 'No way,' they said. 'We don't want them back. They got to learn. They got to stop sniffing.'

In Papunya we found all the Yuendumu young fellows sniffing petrol. Patience yelled at her sons, Austin and Rudy. She growled at them for sniffing and ordered them to climb on the Toyota. The exact opposite happened: they refused to get in, while all of the other Yuendumu young fellows climbed on the back of the ute and refused to get off.

I drove to Papunya Police Station and asked for help. I phoned Yuendumu and was told very clearly to leave the other sniffers in Papunya and only bring Austin and Rudy home.

The police said there was little they could do, as petrol sniffing was not an offence. However, they accompanied us and added authority to Patience's words when she ordered the other sniffers off the Toyota and told her own sons to climb on.

Victorious, we began to drive off towards Yuendumu. But before we had driven 100 metres, Rudy jumped out of the ute and ran back to join his mates. We turned the ute around. Thrown stones ricocheted off the windscreen: we were under attack. While the ute cab offered some protection for me, the passengers in the back had none. Brooke and Patience ordered me to drive out of town before their youngest son Austin jumped out too.

One week later, Papunya community rang us and asked us to

collect all of our sniffers, who they said had been sniffing constantly.

A fortnight after I'd collected the sniffers from Papunya, my wife Vesna and I were packing our bags to head home to Canberra for Christmas. Lloyd dropped round to say goodbye.

'Don't worry about them sniffers,' he told me.' We gonna put them all in bush camp (the ceremony-corroboree place). Really serious business. They're not going to sniff there.'

I went away hoping this would be true.

Despair

'It's got bloody worse!' Ned said as he walked up to me. Ned Jampijimpa Hargraves was a Warlpiri bloke, ten years older than me, who worked at the clinic. I had just arrived back after the holidays to begin my second year in Yuendumu. Some welcome, I thought. All the ex-sniffers had started sniffing again over summer, which meant there were over 60 teenagers getting into it.

In the first week of February two community meetings were held in quick succession. At both meetings, people got up and blamed each other's families for not looking after their sniffers properly. Commitments were made, but very little real action took place.

A lot of the community seemed defeated. I looked at Lloyd: the fire had gone out of him.

'Sorry, *bunji* (brother-in-law),' he said. 'We've tried our best, with football, with [ceremony] business. There's nothing you can do, *bunji*. You can't stop them.'

One respected elder who had instigated the School Council night patrol told me: 'You can't stop them, it's the mother and father's job. But that mother and father in town drinking grog. They're not our family. Don't worry for those sniffers.'

I felt sad. I had read at university about this, about people giving up, about petrol sniffing taking hold and about communities of despair. In the Pitjantjatjara lands people said that 'sniffers were holding communities to ransom'. I remember reading in Ralph Folds' book *Whitefella School* about how students and teachers had been barricaded in the classroom while petrol sniffers pelted the windows and doors with stones. He said that the average life expectancy of an Education Department house in the Pitjantjatjara Lands was two years, due to vandalism by sniffers [Folds 1987, pp. 56–73]. In Arnhem Land, whitefellas were leaving bowls of petrol on the bonnets of their cars to prevent the cars from being damaged by sniffers stealing petrol. South Australian community workers had told me horrific stories of sniffers burning to death when the petrol accidentally caught on fire.

And now it had taken hold in Yuendumu. Ned was right: it had got worse. The leading students in the senior girls' class at school who had never sniffed before, now regularly collapsed on the classroom floor, reeking of petrol, after being up all night sniffing.

2: Yuendumu's Last Stand

Peter Toyne, the School Principal, called a meeting. It was only a small meeting as most people had now given up.

'I've been talking with Peggy,' he told me the day before the meeting. 'Her sons are sniffing and she wants to take them out to their outstation at Mt Theo. She said that if we support her, she will take other kids.'

I remembered Mt Theo and the old man Japangardi with the funny nose and his Series One Land Rover. I didn't know about much about his wife Peggy; to me she was a large middle-aged

Old Japangardi, founder of Mt Theo Program (photo by Frances Mocnik)

Aboriginal woman who looked like she ate a lot. I didn't know she had a tradition of adopting stray kids into her family, that she broke the mould and would take care of anyone, whether they were family or not. She had earned the nickname 'Mother Brown', but I didn't know any of that yet.

Dogs settled next to their owners as we sat cross-legged in the sand, women on one side of the group, men on the other. Peter got up.

'We've beaten petrol sniffing in the past but this time it's different. We've tried to stop it through the families and by running strong recreation and education programs. We've tried to take the young blokes away to other communities. This time it hasn't worked. So Yuendumu is facing a future where its young people will be crazy, sick and poisoned.

'They won't be able to learn Yapa ways or have a Kardiya education. Many will be dead before they are thirty. It's not a problem someone else will fix for us. Government people will not come and sit down here and help, day after day.

'It's not going to be fixed either if Yapa look to whitefellas to fix it, or if whitefellas say it's just family business for the Yapa. We will only fix it if the community decides it is our problem and that we must all work together to fix it now,' he declared.

The meeting resolved to support two outstations, Mt Theo for the male sniffers and Mala Bore for the female sniffers, and to make the youth recreation program stronger.

The idea of the using the outstations was pretty simple. We needed to take the peer group pressure off sniffing. We decided to simply remove the 'ringleaders' or chronic sniffers from Yuendumu and send them out bush. With the chronic sniffers out of the way, we hoped that by running youth activities every night, after school and on the weekends, we would be able to divert the other young people and the 'recreational sniffers' from sniffing.

In the long term it was hoped that we could get the Education

Department to fund a teacher to run a school at the outstations. But right then we had to make do with what we had, which was willing elders. The plan was that the chronic sniffers would simply live at the outstations for a month at a time, giving their bodies and brains time away from petrol. They would live a Yapa kind of bush life, spending their days hunting and learning bushcraft from the elders. No magic processes or programs were proposed, but everyone believed that sacred country was powerful, and that being out bush was healing.

Everybody at the meeting knew the sniffers would be resistant to being sent out bush; there was no illusion that they would come voluntarily. But we had to stop sniffing, otherwise young people were going to die.

Robin Japanangka, the School Council Chairperson, offered $5000 of school money to buy food for the program. Robin was a staunch leader in the face of sniffing. Single-handedly he had continued with the night patrols long after the other elders had given up.

The clinic promised to supply first-aid kits and each organisation said they would lend their vehicles to help with transporting people and supplies. My job was to organise the supplies and shop on behalf of anyone living at the outstations.

This small gathering of people adopted the name 'Petrol Sniffing Working Party' and we committed ourselves to work every day until the problem was solved.

Maiden voyage to Mt Theo

Just over a week after that meeting, Roy Jupurrula, the police aide, and some of the elders drove around the community with the police Toyota and the cage truck and ordered sniffers to get in. The cage truck is like one of those human cargo trucks shown on TV news carrying refugees around Africa. It is the same dimensions as a rigid chassis furniture removal truck. But instead of having van walls of sheet metal, it has walls of steel mesh. It has a solid steel floor and two metal benches that run the length of the cargo space along the side walls. As we pulled up to each camp in Yuendumu, the rear mesh doors flung open, swags were thrown in followed by dogs, billycans, drums of flour, axes and boomerangs, and their owners clambered on top.

Sniffers were cajoled by their family and by the shame of being singled out. Reluctantly they climbed aboard. When there was no more room in the cage truck, private cars were commandeered and they joined the convoy: a motley collection of battered Holdens and Fords snaked its way around the community.

Meanwhile, I was at Peggy's camp, where swags and boomerangs etc. were crammed into the last two rows of seats on the school bus. Compared with the cage truck, the bus was the limousine of the operation: it had doors that opened and shut, all its windows were intact and there were padded seats. When the bus was half full of Peggy's possessions, we began to load her extended family's gear onto the roof – including steel tucker boxes and old Japangardi's two rifles for hunting kangaroo, one of which was held together with red-and-black electrical tape. Peggy's two old aunties, Topsy and Judy, climbed into the bus along with her mother, various in-laws and grandchildren. Peggy's eldest son, Scotty, loaded up his Kingswood ute as well. It had no bonnet and was missing a rear window.

Everyone was excited: 'We're moving back to Mt Theo!' It had just begun to drizzle and the afternoon sky turned grey and dark, but nothing could dampen this family's enthusiasm.

We joined the convoy as it did its final circuit of Yuendumu. There was always one more blanket to borrow from a relative in another household, so gathering the gear for one person required stopping at up to three different houses. Each stop was fraught with peril as the sniffers became increasingly restless at being caged up, so every stop presented an opportunity and temptation to escape. Finally all the blankets were gathered and the convoy headed out west along the Tanami Road towards Mt Theo.

As I drove over the cattle grid that marked the boundary with Mt Doreen Station, Peggy began to tell me *Jukurrpa* information (Dreamtime stories) about the hills and ranges and creeks that we crossed.

'That one over there belong to Jungarrayi and Japaljarri,' she said.

'How do I say that in Warlpiri?' I ask, and then tried to remember my lesson sheets.

'*Yinya ngampu pirli, Jungarrayi – Japaljarri kurlangu. Mai?*'

'*Yuwai Jangala, ngurrju*, you speaking Warlpiri now,' Peggy enthused, pleased with my rough attempt to speak her tongue.

The rain hit the windscreen hard and the clay road turned to mush. At times I struggled to maintain control of the overloaded bus. Old Japangardi sang and another old traditional man, Shorty

Peggy Brown, founder of Mt Theo Program

Jangala, joined him in an ancient traditional song. I don't think I'll ever know enough Warlpiri to be able to grab the old language words out of traditional songs, so instead of translation I had to guess the meaning: 'We're going home'.

After Japangardi and Jangala's singing had gone quiet, Peggy addressed the group of passengers: 'This is how the Nyirripi community started. We going to make Mt Theo a big place, we gotta get shop and school and all.' Then turning to me, 'Yakajirri, you gotta get us a school teacher.'

Japangardi interrupted her to instruct me: 'Don't break any tree at Mt Theo and you gotta make sure no sniffer breaks any tree. That place has got really strong *Jukurrpa*, it's a dangerous place. If anyone breaks them trees there, they might get really sick.'

Carson, Japangardi's fourteen-year-old petrol sniffer son joined in, pleased to have the upper hand on this whitefella who thought he could boss the sniffers: 'You got to be really careful Yakajirri, those trees have really got *Jukurrpa*, but don't worry for those other sniffers, I'll tell them.'

The bus rattled on through the night. I strained my eyes wide open to spot bullocks before I hit them. The rain had stopped and old Japangardi was singing again.

After two hours we turned off the Tanami Road and followed the snaking Mt Theo track, a track that made the corrugated Tanami Road seem like a highway. After an hour of dodging pot holes and wheel ruts I could just make out an orange glow in the distance.

'First!' one of Peggy's grandchildren called out, claiming that he was the first to see the fire light.

'*Ngurrju ngurra*,' Japangardi said quietly as he rubbed my arm and looked at me with his old hunter's eyes, now grey with age. 'Good home.'

'*Yuwai Jangala*, good home Mt Theo,' said Peggy reiterating her husband's sentiment.

Soon afterwards we arrived to welcoming campfires already lit by people from the first vehicles in the convoy. Torch beams bumped around in the darkness as personal possessions were sought, found and fought over, the old ladies haggling with each other: 'That's my blanket! Leave it! You got the 'nother red one, this one mine! My one got the tiger picture on it.'

Old people's swags were rolled out while teenager sniffers chattered excitedly around the campfire, like school kids on the first night of an excursion.

Mt Theo

[Letter to Mr Bell, a close friend I've known since my last year at school. During the time I lived in Yuendumu he worked as an engineer in Kalgoorlie, Roxby Downs, China, and Canberra. We wrote personal letters and descriptions of our lives to each other.]

Dear Mr Bell

I am writing to you from an outstation, 150 km north west of Yuendumu. Its name is Mt Theo and the country looks grand – spinifex plain, lots of ghost gums growing and the round shapes of the hills of 'Puturlu' (Mt Theo).

My bed is rolled out on the red sand and I am sleeping 'warlu wana' (beside the fire). I am surrounded by people who also sleep next to fires, or under 'yujukus' (humpies) or rough bush-made shade shelters. As I began this letter the eastern sky was strong orange – but now the sun is fully up. Flies are buzzing round my face as I write. I have not heard a word of English spoken this morning, only Warlpiri (the local Australian language). One old man, Shorty Jangala, has been singing a traditional song this morning. Windbreaks here are made out of rough and gathered bush materials. There are buildings here, but no one camps in them, by preference because it's nicer to be outside bush way, than in a building. And also for spiritual

Solomon and Andrew Stojanovski (Yakajirri) camping at Mt Theo when the program first started – March 1994

reasons, an old person died sometime back and he camped by those buildings. His spirit is left quiet and the buildings are left alone. We've got a phone box too, with a solar panel on top. There is no other electricity out here.

People have lived here for a long time, this is their country, but I am here for a special reason. The people here have agreed to look after kids recovering from petrol sniffing. I bring petrol sniffers out from the settlement [Yuendumu] and give them to the people here who care for them while they de-tox. The kids learn lots about country and culture here; they go hunting, get bush tucker and the old blokes make lots of boomerang. They chase goannas down holes and dig them out and cook them. I drive out once a week to deliver food and supplies.

The Toyota is bogged at the moment, so I'll have to dig it out soon. I have a bush name: 'Yakajirri'. My whitefella name 'Andrew' has become 'kumunjayi' (a taboo word because someone with the same name has died recently and it would disturb their spirit to mutter their name – so my name is no longer spoken).I asked to be given a new name. One old man, Darby Jampijimpa – who can remember time before whitefellas – gave me that name. Yakajirri was his father's bush name from a long time ago. His father had the same skin name as me, 'Jangala'. Our Dreamings are fire and water/rain. And our Dreaming is also Yakajirri – a little bush fruit.

The world of kinship

As well as my name Yakajirri, I also had a 'skin' name: Jangala, which determined my place in the Warlpiri universe. The Warlpiri kinship system is made up of eight 'skin' groups, with male and female skin names for each group:

Female	Male
Nangala	Jangala
Nampijimpa	Jampijimpa
Nakamarra	Jakamarra
Napurrula	Jupurrula
Napanangka	Japanangka
Napangardi	Japangardi
Nungarrayi	Jungarrayi
Napaljarri	Japaljarri

Males and females in the same skin group are considered to be brothers and sisters. There are skin groups for each member of the family: fathers and mothers, uncles and auntys, grandparents, and mothers- and fathers-in-law. Everyone in Yuendumu has a skin name, and that is the title that most people are referred to by. Even whitefellas are given skin names, so that all the Aboriginal people can orientate the new whitefella in the kinship system.

The Warlpiri kinship system is very complex if you drill down into it, but at a basic level, the kinship/skin name system determines relationships: who a person can ask for food and other things from; who they must avoid (for example, sons-in-law avoid mothers-in-law); who they must treat with respect; who they can tease (e.g. cousins, possible girlfriends/boyfriends); and who they cannot say 'no' to (e.g. people who they are obliged to give things to). For traditional hunter-gatherer life, the skin system was a highly functional social system that resolved potential conflicts in a small-scale society (by avoiding in-laws), and ensured that people were fed and looked after in the harsh desert environment.

Women's Centre Toyota

Each Friday after school, I collected rations from the store and ran them out to Mt Theo. I would usually use the school bus or if I was allowed the school Toyota (though that was fraught with politics), but often these vehicles weren't available so I would have to 'humbug' a vehicle.

The word 'humbug' was first used by whitefellas, then by Warlpiri, to describe what anthropologists call 'demand sharing'. Demand sharing is a social phenomenon in hunter-gatherer cultures where individuals are able to request certain kinsmen share food and other resources with them. These requests cannot be denied and are part of a reciprocal obligation system. Sociologically speaking, this system ensured the survival of the group in hunter-gatherer societies. In contemporary Yuendumu life young people are socialised into a culture of sharing, giving and demanding, that has its roots in the ancient hunting culture of the desert. Humbugging was a part of life at Yuendumu and I had to get hold of a vehicle.

Sometimes Frank at the Mining Company would lend me his Toyota and sometimes I would borrow the Council truck. But that afternoon it had to be the Women's Centre Toyota – the one they used for night patrol. Getting this Toyota was a bit of a process. I would first ask Joan, the whitefella who was the Women's

Centre coordinator. Joan would then refer my request to a group of elderly women who made up the vehicle committee. Like all organisations, the Women's Centre had a 'we don't lend out the Toyota' rule, which was inevitably broken by the very committee members who wrote it. To get a loan of the Toyota, you had to be good at humbugging.

There was a funeral and sorry business going on in Lajamanu, 600 kilometres to the north, and many people had gone to that, riding in the cage truck. One old Jampijimpa man from Mt Liebig had got a ride with the sorry business mob to Yuendumu, but had somehow missed the ride to Lajamanu. He was angry: 'That mob been leave me behind.' He had been stranded outside the Women's Centre with his swag, billycan and boomerangs. He was eyeing the Women's Centre Toyota and insisted he get a ride to Lajamanu. But the Toyota had been promised to me by then to do the Mt Theo run. Joan explained the situation to me. I could still borrow the Toyota, but I had to take the old man with me. After I delivered the rations to Mt Theo, I had to catch up with the cage truck and deliver the old man. He was angry and he was going to hit all the women with his boomerangs if they didn't give him a ride to Lajamanu in the Toyota.

Andrew Cowen, one of the school teachers, and I picked up the Toyota and the old man, and drove to Mt Theo. When we arrived, the young men rushed up to us and presented us with some stone axes they had found while exploring around the outstation. The axes were made of white quartz. My friend Solomon said they must have been left by his grandfather who used to live around Mt Theo in the days before whitefellas.

It quickly grew dark. After the rations were unloaded, Cowen and I sat down for supper with Johnny Hooker Creek and his wife Molly. Johnny and Molly were a sweet old couple who would sit quietly by their fire next to their humpy (which was made out of bush timber and corrugated iron). Johnny and I often shared a pipe of tobacco and drank tea together. Their camp was separated a little from the main camp at Mt Theo, which was a chaotic mix of teenage petrol sniffers, dogs and Peggy's family.

Some nights when I camped at Mt Theo, Johnny would tell me stories of his life. As a kid he grew up with his parents hunting and gathering. He was about six years old when the Coniston Massacre took place. The massacre party approached Aboriginal camps and shot people indiscriminately. This was in 1928. Johnny said his parents hid at Mt Theo; they climbed the mountain which was normally out of bounds and sang the mountain so that it grew taller. That's how they hid away.

As a young man after contact with whitefellas, Johnny got a job working with cattle and learnt how to ride a horse. He travelled widely doing stock work and droving. He was on several cattle drives from the Northern Territory across to Queensland. Once the Aboriginal stockmen's horses were sold or taken by the boss drover, Johnny had to walk back home on foot.

He worked up in the Top End where he had a reputation of being able to ride any 'wild horse'. He says the station-owner's daughter was watching him in the stockyard one day and was clearly impressed. He has a twinkle in his eye as he recalled that yarn.

'Maybe I got white son or daughter,' he said grinning. He never told me if the station-owner chased him away.

In the Second World War, Johnny helped build roads and drive supply trucks for the war effort in 'front line' Australia.

He was sent from Yuendumu to Hooker Creek to build the new Warlpiri settlement of Lajamanu. He was sent away because he had the reputation of being a hard worker, but maybe also because he was a bit of a 'lover boy'. He got his name 'Hooker Creek' from that time.

Solomon's mother, Lucky Nampijimpa Langdon, also lived at Mt Theo. She camped away from the main camp near Johnny and

Molly. She was widowed, but had previously lived with her husband where the main camp was. Because her husband had passed away, the main camp was now a 'no room' zone for her. Under Warlpiri law, when a person passes away, their family must move immediately from their campsite and avoid that place for a long time, to allow the loved one's spirit to settle. The public phone box was situated within the main camp, and therefore was a place where Lucky had 'no room'. I learnt this one afternoon when Lucky's son, Jimmy (who was my next door neighbour in Yuendumu), had asked me to tell Lucky to phone him from Mt Theo. When I passed this message on to Lucky she complained that she could not call Jimmy, as she had 'no room' near the phone box.

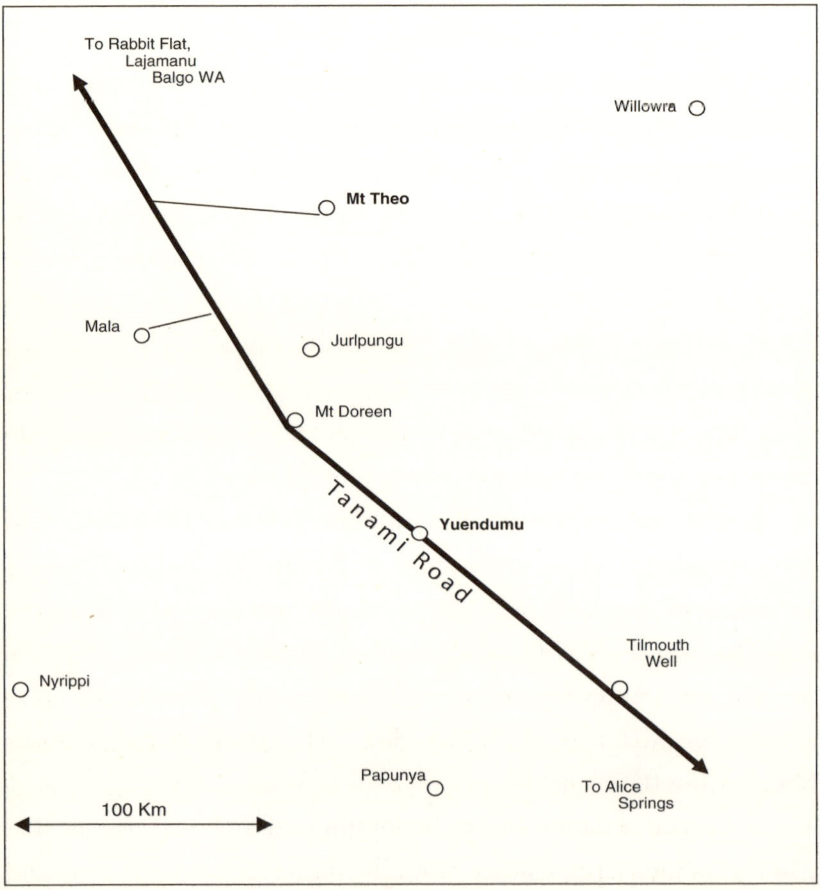

After supper Cowen, the old man Jampijimpa and I got organised to head off. Solomon and Carson (both sniffers) asked if they could come with us for the trip. They promised not to run away. As we left Mt Theo, the other young men, who we left behind, had settled into their swags and were singing love songs to the night.

> *Pina yantarniji* (Please come back)
> *Pina yantarniji* (Please come home)
> *Wangka pina karnangku nyuntuku* (I am calling you back to me)*

We had a cage truck to catch. Joan at the Women's Centre said the cage truck and the sorry business mob were going to camp halfway to Lajamanu. Lajamanu is 600 kilometres from Yuendumu, so I reckoned halfway was 300 kilometres. We followed the Tanami Road west, past the Granites Goldmine, which was lit up like a Christmas tree in the desert night, past Rabbit Flat roadhouse and past the Tanami Goldmine. We then turned north up the Supplejack road. At midnight we found the cage truck, after a 450 kilometre drive and less than 200 kilometres out of Lajamanu.

Small campfires surrounded by families of swags were spread in a broad circle on either side of the road. Snoring bodies slept peacefully under the night sky. Some voices welcomed us to the camp as we unrolled our swags and crashed out.

In the morning my adoptive Warlpiri grandmother, Agie Napurrula, who was travelling with the sorry mob, cooked damper for me and Cowen. Carson and Solomon humbugged breakfast in a similar manner from their distant relations.

We were keen to visit Rabbit Flat (Australia's most remote roadhouse) on our return journey but we had no money. I asked Napurrula if I could humbug her and borrowed $40. This is

* Song written by Lajamanu Teenage Band

Camping on the Lajamanu Road

something that some whitefellas often misunderstand: humbugging works both ways. Whitefellas tend to assume that humbug is a one-way street, of Yapa begging off Kardiya. But Kardiya can also engage in the humbug system. Lindsay Japangardi Williams, the football coach, once described the humbug system to me as 'teamwork'.

The sharing of resources and doing of favours helps ratify relationships. Giving compassionately to another person is a practical expression of your relationship with them. It is an expression of the duty, care and love you have for that other person. Humbugging invites the other person to enter into a sharing relationship with you. Even though humbug will centre around an immediate need (such as 'I want $40 to spend at Rabbit Flat'), it also carries with it an implicit obligation of reciprocity. If you give to someone, they have a duty to give to you too.

At Rabbit Flat we enjoyed spending the $40 that Napurrula had given me before we returned Solomon and Carson to Mt Theo and then home to Yuendumu.

School Toyota politics

Karen Gates did not like me.

Karen was the teacher at Wiylingi Ngurrju Outstation School. Yuendumu School didn't actually have a school Toyota. The Toyota supplied by the Education Department belonged to Wirlinyi Ngurrju School. Its official purpose was to provide transport for the school teacher from Yuendumu, where she lived, to Wirlinyi Ngurrju Outstation, 40 kilometres away, where she taught school.

It's not good to have a bad relationship with anyone. But it's particularly not good when that person controls a Toyota.

I met Karen almost as soon as I moved to Yuendumu. She was in her first year out from teachers college, having abandoned her earlier plans of becoming a nun. Her skin name was Nungarrayi and I was a Jangala. By Warlpiri skin name custom we were an ideal match – we were 'first choice' for each other and we got on well.

We were both new idealistic whitefellas, completely out of our depth in a Warlpiri world. We enjoyed sharing Henry Lawson poems, discussing our reading of Fred Hollows' autobiography and going for starlit walks in the desert night, singing 'sixties folk songs to each other. Because we were 'right skin' it was almost obligatory by Warlpiri custom for us to flirt. Even the act of referring to each other by our skin names was fraught with layers of meaning. The School Principal kept asking me, 'Are Karen and you an item yet?'

Karen and I were never to be: I had already promised myself to Vesna. Like a half-finished soft drink abandoned in the desert sun, the sweet feelings Karen had for me went stale and sour. She left Yuendumu for six months and when she returned to work for Wirlinyi Ngurrju School she no longer liked me. The problem was, Mt Theo needed that Wirlinyi Ngurrju School Toyota.

At the meeting that kicked off the Mt Theo Petrol Sniffing Program, many organisations promised to lend vehicles to support the program. The School Principal and School Council were happy for the Wirlinyi Ngurrju Toyota to be used at weekends and after school to run rations to Mt Theo. But the Wirlinyi Ngurrju School mob was not happy. I don't know how much this was due to Yapa interfamily politics and how much it was due to the 'never was romance' between Karen and me.

What really shocked me though was the comment one old man made at the time. I had asked him for the Toyota. A traditional owner for Wirlinyi Ngurrju, this old man had been a leader in the initial effort to combat petrol sniffing. He was a man of huge ceremonial prestige in the community. He told me: 'There's nothing you can do, we've tried our best, you can't stop those kids from sniffing. They're not our family. Let them die.'

I walked away feeling very sad. Had things really got that bad that people didn't care anymore? He was one of the very people who had inspired me to get involved with petrol sniffing in the first place.

Had I really screwed things up by playing with that boy-girl energy? I love the playfulness of flirting. If I hadn't flirted with Karen would I be hearing those words?

I didn't know. But I knew in a way there was truth in that old man's words. Kids would die and they would die from sniffing. But Peggy still cared and so did Robin and Ned. We could not just let them die. We had to try.

Busy bee

Some whitefellas criticised me for working too hard: I ran around like a blue-arsed fly. I was school liaison officer by day, ran discos and youth activities at night and took rations to Mt Theo and Mala Bore outstations during the weekends.

My day often started at seven a.m. when I would meet Gary the store manager at the shop. I worked seven to eight-thirty packing and organising boxes of shopping according to the individual orders the old people gave me at the outstations. So many tins of meat, so much cordial, three tins of milk powder, Vicks, camp pie, fresh meat, soup mix, flour, cooking oil and laundry powder.

At eight-thirty I went to school to do my day job, which could be interrupted at any time by call-outs by community members to attend to petrol sniffing business. At three-thirty when school finished, I opened the swimming pool for the kids or I took them on an excursion somewhere on the school bus.

After dinner, at about eight p.m., I would put on a disco or basketball or video night. I usually did that with one of the teachers or the Yapa sport and recreation officer.

One of my best whitefella friends said to me: 'I used to do that, put on discos for the kids and everything. It doesn't work, they are still going to keep sniffing – that's why I stopped trying.'

This comment made me feel sad, as I really respected his opinion. I talked to Peter Toyne about it and he told me firmly: 'There is no place for cynics in this community. If whitefellas are going to be cynical here then they are not helping and should leave.'

One of the white school teachers asked me why I was doing so much.

'I feel so honoured to live here,' I said. 'It's such a privilege to live here, to be welcomed here, that I want to put something back into the community to say thank you.'

Photos at the shop

Warlpiri kids are hopeless thieves. Some of the petrol sniffers had broken into the community store. Once inside they had a party, pigging out on chocolate, Coke and cigarettes. They put the music on loud and danced. One of the kids found a Polaroid camera and they took party photos of one another: there was one of Jungarrayi dancing, with a can of petrol under his nose and a freshly stolen Walkman on his head. The party ended just before sunrise when the kids snuck out to go home to sleep, the Polaroid photos left behind, littered like autumn leaves on the shop floor. For many years later, the police in Yuendumu had the photos pinned to a notice board in the police station, under the label: 'Known petrol sniffers'.

One Sunday afternoon Vesna and I arrived back from Alice Springs and unloaded our shopping. Vesna then visited her friend Lucy, while I opened the school pool for the kids. When I got home, Vesna told me we had been burgled. 'The salami and chocolates are gone, and the phone stinks of petrol,' she said.

'Sounds like Austin [one of my teenage petrol sniffing friends],' I suggested.

Later, when I returned after starting the Sunday night movie screening at the school, Vesna told me, 'It must have been Austin who broke in.'

'How do you know?' I asked.

'Well, your mum rang a little while ago. She said she had called earlier in the afternoon and someone answered the phone. She asked where Andrew was, and the thief told her he was at the school. "Where's Vesna?" she then asked.

'"She's up the road."

'"Who are you?"

'"I'm Austin," he said.'

Austin was my most frequent and most honest thief. Once I noticed that $40 was missing from my bedroom drawer shortly after Austin had visited. The next day, while I was cleaning the school swimming pool, he came up to me and asked if he could have lunch with me.

'No, Austin, I don't want to give you lunch until you say sorry and pay me back for the money you stole yesterday.'

'Sorry, Yakajirri,' he said, more as an appeasement than as an admission of guilt.

'Now Austin,' I asked, 'I'm not sure how much money you took – was it two twenties and a five, being $45 you have to pay me? Or was it just two twenties, being $40?'

'Oh, it was only $40,' he said defensively.

Maningrida trip

Not long after the sniffers had broken into the community store and left behind Polaroid photos of themselves on the floor, TJ, the local mechanic, came up to me.

'Have you heard about what's happened in Maningrida?' he asked. 'They used to have a big sniffing problem up there so they replaced all the petrol in the community with Avgas, aviation fuel. You can run a car on it, but you can't get high sniffing it.'

Maningrida is located 500 kilometres east of Darwin and 300 kilometres north-east of Jabiru. It is on the North Central Arnhem Land coast of the Arafura Sea, on the estuary of the Liverpool River.

TJ was a self-educated man, but an educated man nonetheless. He had grown up in Hermannsburg and then had raised his own two boys in Yuendumu. He was one of those whitefellas who was 'here to stay' and even talked about asking the Warlpiri for permission to build a private house on their land so he could retire in the hills near Yuendumu. TJ was also the local Justice of the Peace, and was an integral part of the Yuendumu church. Alongside the Warlpiri church leaders, he would take his turn to preside over services and funerals, and he would sometimes host theological discussion groups with the Warlpiri men at his home.

His wife Helen was amazing. She was quiet and generous, always ready to offer a visitor a cup of Russian Caravan tea (a luxury in Yuendumu) and a biscuit. She had natural blonde hair and a perfect figure. Sometimes when she was walking down the road with her hair out, I wouldn't recognise her from behind and would catch myself thinking: who's that new good-looking blonde girl in the community? Helen and TJ were old enough to be my parents and in many ways were the surrogate mum and dad for a generation of us young whitefellas in Yuendumu.

TJ and Helen were good friends with Mick Jessop, the Council Clerk, and Mick Jessop, in turn, was friends with the store manager, Gary Ulrich. Together this group of whitefellas proposed sending an investigative party from Yuendumu to Maningrida to find out about Avgas.

The store had lost $10 000 in theft and damages due to the 'photo incident' break-in by petrol sniffers. Gary said it made much more sense to spend $10 000 to try to stop sniffing in Yuendumu. Between them, Mick and Gary organised a chartered plane, meals and accommodation for a party of seven of us to go to Maningrida. Ned Jampijimpa Hargraves (health worker), Peggy Nampijimpa Brown (Mt Theo Program), Dee Nampijimpa Granites (Women's Centre Night Patrol), Roy Jupurrula Curtis (police aide), Harry Jakamarra Nelson (Council member), Eddie Jampijimpa Robertson (Council President) and myself made up the party.

The story we heard from Maningrida was that Avgas was an important part of a multi-pronged strategy the community had used to stop sniffing. While Avgas could not be sniffed, they emphasised the importance of engaging the 'at-risk sniffers' in other activities, be they traditional cultural activities, sport, arts or employment.

During our second night in Maningrida we gathered in Harry's room when he told us the following story: 'You know, I think that Australia is the best country in the world,' he began. I had heard whitefellas have this sort of conversation before. Usually the conversation would begin with a statement such as Harry's but before long some politically correct wowser would say: 'Australia may be the best country in the world, but not if you're Aboriginal.'

Yet, here I was in Maningrida, everyone in the group except me was Aboriginal and they were having this very same conversation.

Harry continued: 'When we were coming back from Europe with my father, we stopped at Singapore airport and the soldiers there put the old man's bags through that x-ray machine and found his tins of tobacco and ashes.'

For thousands of years, the Warlpiri have chewed *pituri*, native tobacco mixed with ashes from the Coolibah tree*. Nowadays the Warlpiri who chew tobacco, albeit shop-bought tobacco, continue the tradition of mixing it with ashes. Most people will travel with two tobacco tins, one filled with tobacco and one filled with ashes.

Harry and his father, who was a world renowned artist, were returning from an exhibition of Aboriginal art in Europe. Harry described how the guards at Singapore airport regarded the ashes as suspicious-looking white powder.

'They thought the ashes were drugs or something,' Harry said. 'They were poking old Jupurrula with machine guns and he was shrugging his shoulders, not knowing what all the fuss was about.'

Harry had to convince these suspicious and excited soldiers that this ancient Warlpiri man, who had grown up as a nomadic hunter, was not a drug trafficker. Of course, old Jupurrula's English was not very good and neither was the English of the airport guards.

'And I don't speak Chinese,' said Harry.

The guards in Singapore had probably never heard of tobacco-chewing Central Australian tribesmen, let alone the fact that they blend their tobacco with ashes. How were they to know

---

* Ash for chewing tobacco is called *puna* (one of the names – others are *yurlpulypa* and *yarrminyi*). It is gathered from trees like: Marntarla (Thick Black Gidgee), Karrawari (Coolibah), Ngapiri (River Red Gum,) Yajarnpi (Ironwood), also sometimes yilykinji (Beefwood).

that the ashes did not have some narcotic mixed in with them? It was an ordeal. But after much confusion and delay, they made it back to the plane and home to Australia.

'And that's why I reckon Australia is the best country in the world,' Harry concluded. 'No good them overseas countries, those people have too many machine guns and they are too cheeky.'

I smiled. It reminded me of the story that Dee Nampijimpa Granites told when she returned from an art exhibition in New York. She was feted as a renowned artist, flown in on an airplane and put up at a flash hotel.

'What did you think of New York?' the Australian television journalist asked her, while she sat outside her humpy in Yuendumu.

'Oh, terrible place – all those homeless ones, *wiyarrpa*.'

It was not the Statue of Liberty or the grand buildings of New York that struck Dee, but the poverty.

Compassion is probably the defining characteristic of Warlpiri people. The most commonly used word in Warlpiri rock songs is not 'baby' as it is in mainstream music, but '*wiyarrpa*', the closest English translation being 'oh poor thing'.

I noticed this compassion when I took some teenage petrol sniffers to Adelaide. As we walked through Rundle Mall, they saw a homeless man going through a rubbish bin.

'Oh, *wiyarrpa*,' Lenin, one of the sniffers, lamented. He went over and gave the homeless guy $5.

'We should buy him a feed,' one of the others suggested.

One time I received a brochure from Freedom from Hunger about their annual door-knock appeal. My friend, Solomon, who was visiting me and saw the brochure on my kitchen table asked what it was about. As I explained it to him he said: 'Yeah, really starving buggers over there, that African mob, they don't get sit down money or nothing. You should do that door-knock here in Yuendumu, Yakajirri. Everyone will chuck in for them, poor buggers.'

Yuendumu had its Freedom from Hunger door-knock appeal that year. It had one of the highest donation rates in the country. Compared with the national average of $3 per door-knock donation, Yuendumu had an average donation of $10 – all of this from Australia's 'third world' backyard.

So when Dee Nampijimpa Granites returned from New York the thing she wanted to talk about was the poverty: 'Poor buggers, *wiyarrpa*,' she said. 'Really cold place, *pirriya nganyi* (very cold), snow and all. And all those poor buggers, humbugging for dollar on the street. No swag, no blanket, nothing. Really poor buggers. They got humpy made out of cardboard, no sheet of iron. Really leaky one that cardboard when it rains.'

She contrasted that to conditions in Australia, where no matter how poor you are in Yuendumu, you can always get some corrugated iron to make a decent humpy.

'Good place, Yuendumu,' she concluded. 'Plenty bush tucker, plenty family to humbug for tucker and dollar.'

Avgas was introduced to Yuendumu two months after we first started sending sniffers to Mt Theo and Mala Bore outstations. The effect was almost immediate. The sniffers came back from the outstations to find that there was hardly any petrol in Yuendumu. We went from having more than 60 young people sniffing in February to having six sniffing in April.

At that moment we really thought we were winning; we thought that sniffing was going to be stopped completely. Everyone in the community could tell that the outstation strategy was working.

However, Avgas was not the miracle panacea we hoped it would be. Unlike Maningrida which is isolated by swamps and the sea, Yuendumu did not have an isolated fuel supply. Nearly everyone who has a car in Yuendumu uses that car to drive to town. Alice Springs didn't stock Avgas at its petrol stations so cars returning to Yuendumu would have petrol in their tanks. It took a while for the sniffers to figure this out though.

Hard-core sniffers, desperate for some fuel, walked several kilometres out of the community to various car dumps where they pulled apart a vehicle's fuel lines and drained it of any remaining petrol. They only needed a few centimetres of petrol in an empty soft drink can to get high.

Later they discovered that some contractors who worked in Yuendumu brought their own jerry cans of petrol to run cement mixers. Eventually the sniffers targeted any car returning from town and found a ready supply of petrol to steal. They waited until the community was asleep then crept around the camps with a hose and siphoned fuel.

This undermined any effect Avgas had; in the end it was pointless. People were concerned that Avgas could damage car engines and sniffing continued unabated despite Avgas being sold by the stores.

I'm going to kill you

Dear Mr Bell

I am having a crazy and upset weekend. It's is a pretty hard time for me. In fact just for today I feel that I have 'popped a gasket'.

I have been working with petrol sniffers. Three weeks ago, one of them, Farris, tried to kill me …

… My vision was filled with this youth with bulging bloodshot eyes, anger fuming out of him, nulla nulla swinging and aimed at my skull. I had no way out and no weapon to block the blows of that fire-hardened mulga.

'Farris, you can't hit me,' I yelled. 'I'm your fucking friend. I feed you, I lend you my cassettes, I give you cups of tea. You can't hit me, I'm your friend.'

My barrage of words could not provide an impenetrable force field, but they slowed him down momentarily, long enough for someone to grab him from behind and disarm him. I walked out of the building, desperately wanting to run but trying hard not to. I did not want him to sense my fear. I walked straight home.

'Vesna, we are leaving,' I said as I walked in the house. My newly pregnant bride was terrified.

'We're packing the car now and we're leaving, grab your stuff.'

Before we had finished packing, Farris came with his father to my house to apologise.

'I'm sorry, Yakajirri,' he said.

We sat down and had a cup of tea together. Later that day the Council members took Farris and the other sniffers to Yarripilangu Outstation. They stayed out there for a few days. Meanwhile Vesna and I had gone to Alice Springs where we spent a week living in a friend's backyard and painting artwork on our tandem bicycle.

The Yuendumu Council Clerk and Council President rang me: 'Please don't leave this way,' they said. 'We know you really care for those sniffers … we want you to come back.'

'I want to come back too,' I said. 'But I want to send a message to the community that attacking my wife is unacceptable. I won't put up with it.'

It was pretty scary, man. Vesna is finding it hard living in Yuendumu and I don't know how to make her happy. We had a big fight on Friday night about lots of issues, like how we relate to people, to our home, to material possessions.

It's like a three-way cultural tug of war between Vesna's Yugoslavian culture, my swagman culture/Australian culture, and Aboriginal culture, plus it's a tug of war of ideas … hippy ideas, Buddhist ideas, Christian-Jesus Christ ideas … you know, about 'giving all your possessions to the poor', Gandhi's ideas, greenie ideas. Geez man, I think too much.

Anyway, we sort of came to a resolution to leave Yuendumu and move back to our own country …

Well, I was pretty sad that Friday night. I took my map and tobacco over to my mate Dave's house. He had some strong Polish alcohol. Man, that stuff's so strong you could run aeroplanes on it. I only had half a glass. I was feeling reckless … I never drink in Yuendumu, I respect that it is a dry community. But because I thought that I was leaving, well, what the heck. I looked at the map of my own country. The Shoalhaven River, Deua Wilderness, the forests. Places where I have walked and camped. Orchards where I've picked fruit. Waterholes and waterfalls where I have swum.

Yeah, it's good country. But I really want to live in Yuendumu, you know, live out the visions in my head, to live the Dreaming, to follow the calling in my heart, to learn.

I was pretty sad and pretty drunk. I've never been that drunk before. I went for a walk around the community and found my friend Solomon. He was straight and sober, it was two a.m., the place was dead quiet and everyone was asleep. I told Solomon. I said: 'I love Yuendumu, I love my wife. But Vesna is singing me back to my own country. I don't want to leave, but I want her to be happy.'

We talked lots. Next day I went out hunting with Long River and his wife Napaljarri. We saw emus, we drove a long way. We got bush honey and chased plenty *marlu* (kangaroo).We shot one kangaroo, went back and got the women, cooked him up that *marlu* – cooked him in the ground with ashes. Tasted plenty good. Drove home, pretty country, visited outstations that run on solar power. Sunlight makes golden on spinifex. Cold Chisel music on the car stereo. Nothing could be more Australian.

Love, Yakajirri

Missing person, missing soul

It was 1977. Fatty Forster had just touched the dry grass I was holding with a lit match. 'We'll smoke him out,' he said.

We were both nine years old, trying to coax a blue-tongue lizard from its hole. It was a blue-sky day on one of those grassy hillside paddocks that form a patchwork between the suburbs of Canberra. I grew up building cubbies in the backyard, wandering the bush with friends and catching lizards. Many years later, when I moved to Yuendumu, I remember thinking to myself that Warlpiri kids grow up catching lizards too.

The Aborigines that I learnt about as a kid came from the mythologies of schoolbooks and television. At school we learned about the explorers and pioneers who seemed to always have an Aborigine as their rescuer or guide. The real Australian bushman (our outback hero) was one who could track and live off the land just like a blackfella. It seemed Aborigines were the yardsticks that white Australians were measured against.

As we gathered around the television after school to watch 'Skippy', we were presented with images of noble, mysterious and wise Aboriginal people who knew the land and animals intimately. In the evening, naturalist Harry Butler on his 'In the Wild' TV series would tell us: 'I learned everything I know about the bush from the Aborigines'.

In 1983 I was fifteen years old, failing Year 10 and hating the selective private school I attended. I was ready to drop out.

My parents sent me on a school excursion to Central Australia as a bribe to keep me at school until the end of the year. We had a few days stopover in Alice Springs where the students were given permission to explore the town. Walking along the dry Todd River bed as a lonely and confused adolescent, I saw groups of people gathered around campfires and they invited me to join them. They waved and called out: 'Hello, come over here. What's your name, boy? Where are you from? Sit down.'

All of a sudden, for what seemed the first time in a long time, I was being welcomed. No one was judging me for my clothes, my hairstyle, my parents' car, or what my dad did for a living. I didn't have to act cool or smart and I didn't have to try to make up clever conversation. I was welcomed just as I was and the people who were giving me this welcome were the Aborigines; the people of the deep Australian mythology, the ones who held the very heart of my country in their Dreaming, the yardstick that heroes were measured against. The welcome and the simple invitation to be in their company was such a contrast to the materialistic culture of my peers from school.

Our school trip continued to travel across the Western Desert from Ayers Rock through the settlements of Docker River, Giles and Warburton. I met and saw people who lived in humpies, not houses, people whose simplicity of material life seemed elegant and liberating compared with the consumerism of white culture.

The Giles Weather Station meteorologists told us a story of how only a few days before our visit, a bush blackfella had walked into the station.

'Where have you walked from?' they had asked him. He pointed to the south and then swept his arm across the horizon. The whitefellas could just make out the faint signs of smoke from his trail. They told us that his path to the weather station was marked out in an 80-kilometre arc of hunting fires.

To the north of the weather station were a group of Pintubi hunters who lived a completely nomadic life, and who hadn't made contact with whitefellas. Those hunters walked into an Aboriginal settlement fourteen months later. After living there for a while, one of them picked up his spears and walked back into the desert.

The desert holds secrets and the desert also welcomes. I was standing on the outside of another culture, another world. I had met people who knew how to live in Australia, as real Australians. People who could live off the land, people who were not caught up in all the trappings of Western society. I remember thinking: this is where I want to live.

A decade later, just after my 25th birthday, having completed a degree in Anthropology, I began my life in Yuendumu.

At the end of my second year in Yuendumu, following the 'I'm going to kill you' incident, Vesna and I moved back to Canberra. But for me, even though my body had relocated, my soul remained deep in the desert. My parents, in-laws and Vesna all wanted me to live a nine-to-five mortgaged life in the suburbs.

'You get nice government job in office,' my Yugoslav mother-in-law told me in broken English. 'No very hard work and wear nice suit clothes.'

'I don't want a hard life in a dusty place full of rubbish and humbug. I want to have a relaxed life, I want the finer things,' my young bride pleaded.

'You're married now, you have a responsibility to your own family to settle down and think of what's best for them,' my father advised.

'Yes, it must be so hard for her out there,' my mother chimed in. 'Why don't you stay here in Canberra?'

But the desert called me more strongly. My Warlpiri friend Gordon and his band 'Black Storm' had a song that I played over and over again on our car stereo:

Dusty wind blows through my soul
Spirit's calling from this land that is old
And the desert keeps on calling me
Calling me
I am the land, I am the sea

Can't you hear it calling me
Can't you hear it calling me home?

On a morning off from work I sat up on Red Hill looking over the suburbs, out at the mountains west of Canberra and I could feel the call. My heart was being torn apart by my duties and loyalties to Vesna and family, and my own yearning for the desert. My mind could not reconcile my Christian ideals of being liberated from materialism, with the values I would have to assume in order to worship the 'money god' and take on a mortgage for $100 000 just to get a house in the 'burbs. How could I do that when some of my Warlpiri friends raised their families in humpies? How could I justify that level of materialism in my life?

It was rare for me to drink back then. Friends of mine said they could count on one hand the number of times they had ever seen me with an alcoholic drink. Any other normal Australian bloke would have walked off to the pub to escape his problems. I walked off to the mountains.

I walked away from my life for 30 hours. I tried riding my bike but the gears stuffed up and I cut my hand trying to fix them. Ouch! Pissed off, I dumped the bike on the hilltop and just walked away, like a snake shedding its skin.

No possessions, no money, just me. I humbugged a bum at the bus stop for twenty cents to buy a box of matches. Now I had fire. It felt good to be free.

I dreamt of walking forever, completely walking out of my whitefella life, no bank cards, no ID, nothing. I thought about walking all the way across the country; giving my life up to faith and the generosity of the road. I was going to find those people, those Pintubi, the ones who still knew how to live without all this suburban crap. I dreamt that one day I would be a hunter-gatherer myself and that I would tell my honey-skinned children: 'I was a whitefella once.'

I walked west for a day and half, hitchhiking part of the way. I got as far as Batlow and then I called Vesna.

'I'm sorry,' I said. 'Can you come and get me?'

I had no idea what chaos had ensued in the 30 hours since my departure. I had never been late for work before. I was always a reliable man. I was due at work that afternoon and I didn't show up. My boss rang Vesna. Worried, Vesna rang my friends. My friend Mr Bell who knew about my heartache said to her: 'I bet he's up on Red Hill. I'll go look.'

He came back ashen faced. 'I found his bicycle,' he said. 'Andrew would never leave his bicycle.'

Someone contacted the police. The police found the blood on the bike from where I had cut my hand.

That night all my friends in Canberra gathered together with the police search and rescue team and combed the gullies and fallen logs of Red Hill, looking for my injured or dead body. Police helicopters with powerful search lights scanned all over the hill.

'If it was one of us, you can bet Andrew would be out here looking,' my friends told each other. Even one of my old school teachers joined in the search.

My friend's father, Doc Pilko, searched with my dad. 'Look up in the trees, Bruce,' Doc said. Their torch beams traced up dead and ageing eucalypt limbs. My father was looking for his own son's body hanging from a tree. They searched all night long.

The next night my dad was about to go on television. He was going to appeal for people to come forward who might know anything about the disappearance of his son. That was when Vesna got my phone call.

'We thought you might be here, in the mountains,' said Doc's daughter, Nikki. Nikki, Vesna, Vesna's sister and Mr Bell came out to Batlow to collect me.

'We were up on that hill. Everyone was searching for you there, but some of us looked out, thinking: I bet Andrew's out there in the mountains.' Nikki grinned and looked at me.

'We know we pushed you too hard, Andrew,' Vesna said.

I looked at her sadly. A lump welled up in my throat, making it difficult to speak.

'I've got to go back to the desert,' I said. 'It's my Dreaming.'

'I'm going to come back with you,' she said.

Brushing away the tears, I smiled and looked at my heavily pregnant wife. She smiled back and added, 'Maybe we can raise little white Warlpiris.'

Two weeks later Vesna gave birth to our first child. For me, meeting this new baby was like falling in love all over again. We named her Deua, after our favourite river country.

3: On Fire Again

It was a Sunday afternoon at the end of the July school holidays. We had just moved back to Yuendumu after six months in Canberra where Vesna had given birth to our daughter Deua. I was glad to be home.

Our house was behind the school and when we sat on the veranda we could see into the school grounds. Some young kids came up to me and said, 'Hey, Yakajirri, those kids are sniffing petrol over there.' I was grateful that they told me but I did not know what to do. I had been back only a few days and no one had yet given me authority to deal with petrol sniffers. I went inside for a cup of tea and then came out again to have a smoke with my neighbour, Tarryn McKell.

Ker bang!

A burst of flame leapt out of the old air-conditioning unit the kids had pointed to when telling me about the kids sniffing. Someone covered with flames climbed out of the air conditioning unit. I ran to the toilet in our house where we kept a bucket full of water (because the toilet did not flush properly) and ran outside. A boy lay writhing on the ground, his friend throwing sand on his burning body to put out the flames. I doused him with water and ran back to refill the bucket. Tarryn ran next door to Lucy's house to phone the clinic. Both boys were severely burnt.

At the clinic, the nurses and the Aboriginal health worker, Ned Jampijimpa Hargraves, treated the burnt boys while their families gathered outside and wailed. They hoped the boys would live but knew the odds were against it. Toupe, the boy I saw on fire, was literally cooked. It was the same look as meat cooked in a fire; his flesh hung off him in chunks.

While we were waiting for the Flying Doctor to arrive, Ned looked at me and said, 'So how long are you back for this time?' He expressed it in the tired tone of someone who was sick of whitefellas coming and going and treating Yuendumu like some short-stay holiday camp.

The boys were airlifted to a hospital in Adelaide and people anticipated the worst. Toupe had burns to 70 per cent of his body and the doctors didn't expect him to live. Miraculously he survived. Ten years earlier Toupe's chances would have been zero, but medical science is a great thing. The other miracle was that sniffing stopped instantly in Yuendumu. Stories flew around the community that if the boys died then the petrol sniffers would be blamed and would be punished by payback (spearing). Suddenly no one wanted to sniff anymore. Petrol sniffing stopped for nearly six months, until Rudy got out of jail.

Rudy did not know or feel the shock in Yuendumu after the accident, so when he got out of jail in December, he came back and did what he was used to doing, sniffed petrol. He got his younger brother Austin and his friend Lenin to sniff with him. The accident had happened a long time ago now and no one had died so there was no payback.

Warlpiri father

Shortly after the fire, Ned adopted me into his family. He was Jampijimpa and I was Jangala. Skin name way it made sense; under the classificatory kinship system, Jampijimpa was Jangala's 'father'.

Ned was a skinny blackfella with a bung leg. From when I first

Andrew Cowen, Solomon, Carson and Andrew Stojanovski (Yakajirri) at the Lajamanu Turnoff

Johnny Hooker Creek and Peggy Brown

Collecting firewood at Mt Theo

Old Jangala – Number one spear thrower in Yuendumu

The end of sniffing

Traditional land management – burning off the spinifex at Mt Theo

Yakajirri and Johnny Hooker Creek telling the Mt Theo Story at Uluru

Jaru Pirrjirdi excursion

met him I remember that he drove a hard bargain when I tried to buy pushbike parts from him. Later that summer he humbugged me for paint supplies from the school art room to take out to business camp.

Ned walked with a heavy limp, a result of having polio as a child. Polio had been wiped out in suburban Australia and only really old whitefellas remembered it. I would sometimes look at Ned limping around the community and think, 'That guy would have been stuffed in the old hunter-gatherer days', but then I would correct myself, remembering that polio was a disease that whitefellas brought to his country.

Ned was a relatively young man, in his early thirties, only ten years older than me. He was such a charismatic individual that people usually did not notice the limp, it being overshadowed by his personality. Having spent much of his childhood in hospitals and foster homes, Ned knew about whitefellas. He knew our culture backwards and could play us like a charm.

He was an activist, an organiser and a rock and roll singer. His mother-in-law told me the story of this young man who courted her attractive and popular daughter.

'Really good singer,' the daughter would tell her mother.

Up on stage Ned had fronted the band. He won the girl ahead of all the other guys. Warlpiris know how to sing people, they know all about love magic.

Though he had never played football in his life, Ned was a convener of Yuendumu Sports Weekend and was the person who organised and coordinated the local 'Tanami Football League'. He's a highly intelligent fellow. Government people love him: he's articulate, literate, and very entertaining. He's a man they can talk turkey with.

Ned was a rescuer. Many tourists who have broken down on the Tanami Road, who have hit a bullock or rolled their four-wheel drive have been rescued by Ned. It will be Ned who pulls them out from the wreck of their overturned car. I'm sure that Ned's random acts of kindness, coupled with his excellent English and good humour, have done much for the cause of reconciliation.

He is a restless character though, and I guess it is that part of his personality that drives him to be an activist. He is most certainly a key character in the success of Mt Theo. A whitefella school teacher once described Ned to me in the following way: 'When you are driving down the road, you might see a group of Yapa, sitting in the shade next to a broken down car. As you drive on further and go over a rise, a few clicks down the road, you will see this skinny black fellow with a limp and a flat tyre under his arm, walking back to Yuendumu to get it fixed: that will be Ned.'

Sniffing is back

On Monday 11 December I found Flint (one of the boys who had been burnt in July) sniffing with Rudy, Austin, Lenin and eleven other young people. Some smoked cigarettes while others stood next to them, Coke cans full of petrol pushed under their noses. When I growled at them and reminded them of the fire in July, they replied to me that Toupe was okay now.

I couldn't believe it. What sort of education did these kids need? Flint had also been burnt in that fire. People thought he was going to die from his burns. Now he was sniffing again, next to people with lit cigarettes. Austin and Lenin had been right there when the fire happened.

I decided that Rudy, as the eldest, needed to know that the petrol burning tragedy was real. He should see Toupe. Flint sniffing sent a message to young people that being burnt while sniffing can be a survivable experience and worth the risk.

I decided to take Lenin, Austin and Rudy down to Adelaide to see Toupe. As ringleaders of the sniffers, they needed to know about the very real danger that comes from mixing petrol and fire.

I hoped to reawaken the feelings that made everyone abandon sniffing following the fire in July. I also thought it would be good for Toupe to have his friends visit him, to show him that people in Yuendumu still cared for him.

I went around Yuendumu to raise money for the trip. All the different organisations chucked in some cash to pay for food and fuel. I was all set to leave on Friday, after school broke up for the Christmas holidays, but then my car got trashed.

I had lent the car to some friends on Thursday who were driving to Alice to catch a plane. About 100 kilometres before town the radiator hose burst, so my friends had to abandon the car and hitch into Alice to catch their plane.

When I arrived back at the car I found all the windows had been smashed. Someone had tried to rip the stereo out, it was damaged and the speakers were gone. I was really upset and all the racism in me boiled to the surface. Anyway, the car had not been set on fire and it had not been stolen, though I think that was because people could not work out how to steal it.

I began to refit the radiator hose when Lloyd Jungarrayi Spencer came along and consoled me. 'Don't worry, *bunji* (brother-in-law),' he said, emphasising our close relationship. 'People smashed my car up too before, that Burumbella mob.'

I was pretty confident that no one from Yuendumu would smash up my car as they would recognise it. Most probably drunks had done this, after all, it was a Thursday (pay day).

I still had the big plan of taking Rudy, Austin and Lenin down to Adelaide, and after organisations had donated money, I felt obliged to do the trip. But I had no car.

My friend Blair who worked for Tangentyere Council in Alice persuaded his boss to lend me one of their night patrol vehicles. I drove straight back to Yuendumu to pick up Rudy and the others. Perry Japanangka, a traditional owner for Mt Theo, accompanied me on the trip to Adelaide. Perry had just got out of prison himself.

He was full of the spirit of personal redemption and advocated abandoning all substance abuse; he even criticised me for smoking. He was keen to help the sniffers find redemption too. Prison must have been good for him – he looked like he'd come off a health farm.

It took us a night and a day to drive to Adelaide. When we went to see Toupe in hospital, the nurses had dressed him in his best to receive his guests. I had hoped that the sight of Toupe's horrific burns would be sufficiently shocking to put Rudy and the others off sniffing. Instead, the picture of Toupe with his wounds carefully hidden beneath his new trendy clothes may have even had the opposite effect, proving to the others that petrol sniffing and being burnt while sniffing is survivable. Toupe looked all right. He was confined to hospital, but everyone, including the nurses, put on cheery faces to make the visit from his friends a positive experience.

When we returned to Yuendumu, Rudy and the others returned to sniffing.

I did not take school holidays that summer. Sniffing grew worse and I knew it would grow further if there was no school holiday program. Vesna and our daughter Deua went to Canberra for Christmas while I spent summer in Yuendumu, running the swimming pool and disco.

Fire ceremony

My ears were filled with the songs of clapping boomerangs and the women wailing and singing. I was painted up in red ochre and white feathers and I wore a red loin cloth. Robin Japanangka decorated me.

I had gone to the ceremony every afternoon it was on, sometimes taking old Darby Jampijimpa with me in the car. The ceremony ground is just next to East Camp, a large humpy camp. I took my boomerangs with me each afternoon.

One afternoon old Jupurrula, Harry Nelson's dad, asked how much they were going to get paid for doing this ceremony. The last time this ceremony had been performed, a documentary team had filmed it and had paid the participants. Harry said to Jupurrula that they were not going to get paid because they were doing the ceremony for themselves, as Warlpiri, for Yapa business, not for a film crew. 'Surely you can get some whitefella to pay us?' Jupurrula queried in response.

On Saturday afternoon I went to the ceremony place with my boomerangs and I sat next to Darby. The men were singing and the women were dancing (I think they were dancing – we weren't allowed to look at them). Old Strongarm, who was drunk, turned up and started yelling at people and arguing. He argued with Purlka Pawu Jakamarra, the boss of the ceremony, and he argued with some women, then he looked at me and said, 'You shouldn't have white people at this ceremony. This not his culture, he's got no Dreaming.'

Yakajirri getting painted up for a ceremony

He kept on about my presence. I didn't want the focus of the argument or ceremony to be on me so I picked up my boomerangs and walked away. All the Yapa called out for me to come back and sit down. But I walked about 150 metres away and sat down behind some bushes. I could hear Darby and Agie Napurrula (my adoptive grandmother) and lots of Yapa calling out, 'Yakajirri, come back here!'

Hogan Japanangka came and sat with me and then Purlka Pawu. We waited for all the commotion to die down. When things were quiet we returned to the ceremony place but the ceremony had been aborted. The others were sitting in a group and they called me over. They said I should be at that ceremony and that drunks shouldn't interrupt ceremonies. They said, 'Yakajirri you are a good man, good helper for Yapa people, worrier for petrol sniffers, interested in learning Yapa culture. We want you at the ceremony. We have growled at Strongarm and he's got to say sorry for you.'

Afterwards, I visited two white women who had been at the ceremony. Both were studying for PhDs in anthropology. They were told to leave the ceremony when the trouble started. They were worried Yapa didn't want Kardiya at the ceremony and were worried that Old Strongarm was articulating a commonly felt feeling. I didn't necessarily agree with this analysis in light of what so many Yapa had said to me. One of the women suggested that Yapa had said those words to me because they were shamed at Strongarm's behaviour, but it didn't really mean they wanted whites at the ceremony.

Later I talked with lots of Yapa, all of whom said it was good that I went to ceremony. Harry Jakamarra Nelson advised me to wait a while until things had cooled off. By Sunday night, Harry said that things had calmed down enough and I was invited to attend. Strongarm left Yuendumu shamed and didn't return until the commotion had died down; he and I had been the talk of the town for the previous 24 hours. It was affirming that so many Yapa wanted me at the ceremony.

On Sunday night people were painted up and there was a big totem pole in the ceremony ground. People were going to sing and dance all night. I was told to spend the night there, but just before midnight, all the people who had daytime jobs were allowed to leave and I was given a ride home. I left my boomerangs with Jakamarra. I had to sit in one spot all night; I wasn't dancing and I had found it a struggle to stay awake.

On Monday Rex Japanangka Granites instructed me to bring some red loincloth with me and to go to the ceremony early. I went with Rex's brother Robin at about five p.m. Robin decorated me in ochre and feathers. There wasn't a lot of ochre left, as everyone else was being painted up too. So even though I had my torso covered with ochre, parts of my legs, arms and face were still white. Robin said that this wouldn't do, so he got a jar of black paint and painted my legs, arms, face and hair black, so that I wouldn't stand out. My feet were left white.

I was wound up from all the painting and preparation for the big ceremony. At the central ceremony area there were lots of people and we arrived in the dark. As the men began to dance, showers of sparks were sent up into the air. I was mentored through the first part of the dance by three Japanangkas: Robin, Rex and Hogan. They gave me instructions all through the dance and told the Yapa that it was me, 'Yakajirri', because people didn't recognise me in the dark, decorated and painted black.

When I finished my dance everyone clapped and made appreciative noises. 'You winner, Yakajirri,' they said, and 'Really good one.' All the Japangardis, especially the ones from Willowra said, 'You got to give me your daughter, Yakajirri.' (Japangardi are the first choice skin group for my daughter to marry into.) Old

Strongarm stood right next to the spot where I was directed to sit down. He shook my hand and said sorry. Yapa later told me he was really happy I danced.

The next stage of the ceremony was about to begin; my grandmother Agie Napurrula gave me some really green branches to use to protect myself from the fire. Old Darby got up and went to the side of the circle where the watchers were. Some people indicated for me to follow him but Robin called me back and said,

'He's got to go through with it and learn the hard way.'

All of a sudden the sky was filled with sparks and flying burning branches. We huddled together and I used the green branches Napurrula had given me for protection. As the fire rained down all around we felt the sparks hit us.

Filled with excitement, I can't remember whether the women were still singing and clapping their boomerangs. The flames leapt high and the scent of eucalyptus smoke was pungent in the air. My strongest feeling was of total sensory switch-on, with all my senses filled with the experience. It was amazing to be there and be part of it, and even more amazing to be a white man in an Aboriginal ceremony of such power, ancient and of this land.

For the next three days many Yapa congratulated me for dancing and getting burnt and being part of the ceremony. I was respected for that. People said, 'All the Yapa are talking about you, Yakajirri, and they're really proud of you.' It was a fantastic experience, one I had waited for all my life. To be part of a real Aboriginal ceremony made my spirit feel so alive. Happiness filled me at that ceremony. I thanked God.

The invitation

During that summer my Warlpiri father, Ned Jampijimpa, invited me to be initiated as a Warlpiri man. I considered this invitation a great honour and gave it very serious consideration.

There was the obvious attraction, wanting to be part of the tribe. The temptation was even stronger during summer when most other whitefellas had left and ceremony business was the dominant agenda in the community. I was seeing the men of the community painted up and covered in ochre, knowing that they disappeared to 'business camp', to a place where the uninitiated are forbidden to go. I heard the triumphant calls of the posse of secret business men as they seized the boys to make them into men, knowing I was missing out. I was being turned away from ceremonies when the women and children were also sent home, because I was not really a 'man'.

Despite living in Australia, loving this country as an Australian and loving the bush, I always felt there was something more to it, something deeper. It's hard to explain in words, but I sensed that Aboriginal people were more deeply connected to this land, connected to its spirit, its power and its Dreaming.

I often thought about the temptation to become a hunter-gatherer, to shed my clothes, like a snake sheds its skin, and to live with the last of the nomadic Pintubi. To be with people who really know how to live: people without any props, without cars, shops and money. People who don't even need matches, who can make their own fire. I envied these people and their knowledge. They somehow seem more alive, more independent and more human. I wasn't a hunter-gatherer yet, but here was an Aboriginal man inviting me to join his tribe …

Sometimes I was pissed off with Vesna and what I saw at the time as her consumerist and racist ways. She didn't want to live in Yuendumu and she didn't want to live like Yapa. In hindsight, Vesna wasn't racist. Other white women described her behaviour as 'nesting'. With a young baby she was very protective of our home space, our privacy and maintaining hygiene. This was difficult in a community with Third World health conditions and at odds with having a husband who wanted to welcome Yapa into the house in the same way Yapa had welcomed him onto Warlpiri land. To try and create a germ barrier, Vesna insisted on having one set of cutlery for the 'family' and one for visitors. Of course the family got the 'good' set. This reminded me of too many racist stories from the old station days I read about, where whitefellas drank from fine china and offered the blackfellas a broken cup. It stank of racist standards.

I was also pissed off with my family for always pressuring me to give this 'desert thing' away and live in the city. I knew if I said 'yes' to Ned's invitation then I would pass the point of no return and my life would be forever changed. I was afraid: not just of offering my body to men with stone knives, but of handing my whole life over.

'Don't worry Yakajirri, we'll be with you each step of the way. We'll look after you,' Ned assured me.

But weighing more heavily on my mind were the serious consequences of becoming a Warlpiri man. One of the reasons whitefellas are useful in Aboriginal communities is because they have 'diplomatic immunity' to the kinship obligation and clan system. Unlike a Yapa, a whitefella is seen as non-aligned with any clan group. They are seen as neutral, much like Switzerland. This neutrality allows whitefellas to manage and look after resources on behalf of the community without any accusations of bias. The general feeling is that whitefellas distribute and manage those resources fairly for all people. They have the best interests of the community at heart, as opposed to the best interests of a particular clan. Whitefellas are useful for 'policing' as well, like being the home liaison officer for the school. A whitefella can carry out this role without the accusations that would befall a Yapa person, that one clan interferes in the family business of another clan.

If I became a citizen of the Warlpiri nation, I would no longer have my diplomatic immunity. I would no longer be seen as neutral and non-aligned. Instead, I would have serious obligations to the people who initiated me. I would be aligned to a particular group of people, to a particular skin group and clan. I would also have serious, non-negotiable avoidance relationships. There would be people who I wouldn't even be allowed to be in the same room with, let alone speak to. There would also be people who I was absolutely obligated to, people who I couldn't refuse, no matter how unreasonable the request.

Another white man, Marlon, told me of his experience in business camp. Marlon had trained to be a monk. He was a serious and principled man, who had seen firsthand the destructive effects of alcohol on Aboriginal communities. Marlon had been initiated. He described one time at business camp in Jilliga when some of the men (who he was obligated to) asked to borrow his car so they could do a grog run. Jilliga is 400 kilometres from the nearest liquor shop. It is illegal to bring alcohol into Jilliga. When grog is carried, there is the risk of having the vehicle seized by the police. People get murdered in Jilliga during fights and riots fuelled by alcohol. But despite this, Marlon couldn't say no to the request. He was initiated so he was obligated and there was nothing he could do about it.

They say most whitefellas who get initiated end up either going mad or leaving the community because the pressures and conflicting obligations are too much. It is extremely rare to find an initiated white man still living in a remote community, let alone performing a whitefella role that requires diplomatic immunity. I knew that if I joined the tribe and became a man, my usefulness to the community would be reduced. I could no longer be an impartial resource manager or an effective anti-petrol sniffing activist. There would be some sniffers who I would be under obligation to and others who I could not even speak to.

I find it interesting how governments, policy makers and community workers assume that if only Aboriginal people were trained well enough, then they could take on all the roles whitefellas currently perform in communities. I often wonder how many of these policy makers have seriously considered the complexities involved for Yapa to perform these roles when they have no diplomatic immunity. I wonder if any of the policy makers would themselves be prepared to undergo initiation and then perform a neutral role, while also seriously fulfilling their cultural duties of obligation and avoidance. When I consider the complexities involved, I am amazed at the fine balancing acts many Aboriginal people already achieve.

I talked with my father Ned about this: 'Ned, I think you Warlpiri actually like having whitefellas do certain jobs in the community, like shop manager, because it avoids all the arguments and fights and conflicts of interest that would arise if a Warlpiri person did it. I don't think it's that Warlpiri don't have the knowledge and skill to do those sorts of jobs, I actually think that Yapa don't want Warlpiri to do them.'

'Shhh,' said Ned. 'That's our little secret.'

Vesna and Deua came back to Yuendumu after the summer holidays. The lifestyle I had adopted while they were away was at odds with having what Vesna saw as a normal (whitefella) family life. While I may not have taken up Ned's invitation, I still aspired to live more like Yapa who inspired me with their generosity. Vesna found the whole experience stressful.

Washing machine humbug

Lots of our neighbours knocked on the door to ask if they could use the washing machine. I had lived without a washing machine myself and know what a convenience they are if you can use one instead of having to wash by hand. Members of the School Council also asked me if they could use our washing machine.

Sometimes people brought their own washing powder, but mostly they would use whatever washing powder was there. Vesna became upset about our house turning into a laundromat.

The person who had asked to do the washing would arrive, usually with one other adult for company and three or four small children. The washing, two or three huge garbage bags, would be brought in and the group would then settle in the lounge to watch TV and drink cups of tea while the machine went through its many washing cycles. The kids explored the house, climbed into cupboards and emptied drawers to see what interesting things a whitefella might have at his camp. A jar of peanut butter would be found and a small hand would dart in and grab fistfuls out. After two or three hours the washing would be done and the washing party would go home. The house would be in a state of uncompleted exploration – the kids had left things where they fell. The two bottles of Dynamo and box of Omo that Vesna had planned to use over the next four weeks would be all gone. Any delicacies she was saving in the fridge such as sticks of salami or chocolate were found and eaten. The supermarket was 300 kilometres away. Vesna told me that in her Yugoslavian culture, it was an honour to have guests, but after a laundry visit she felt depleted and used.

What to do as a whitefella, a guest of this Aboriginal community and a representative of the white race, of the invader culture that had taken over Aboriginal people's country with decimating effects? I had learnt too much at university. I knew about colonialism. I knew that the wealth and privilege which we enjoyed as members of white Australian society was built on an invasion, on theft. I knew how Aboriginal people had fared as a result. The old saying about Australia's wealth used to be: 'Australia rides on the sheep's back'. Yeah, and the sheep grazed on country that Aboriginal people were forced off at gunpoint, their waterholes poisoned and their children taken away.

I was a guest in Yuendumu and my hosts were asking me to

share something that I had: a washing machine. The washing machine came with the house, the house came with the job and the job was given to me by the Aboriginal School Council. It was a rare opportunity and a privilege to live and work on the frontier, to get to know the people who still knew about the real Australia. I felt forever grateful for this privilege and for the welcome and friendship people offered me, despite the fact that I represented the invader race. In the face of all this, it seemed a small way to express gratitude, the sharing of a washing machine.

Beyond the 'duty statement' – bicultural partnerships

Our house was a place of endless cups of tea with so many visitors that it earned the nickname: 'Dog Ear Café'. Other whitefellas who were stuck for accommodation in Yuendumu refused to take up our offer of the spare bedroom because we would have sniffers coming over for breakfast. 'It's too extreme,' they complained. Maybe it was for them, but Warlpiri live in open households with up to 30 or more extended family. In contrast to my Yapa neighbours, our life wasn't that extreme. And I wanted to reach out to those sniffers. I'd much sooner have Austin having breakfast with me and watching TV in my lounge room than sniffing petrol.

In hindsight such generosity integrated me with the Warlpiri community and really helped my role as a community worker. Our open house served as a base for building relationships with Yapa that were intimate, that were far beyond professional. I'd seen whitefellas like the Toynes and Frank and Wendy Baarda do that too. They had succeeded in creating empowering partnerships with Yapa such as the school's bilingual program that Wendy worked on. It seemed that opening your house was a way to cross the cultural divide.

Those other 'professional distance' whitefellas who live in

The menu at the 'Dog Ear Café'

houses and don't let blackfellas in the door, who don't match the same level of commitment that Yapa people like Peggy Brown have, are the reason why so many programs on Aboriginal communities fail. When you join the cause it has to become your whole life, and then it can really work. But Vesna wasn't happy with our life and wanted me to find a job in the city.

As well as my continuing personal dilemmas, sniffing was growing out of control. People had talked about reopening the outstations and taking the sniffers out there, but most of the elders were tied up in ceremony and sorry business. No one seemed to be ready to go.

I had applied for funding to support the outstations under the auspices of the school, and had received permission through the School Council and the Education Department to use the school bus and Toyota to support the program. By the time the elders were prepared to move back to the outstations, the school had a new Principal, and that seemed to make things even more difficult.

Not the school's role

I didn't get on with the new School Principal, Dr Howitt. He often told me the petrol sniffing program should be a council responsibility, not a school responsibility. He seemed concerned that the program was taking too many resources away from the school, in terms of my time and in administration of grants and use of vehicles.

The previous school principals such as Peter Toyne had really supported me. They saw solving the petrol sniffing problem as part of the liaison officer's job because petrol sniffing directly impacted on the students. They released me from school duties to work with the community to stop sniffing. Howitt didn't have that history so it's possible he couldn't appreciate my involvement.

All of a sudden I had two jobs, the liaison officer for the school as defined by Howitt and my work outside school on petrol sniffing, supporting the outstations and putting on youth activities. I was getting really worn out. Howitt wasn't trying to stop the program, nor did he undermine it, so I didn't want to fight with him. He just held the view that the petrol sniffing program was not the school's role.

It was difficult and frustrating. I believed in stopping petrol sniffing. I really believed in it. Did Howitt think I was going to give up trying to stop sniffing, just because he said it was not the school's responsibility?

Does the issue of petrol sniffing suddenly become less important because we get some new whitefella Principal at the school?

Were kids less vulnerable to its dangers?

I had faced down death many times in the line of trying to stop sniffing. I had seen my family terrified when sniffers tried to smash down the door of our house. I had given my all to this cause. I had seen Toupe and Flint severely burnt right in front of my eyes. I had heard too many stories and read too many reports about the tragedy that sniffing has wrought on Aboriginal communities. I knew that sniffing killed kids.

I had people by my side, my best friends, Ned, Robin Japanangka, Peggy and Johnny Hooker Creek. They too had all faced death in the campaign to stop sniffing. Was I going to let them down and give up just because of a school principal who had some different ideas?

I hated feeling uncomfortable around Howitt, like a naughty child who was doing the wrong thing.

Organised

The petrol sniffer outstation program started up again in May. Before then, community members were tied up with sorry business and that fire ceremony. Meanwhile we had 60 young people sniffing. Youth activities continued every evening, on weekends and after school. The activities were not run just by me. Most of the football stuff was organised by Yapa.

Working on the vegetable garden at Mt Theo 1994

Initially, Mt Theo was opened for the males and Mala for the females. This changed when some traditional owners for Mala, whose nephews were sniffers, insisted that these males stay with them at Mala. As a result, the outstation a young person was sent to was no longer determined by gender.

Once the outstations were open, the sniffing numbers dropped dramatically. I had written a list of everyone who I had found sniffing and had started to talk to the families of each and every sniffer. These conversations took place at people's homes, sitting outside by the campfire. I would outline my concerns about sniffing, about how dangerous it was. The family and I would then discuss what they thought was the best plan of action to stop the young person from sniffing.

The discussions had a positive effect; even though most families already knew that their teenager was sniffing, having a whitefella come and talk about sniffing combined with the threat of sending the sniffer to an outstation seemed to be a catalyst for action.

'You don't have to take Rina,' her father told me. 'I don't want her to go. I'll give her a hiding if she sniffs again, but give her one more chance.'

Most of the young people who were recreational sniffers stopped sniffing. They either didn't want to be forced to go to an outstation for a month, or they didn't want the other sort of treatment their family suggested. This left only the chronic sniffers to deal with. Rounding up these sniffers was an ordeal. Nearly all of the chronic sniffers were males who had gone through initiation, and were therefore considered men. As such they thought that they had the right to sniff.

Personal autonomy and the right to sniff

An aspect of Aboriginal culture that is well documented by researchers such as Maggie Brady is the right to personal autonomy:

people have the right to do with their own bodies what they choose. It also means that people in the community are reluctant to impose their will on another individual (Brady, 1992, pp. 72-5).

In terms of petrol sniffing, this aspect of Aboriginal culture makes it hard for families to stop their teenage children from sniffing. When discussing sniffing with families, parents often say: 'That kid won't listen to us … he doesn't want to stop sniffing and we can't force him.'

Non-Aboriginal people can find avenues to control their children's behaviour through sanctions such as grounding or imposing curfews. However, such sanctions are so foreign to Aboriginal child-rearing practices that they are considered inappropriate and unworkable in the context of most Aboriginal families. The young people know they have a right to personal autonomy in their own culture. They know that their parents feel uncomfortable forcing them to do things against their will. When parents do try to force their child to stop sniffing or to go to an outstation, the child will often react in such a violent way that the parents will quickly back off. Maggie Brady states: 'Put simply, drugs enable individuals to exploit this finely balanced [social] system … sniffers of petrol … are able to transform notions of personal autonomy … to their own ends. At their disposal are communities of people who have been socialised into the belief … that to remonstrate or dissuade them from drug use is to interfere with their right to do what they please with their own bodies … petrol sniffers exploit the "loopholes" in what is, for the most part, a highly workable social system.' (ibid., p. 74)

The violence and disruption to family life associated with petrol sniffing was of great concern to parents who would frequently seek me out and say, 'That kid was keeping us up all night sniffing petrol, running around with a knife and axe. Please take him to Mt Theo.'

When I went to collect the young person I would nearly always go with a Yapa member of the Petrol Sniffing Working Party. This would usually be Ned or Robin Japanangka, but many other Yapa helped out. When we arrived at the sniffer's home, the parents would cajole the young person to get in the car and go to Mt Theo. Sometimes the young person would come easily, but it was equally likely that they would refuse to move. In the face of point blank refusal, most Yapa parents were at a loss, because it was culturally wrong for them to physically manhandle their teenage children to force them into the car. The young people, being aware of this dilemma, would either continue to stonewall their parents or simply walk away. Occasionally they would pick up a weapon, such as a rock or iron bar.

In exasperation the parents would say, 'That kid won't listen to us, get the police.' But sniffing petrol was not against the law.

Solutions: the courts and the police

By October we had started using court bonds to deal with sniffing. Most chronic sniffers usually ended up committing some type of criminal offence, typically assault or theft, and got in trouble with the law. When they did, Peggy and I would go to court with them and ask the magistrate to put them on a good behaviour bond that forced them to live at Mt Theo. Mt Theo was the preferred outstation because it was fifty kilometres from the main road and therefore it was very hard to run away. Mala was only twenty kilometres from the main road and sometimes sniffers would walk those twenty kilometres and then hitchhike to Yuendumu.

The bond conditions gave the police the legal authority and obligation to assist in sending young petrol sniffers to Mt Theo. Having a police officer verbally tell a young person that they had to go to Mt Theo made sniffer round-ups a lot easier. It helped to overcome the complexities associated with the young person's cultural right to personal autonomy. The sniffers recognised that the police had authority over them that their parents did not. This greatly reduced the level of confrontation associated with taking young people to Mt Theo, as not only did they accept the authority of the police but most who had been through the court were relieved to go to Mt Theo instead of jail.

We would usually request a clause in the bond conditions that gave us the legal flexibility to direct the young person to move back to Yuendumu if they gave up sniffing. Having wording such as: '*... reside at Mt Theo or elsewhere at the direction of the outstation manager*' meant that before the bond expired, we could reintroduce the young person to Yuendumu and observe their behaviour. If the young person sniffed again then we had the legal authority to force them to go back to Mt Theo. However, if the young person no longer sniffed then they could remain living in Yuendumu while being monitored for relapses.

The limitation of the court bond strategy was that not all the young people who sniffed petrol had been caught committing crime. Some chronic petrol sniffers we had no legal power over.

Occasionally some older police officers would help us with the sniffers who were not on bonds. These experienced police would bluff and intimidate, and despite having no legal power to do so, they would tell the sniffer that they had to go to Mt Theo. However, given that sniffing was not an offence, many police were reluctant to direct young people in this way.

The lack of legal authority over sniffing was the biggest gap in the program. What we really wanted to do was nip petrol sniffing in the bud. As soon as a young person started sniffing petrol, we wanted to be able to stop it, but we did not have the power.

Rogan started sniffing recreationally when he was thirteen. He refused to go to Mt Theo, his parents could not force him, and since he had not broken the law the police could not force him either. So he stayed in Yuendumu and sniffed more and more, assuming the status of a 'king sniffer' when the other chronic sniffers were removed to Mt Theo.

He got deeper and deeper into petrol sniffing. He began to hallucinate and see devils. He started walking around at night with a knife and an axe, sniffing petrol and threatening people. He recruited other young people to sniff petrol with him. By the time he was fifteen he was in prison, serving time for numerous assaults, including a stabbing, punching a nurse, escaping from custody and throwing petrol on a police officer.

Why do kids sniff in Yuendumu?

The two most commonly stated reasons (that the kids who sniff immediately give) are boredom or peer group pressure. There are, however, many factors that affect an individual's decision to sniff petrol.

Pro sniffing forces

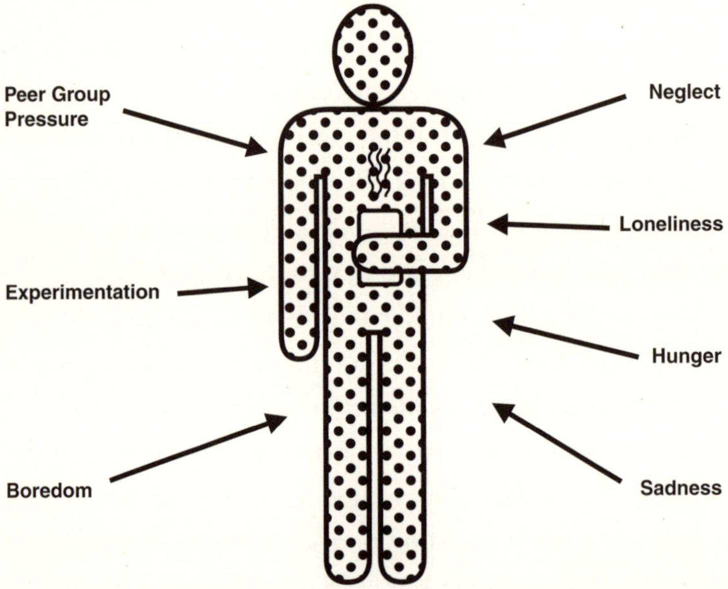

The kids who tend to be the most chronic sniffers are those who are often the abandoned children or street kids of Yuendumu. Many of the kids living at Mt Theo fall into this category. These kids carry with them a lot of personal hurt and have significant members of their families and role models (often their parents) who live lives of chronic substance abuse.

One of the continuing problems with the program had been with parents or relatives of the young people giving them lifts back to Yuendumu before enough time had passed to break the habit of sniffing. When family visited the outstations, sniffers often put immense pressure on them for rides back to Yuendumu. Frequently the sniffers would threaten violence or self-mutilation. Their family, feeling either overwhelmed with compassion or intimidated by the violence, often gave in to this pressure.

Chronic sniffers

The kids who tended to be the most chronic sniffers were often the abandoned children or the street kids of Yuendumu. Kids whose parents had either died, or who were alcoholics in Alice Springs. Stopping these kids from sniffing was really hard. This was for two reasons: the emotional damage these kids carried with them, and the lack of close family who could stop them sniffing. There was no one to say: 'The buck stops here for this kid.' These kids sniffed at every opportunity and many sniffed for years. The fact that most of them survived their teenage years without any long-term medical damage is probably because we consistently took them away from petrol. Some of these most chronic sniffers spent more than six months of each year at Mt Theo. This alone would have reduced their petrol intake by half for that year. Their diet improved too – simply by being providing with three meals a day, which was something they often did not get as a petrol sniffer in Yuendumu.

For these chronic sniffers, Mt Theo was like a second home; for some, it was their most consistent home.

Profile of petrol inhalation: petrol intake of a sniffer

Left alone in Yuendumu with their sniffing going unchallenged and unchecked

Involved in the Mt Theo Program and the Youth Program

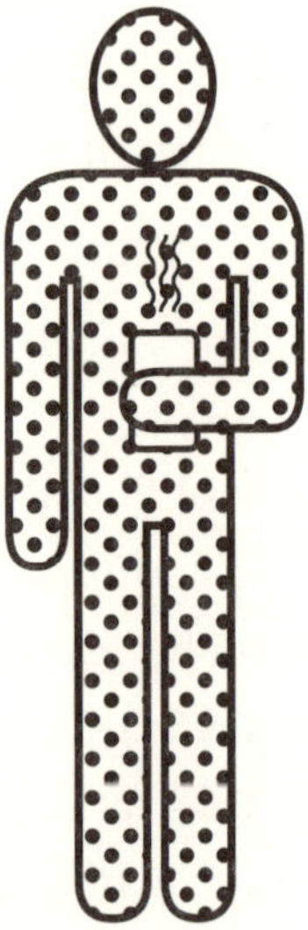

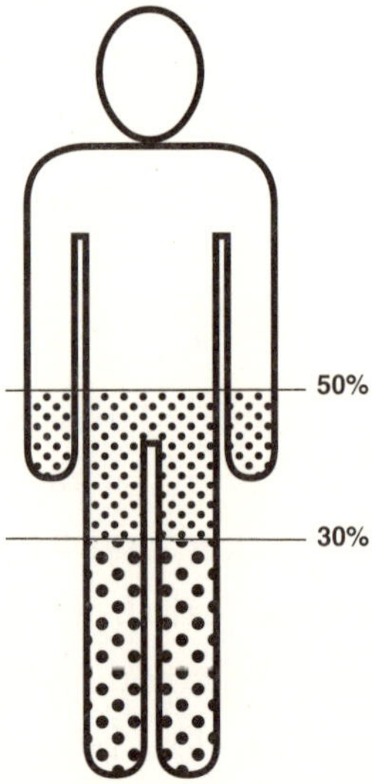

Pattern of Petrol Sniffing

A young person who is a chronic sniffer may be sniffing petrol for as long as 12 hours a day, 7 days a week. Sometimes kids go to sleep with a can of petrol under their nose.

Petrol inhalation reduced by over 70%

Explanation:

1). For over 6 months of the year the young person is kept away from petrol. This means the amount of petrol the young person is able to sniff is reduced by 50%.

2). During the months the young person is living in Yuendumu, because of proactive anti petrol work, the young person only sniffs at night and interrupts sniffing to take part in activities such as discos, football, swimming, basketball and billiards. So instead of sniffing for 12 hours a day, the young person may only sniff 4 hours a day.

Combined, the two points above mean an overall reduction in that young person's petrol intake of approximately 75%.

4: Economics, Adventures and Gender

Economics for non-Aborigines

Living in Yuendumu is like living in two worlds. Yapa and Kardiya perspectives on time and economics often seem at odds with each other. This has a significant impact on community programs and can make resource management problematic. While Kardiya see having money accumulate in the bank as a good thing (running a surplus, having cash assets), I have heard Yapa refer to the same thing as a waste (the money has not been spent therefore has no purpose or use). Kardiya refer to Yapa as wasteful, and Yapa say Kardiya are greedy and stingy.

I have thought hard and had lots of conversations about this issue. Paul, a whitefella from Nyrippi, gave me a short spiel on the differences between the hunter-gatherer attitudes to time and material possessions, and the European ones, based on the European need to store food in barns in order to survive the bitter cold winters in Europe. That conversation made me think a lot about where we had come from and where Yapa had come from.

As whitefellas, who originally came from Europe, our culture over the last 5000 years was mainly an agriculture-based culture, where most of us tilled the soil and farmed. As farmers we had to plant in spring, water our crops through summer, harvest in autumn and store our food in barns so we could survive the bitterly cold European winters. In effect, we grew accustomed to deferred gratification, working in spring so we had food to eat in winter. We also developed the idea of saving – storing food in barns and meting it out little by little through the winter to make it last. If we didn't work at planting and looking after our crops, if we gave our food away and did not save enough for the winter, or if we ate it all at once, we wouldn't have survived those cold winters when snow covered the ground, and we as a people would have died out. These ideas of planning and working for the future, of saving and storing up for the future, were necessary for our survival.

Sometimes crops failed, causing famine, and the only people who would survive were those who had enough food in their barns to last two years. So we would work towards something two years in advance. But if you look back at our ancient dreamtime stories, like the stories in the Bible, there is evidence of famines that lasted even longer – sometimes up to seven years. Joseph and his coat of many colours is one such story.

Joseph was a dream interpreter. He was a Jew who had been sold into slavery in Egypt by his brothers who were jealous because he was gifted and their father's favourite son. In Egypt, Joseph interpreted the pharaoh's dreams. The pharaoh had a dream of seven fat cows followed by seven skinny cows. Joseph told him that it meant that there would be seven years of bumper crops followed by seven years of famine. Joseph advised the pharaoh to build huge food storehouses to store the bumper crops in so that there would be enough food stored to feed the Egyptians during the seven years of famine. This meant they planned, saved and worked for survival fourteen years into the future.

Sure enough, the famine came and people in all the countries outside Egypt starved. During the famine, Joseph's Jewish family came to Egypt and begged for food because the Jews were starving. As a result of Joseph's esteemed place as the pharaoh's advisor, the Jews were allowed to live in Egypt and eat the stored food and therefore survived. However, it came at a huge cost as the Jews were subsequently enslaved by the Egyptians for hundreds of years and weren't set free until many generations later when Moses led them out across the Red Sea.

What does all this mean? It means that deep in our cultural psyche as whitefellas is the idea that if you don't work and plan for the future, and if you don't save and be careful with your resources, you as a people, will be wiped out or become slaves.

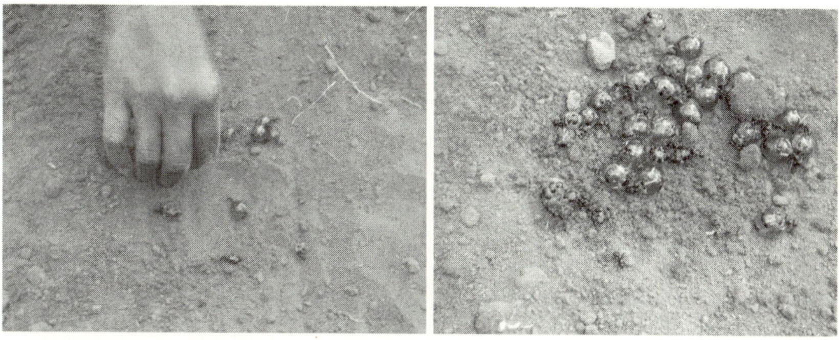

Gathering honey ants

Cross now to the hunter-gatherer way of life of Aboriginal Australians which has existed for 40 000 years. Australia, the world's most arid continent, had no grains suitable to grow as crops and no suitable animals to herd. Imagine you are a Warlpiri living in pre-contact time, in the Tanami Desert. You are out hunting and get a big kangaroo with your spear. You do not have a fridge. You have no way of storing the meat. If you do not eat that kangaroo within a few hours the meat will spoil and be wasted.

There is no way one person can eat a whole kangaroo. So what is the most economically sensible thing you can do with this resource? The smartest thing you can do is take the kangaroo back to camp and share it with your group of, say, eight people. That way, if everyone eats as much as they can while the meat is fresh, they can get the maximum nutritional value out of it.

Tomorrow you go out hunting and you're unsuccessful. Kangaroos are hard to catch and it is unrealistic to expect to get one every day. That evening you return to camp hungry.

But usually someone within your little group of eight has been successful and has speared a kangaroo. What are they going to do? You shared your kangaroo with them yesterday, so they'll now share their kangaroo with you today, because they 'owe' you. If you had not shared your kangaroo yesterday, no one would be obliged to share food with you and you would go hungry. So sharing actually helps ensure your survival into the future.

This is the way Warlpiri economics works: immediate consumption so that food does not spoil and so that maximum nutritional value is gained, coupled with sharing, where you invest in relationships of mutual obligation to ensure your survival into the future.

Many Warlpiri people still relate to resources such as money in the same way today as the kangaroo would have been treated. Money is immediately consumed and shared or, to put it another way, 'invested in relationships'.

The custom of sharing resources was so critical to hunter-gatherer survival that it is enshrined in Warlpiri law. The rules in Warlpiri law about sharing are so strict that people aren't allowed to refuse to share, especially with certain kin. In short, they can't say no to requests for food, money or other resources, including cars.

What about work?

What if you as a whitefella buy your flash four-wheel drive and go off on a desert safari and your car breaks down in the bush. What would you do? Would you run around in the desert sun and exhaust yourself? If you do that you might die. If you open your glove box and read your *In an Emergency Handbook*, it will tell you: 'If you are stranded in the desert, ration your sweat. Do not move around or use up energy and water unnecessarily. Find some shade and sit down and rest.'

That is the way to survive in the desert, by using up the least amount of water and energy that you can. As a hunter-gatherer, it is crazy to run around and work if you don't need to.

What motivates people to work?

As whitefellas, we all think people go to work because they get paid, right? Not exactly. People like to get paid, but money is not the only motivating factor to work. Individual financial wealth is hardly the only factor motivating a Warlpiri worker either. Say you are a Warlpiri person and you have a job that gives you $600 a week take-home pay. Meanwhile everyone else in your family is unemployed, getting $400 a fortnight unemployment benefit (which Warlpiri describe as 'sit-down money'). You have about eight people living in your household. As soon as your $600 is in your hand, there are eight people who you are obliged to distribute it to, in the same way that you would have had to distribute a kangaroo. When they get paid, they also have to share their sit-down money with each of the others.

Because all your pay is immediately shared, having a job does not bring much financial benefit to you as an individual. In a household of eight people where seven of them may get sit-down money, one individual bringing home a wage does not make a huge difference to the overall household income. This is the reality of how people live in Yuendumu. Warlpiri in the desert communities do not get jobs and then move into single-person apartments and keep all their money to themselves, like a whitefella in the city might. Warlpiri wage earners live with extended family. They are enmeshed in a network of strong obligation kinship relationships, which require them to distribute whatever income they have – obligations that prevent the accumulation of individual wealth.

So why else do Warlpiri people work? The reasons for having a job, apart from earning an income are: fun, meaning, a purposeful way to spend time; access to resources such as vehicles; office space, telephone, perks such as trips; status and self-esteem. People also work because they value their relationships with their boss, co-workers and client group. I believe this was and is the key motivating factor in the Mt Theo Program.

In the old anthropological texts that I read at uni, there were stories of individual Aboriginal stockmen who would be the hardest working, most reliable stockman on a cattle station. However, when their boss left the station, the Aboriginal stockman would no longer be interested in having the job. Why? Because the thing that he appreciated the most about the job and what motivated him to be a loyal and reliable worker, was the valued relationship with a particular person, his boss.

This idea was reinforced to me many times by Peggy Brown, the founder of the Mt Theo Program. The relationship between co-workers was the most important factor motivating people to work on the program. This idea flies in the face of the whitefella belief that staff can turn over and everything will be all right if another skilled worker is recruited. In the Warlpiri world it is not just a worker's skills that matter; the relationship matters more, for example, how that person treats Yapa, if they are kind, if Yapa feel connected to them and obliged to them.

The everything story

Every second Friday school finished at midday. On these short Fridays many school teachers took the opportunity to go to Alice Springs while I took the opportunity to do a ration run to the Mt Theo and Mala outstations. At this stage both outstations were looking after petrol sniffers.

After dropping the rations at Mt Theo, I drove south to

Mala 100 kilometres away. At Mala, Teddy Gibson (Gibbo), who was the senior man there, said, 'Yakajirri, when you get back to Yuendumu, can you ring Mundy [the Council Clerk at Nyirripi] and ask him to sign my dole form for me?'

Gibbo was a Nyirripi man who volunteered to look after sniffers at Mala. They weren't his kids and he worked unpaid. At this time Mala's only form of communication was a two-way radio, so Gibbo couldn't make the phone call himself. Nyirripi was 200 kilometres away.

'Sorry, Gibbo,' I told him, 'I can ring up, but I don't think Mundy will do it. He's a whitefella, and whitefellas have got really strong law about that. We're not allowed to sign other people's signatures. It's against the law. I can ask, but Mundy won't sign the form. If he signs your signature on your dole form, he could be sent to jail for fraud. I don't think he will do it. If you want I can give you a lift back to Yuendumu and you can get someone to take you to Nyirripi.'

'Can you drive me to Nyirripi in this Toyota?'

'Sorry, Gibbo, the school won't let me drive this car to Nyirripi. It's hard enough to get permission to use this school Toyota to run rations.'

'What about your private car, then? If I pay you for fuel, can you drive me to Nyirripi and then drop me back here at Mala?'

'Sure. If you get me some money for fuel we can do that tomorrow.'

I took Gibbo back to Yuendumu with me. We arrived at about 8 o'clock. I went off to run the disco and Gibbo went off to win money playing cards. At about ten o'clock, Gibbo turned up at the disco with a fistful of twenties he had won and he gave me the money to pay for fuel.

A student doctor from Switzerland called Yuri was helping me out at disco. 'Do you want to come on an adventure with me tomorrow?' I asked and I told him about the trip.

The next morning after fuelling up my little Subaru, Gibbo, Yuri and I headed off for Nyirripi, 160 kilometres south-west of Yuendumu. The fuel tank in the Subaru had a crack in it, and halfway there, I noticed that the fuel gauge was dropping faster than it should have been. I had some blue and white goo, which the Mining Company Store sold for temporary fuel tank repairs. I got underneath the car with the goo to fix the tank. As I was pressing it onto the leaking tank, I burnt my wrist on the car's exhaust pipe. I showed the burn to Yuri. He took out a bandanna, soaked it in water and applied it to my wound.

When we arrived at Nyirripi the whole town was in sorry business. They had just received news that morning that a relative had passed away. Gibbo had to pay his respects. Everyone was wailing and mourning. Yuri and I refuelled the car at the local store. Gibbo and I then headed off to find Mundy, the Council Clerk, to get Gibbo's dole form signed. When we found him, Mundy explained that he knew that Gibbo was living at an outstation, so he had already signed Gibbo's dole form on his behalf. So much for my big rave about how us whitefellas have really strong law about that sort of thing!

Gibbo told us there was a back road from Nyirripi to Mala, a shortcut that was only 100 kilometres long. The road went through Pirlinyanu and Nginyirripalangu. The alternative was to drive back to Yuendumu and then to Mala, a trip of almost 300 kilometres.

'It's a good road, no worries,' he said.

The road was much further than 100 kilometres, more like 200. It skirted through some beautiful virgin country. There was plenty of game and Gibbo managed to shoot some kangaroo and bush turkey to take with us to Mala. The road was not as flash as I had been told. It was overgrown with spinifex and hidden in amongst the spinifex clumps were *mingkirri*, rock-solid termite mounds. All of a sudden a huge *mingkirri* appeared in front of the car. I was travelling at about 80 clicks and dodged the car to the side to avoid hitting the *mingkirri* and have it take out my radiator and sump. Suddenly, hidden in the spinifex of my detour were more *mingkirri*. As I swung the steering wheel back and forth in rapid succession, dodging termite mounds, the car began to fishtail.

Two weeks earlier, three cars from Yuendumu had been involved in rollovers. In one accident a person had been killed and two others had had their backs broken. The driver from another rollover described to me that his car had rolled when he suddenly swerved to avoid an object on the road, exactly what I was doing now. This was not the place to have an accident. We were at least 150 kilometres from Nyirripi and even further from Yuendumu.

The young Swiss doctor thought his life was going to end in outback Australia. The swerving Subaru had left the road and was plunging through the scrub. 'Bugger it,' I thought. 'Best thing to do is let the car have its head, hold it in a straight line and slow it down.' As the car clanked over termite mounds that struck the undercarriage, I was reminded of Mike Harries' yarn about how one of his mates had had his whole diff taken out by a termite mound.

Apparently this fellow was flying along the Papunya road when his car took off in the scrub over termite mounds. After the car finally came to rest, the bloke thought he was bogged, as he was giving it heaps of throttle and getting nowhere. It was only when he got out of the car that he discovered the whole back axle was missing. It lay 50 metres away in the scrub, taken out by a termite mound. Thankfully that didn't happen to us. We continued to drive on to Mala, albeit at a more cautious speed.

At Mala, we brought with us the sorry business news from Nyirripi. Everyone began wailing and mourning. After a period of time, Patience Napaljarri River approached me and said: 'You've got to take me to Yuendumu for sorry.'

'No worries,' I replied. 'But Austin (Patience's petrol sniffer son) has to stay.' Patience said that was okay by her. But it wasn't okay by Austin.

'You can't leave me here like a fucking dog,' he yelled. 'This is not my country, I got no family here. If my mother's going, I'm going too.'

'No, Austin,' I explained. 'I can't take you back to Yuendumu. You have sniffed too many times. I don't want to see you get burnt like Toupe or die like those Pitjantjatjara sniffers.'

Austin picked up an axe.

'I'm not fucking staying here, no mother!' he yelled. He started circling me and the car. 'I'll smash your fucking car. I'll fucking smash you, you white cunt.'

Gibbo's rifle was still in the car and I didn't want Austin anywhere near it. I can negotiate withc axes but not guns. I reached into the car and pulled the bolt out of the rifle and stuffed it in my pocket. I then stuffed the ammo in my other pocket.

'I don't want to stay here, no fucking mother!' Austin yelled. I turned to face him.

'Okay Austin, what about Mt Theo? Will you stay at Mt Theo? Your mates Brando, Vasco and Lenin are at Mt Theo. Will you go there?' I asked.

'Yeah, I'll fucking go Mt Theo, not this place,' he replied.

Patience and Austin packed their swags and stuffed them into the car. I wasn't sure I had enough fuel to get to Mt Theo and back to Yuendumu, given the leaking fuel tank and the fact that Gibbo's estimate of the Mala-Nyirripi road was 100 kilometres out.

We drove to Mt Theo via Yumurrpa, which has a tank you could swim in that is fed by an underground river. Never one to pass up the chance of a swim in the desert, Yuri and I got out for a quick dip.

When we arrived at Mt Theo, Patience told of the sorry business news from Nyirripi. Everyone began wailing and mourning. Peggy said that her husband, Old Japangardi, had to go to Yuendumu for sorry. The problem was that Japangardi and Patience had 'no room' with each other.

Under traditional Warlpiri law, many people have avoidance relationships. The one that most Kardiya are aware of is mother-in-law and son-in-law avoidance. (Which makes complete sense to whitefellas: if you never have contact with your mother-in-law it's easy to avoid arguments.)

'No room' meant Japangardi and Patience had an avoidance relationship. Due to custom, they were not meant to speak to each other, make direct eye contact or even be in the same room together. Yet here they both wanted a lift in the same car to Yuendumu. They were definitely not meant to travel together. Peggy came up with the innovative solution of putting Patience in the cargo area of the station wagon, while Old Japangardi sat in the front passenger seat.

Fearing I would run out of fuel on the way back, I rang Yuendumu and explained I was at Mt Theo and would be taking the shortcut home through Jurlpungu. I asked Vesna to worry for me if I didn't make it back, explaining I was low on fuel. When I got back to the car, I told the Yapa about what I had said in my phone call.

'We can't go that way,' Patience said. 'I've got no room in that country.'

The shortcut ran through Banana Bore, country where Patience's deceased husband had been a traditional owner. Due to his recent death, Patience was not allowed to go anywhere near that country, out of respect. We had just solved one avoidance relationship issue and now we had another. Patience had an avoidance relationship with the road.

I rang back to Yuendumu explaining that we would not be travelling on the shortcut road and would have to come home the long way. And yes, I expected to run out of fuel.

By the time we crammed in everyone who needed to come back for sorry, we had eight people (not counting children or dogs) in my five-seater Subaru. To try and stretch the fuel out, I drove at 60 kilometres per hour in fifth gear. Halfway down the Tanami Road, the car was rattling apart and we felt every corrugation. Even the screws that held the cassette player to the dashboard were rattling loose.

A big goanna, a perentie, dashed across a creek bed in front of us. I pulled up and everyone piled out of the car to give chase. The goanna ran up an old ghost gum and everyone hurled sticks, rocks and boomerangs at it. Eventually Stephen Brown, Japangardi's youngest son, shot it with a rifle. The inside of the car was so cramped with humans that there was no room for the huge goanna, so it was tied to the roof rack. At times during the trip home its head or tail would bounce off and fling into an open window.

We arrived in Yuendumu without running out of fuel. Yuri asked me for his bandanna back but I couldn't find it anywhere in the car. 'I'll buy you another one,' I said.

'No, don't worry about it,' he replied. He seemed upset about it, but said nothing more. Maybe his girlfriend had given it to him or something.

Because of sorry business, the Saturday night disco was cancelled and I spent the night doing a uni essay on the computer. I printed out my first draft and then proceeded to check it. After I had perfected it, I was in the process of saving it from one disk to another backup one, when an error occurred and wiped both my original and backup copy of the essay. I had to drive into Alice the next day and spent most of Sunday afternoon in at the Todd Tavern with my laptop, drinking beer and retyping the essay from the first draft version I had printed out.

On Tuesday afternoon I got a phone call from Peggy saying that everyone had to come back from Mt Theo 'today' for sorry business. She said everyone had to come back from Mala too.

'It can't wait until tomorrow, we want to come to Yuendumu today,' Peggy ordered me.

After school, I borrowed the cage truck and took my baby daughter Deua with me. Driving out of Yuendumu, I invited Mia, one of the Catholic nuns, to come for the trip. Mia was a beautiful-looking Indian woman who worked as the school secretary. She had the Warlpiri skin name Nungarrayi and I was a Jangala. By 'skin name' custom we were an ideal match –'first choice' for each other. I used to tease her sometimes: 'Oh, Mia, we both missed out. I married Vesna and you married God. Well, maybe next lifetime.'

I wasn't the only man in Yuendumu who thought this nun was beautiful. Dr Howitt, the righteous School Principal, seemed to think she was all right too. As we drove to Mt Theo that evening, I tried to ask Mia about what it was like living a life committed to God. I asked because I was struggling to reconcile my Christian non-materialist ideals with my responsibilities as a father and breadwinner. But Mia was quiet and not that forthcoming. I was not aware that she might have been re-examining her own life then.

We arrived at Mt Theo just on dark and it was then that Peggy said we had to camp the night.

'But you said you wanted to go to Yuendumu today,' I protested. I was not prepared to spend the night at Mt Theo with no swag, one young breastfeeding baby and a good-looking nun.

'No, no,' Peggy countered. 'You gotta listen to me. We're not travelling night time. Too many spirits.'

I rang home to explain the situation to my wife. I asked her to tell Principal Howitt that his secretary and his liaison officer would be late for work the next morning.

Peggy and the old people at Mt Theo made up two beds for Mia and me. This probably meant that other people would have to sleep closer together and share blankets. Both Mia and I were impressed by their generosity. As the night wore on Deua became restless for her mother or, more importantly, breast milk. I walked around with her cradled in my arms, beneath a blanket of stars, singing 'Starry Starry Night', trying to sooth her back to sleep.

At midnight Vesna and Howitt turned up in the school Toyota.

'He said he was worried about our baby,' Vesna told me. 'But I told him you would do fine. He was insistent though and he seemed very taken aback that you had taken his secretary to Mt Theo.'

Mia and Howitt married three years later.

In the morning, all the Yapa piled into the cage truck. We headed off towards Mala, via Yumurrpa, where I insisted on stopping and having a swim. The Warlpiri saw me duck-diving in the milky brown tank water.

'What are you looking for, Yakajirri?'

'I'm searching for that Swiss doctor's bandanna. I think I lost it in here.'

'Can't you buy him another one?'

'No, this is a special one; I think his girlfriend gave it to him or something.'

I eventually found the bandanna and yelled out a triumphant 'Yahoo!' When I gave it back to Yuri he confirmed it had indeed been given to him by his girlfriend just before he came to Australia. She had since broken up with him and it was all he had left of her to hold onto.

Gender relations

There is continuing romantic tension between the sexes in Yuendumu. Children as young as five tease each other about boyfriends and girlfriends. They point at a girl and a boy and make the Warlpiri hand sign for husband and wife, which is a simple gesture of twice clapping your right palm across the back of your left hand. This teasing continues throughout childhood and adult life.

When delivering rations to Mala Outstation, my 65-year-old

'grandmother' Agie Napurrula used to tease me. Part of my job was to write down each person's requests for shopping. I had a standard list people would choose from and add to. One day, as I sat at the outstation with my clipboard and pen, reading out the items on the list (bread, flour, vegetables, milk), Napurrula began brushing her hand over her breast several times and called out, 'Yakajirri, I got no *lampurnu.*' Giggling, she continued, 'You gotta bring me two *lampurnu* next time.'

The Warlpiri translation for the English word 'milk' is *lampurnu. Lampurnu* is also the Warlpiri word for breasts. This double meaning was a constant source of humour. Of course, the two meanings make sense when you remember that in the time before whitefellas introduced cows into Australia, human breasts were the only source of milk.

This sort of teasing is a recreational pasttime in Yuendumu. In the Warlpiri skin system, there are several 'skin' groups who you are encouraged to tease, these being the groups who are your first-, second- and third-choice partners. For me these were the skin groups of Nungarrayi (ideal wives), Napanangka (female cross-cousins), and Napurrula (maternal grandmothers).

There are also skin groups which are taboo to flirt with and tease, people who you must always treat with proper respect: these are mothers, daughters, nieces and sisters. There is also the ultimate taboo group, mothers-in-law, who you are not even meant to talk to.

Old Nellie, who lived at Mt Theo, used to flirt with me. She was Peggy's mother; she was blind and crippled with old age. But none of that mattered, because she was a Nungarrayi.

'Yakajirri, Jangala,' she would call out, emphasising my skin name, which tagged me as her ideal choice for a boyfriend. 'You a lover boy. Come here, lover boy, Jangala.'

Everyone witnessing this scene would start giggling and tease us both.

'Go on, Yakajirri,' Peggy would call out. 'She's your right skin.'

Playing along, I would rush over and give Nellie a brief kiss on the cheek, creating instant applause and raucous laughter in the group.

Alongside this flirty energy sits gender separation. At disco, church and council meetings, males and females will congregate at opposite sides of a room. Rumours of love affairs go around constantly and, in a community where nearly everyone can track and recognise each individual's footprints, it is almost impossible for secret lovers to go unnoticed.

Warlpiri find the idea of platonic relationships between male and female almost ludicrous. If a man and a woman are seen alone together, it is assumed they must be lovers. This can mean that a lot of behaviour, which whitefellas might find innocent, is interpreted differently and charged with sexual suspicion. Nearly all Warlpiri girls from fourteen years of age upwards are either 'married' or promised to be married. The newcomer whitefella who innocently and charitably gives an unaccompanied Warlpiri woman a ride to town (or anywhere for that matter) leaves himself wide open for gossip. The gossip can lead to trouble; big trouble in a culture where jealousy frequently leads to violence.

'See that Kardiya,' an ancient *tjilpi* (elder) told me once. 'I been give him hiding when he was a young fella, he been chasing my wife.'

The incident that sparked the Coniston Massacre was a reaction to jealousy. In 1928, Fred Brookes, a whitefella dingo trapper who was camped east of Yuendumu, had two Warlpiri girls 'working' for him, doing washing and other duties. 'Bullfrog', husband of these women, was jealous. Maybe that whitefella was a lover boy, which is what the Warlpiri believed.

Warlpiri say Bullfrog was gripped by jealousy. He killed that dingo trapper. He chopped him up and hid his body in rabbit holes. With tension already existing on the frontier, the whitefella police posse sent out to arrest Bullfrog became a revenge party, shooting and killing Aboriginal people indiscriminately. Estimates of the death toll from the ensuing Coniston Massacre range from thirty into the hundreds. It has been called the last act of the frontier war.

'See that whitefella over there,' Ned said to me with disgust as we sat in the shade outside the Mining Company Store one day. He was pointing to a handsome bare-chested white man who was strutting, showing off his well buffed torso. 'He's done nothing for our community. All he's ever done is screw our women.'

These warnings were strong enough for me. There was no way I was going to get involved with a Warlpiri girl.

Five naked Nungarrayis

While I was away from Yuendumu on holidays, I met an impressive young white woman named Imelda who drove an old canvas covered ex-army Land Rover. She was living at a forest blockade in East Gippsland where she volunteered for the environment movement, in the role of 'police liaison'. An intelligent and articulate person who appeared to know a lot about the law, Imelda was able to skilfully negotiate in the emotionally charged atmosphere of an anti-woodchipping protest.

Following another round of violent conflict (on the previous day a logger had gone psycho and stormed the woodchip mill protest, armed with a chainsaw running at full revs), Imelda and I were sitting by a smouldering campfire in the forest mist. She asked me where I was from and I told her about Yuendumu.

'I know Yuendumu!' she exclaimed. 'My dad used to work up there.' It turned out that her father, who was now a judge, had been a lawyer for the Warlpiri during their land rights claims. We were both excited to find this connection.

'What was your father's skin name?' I asked.

Imelda could not articulate a name straight off, so I recited a list of the eight Warlpiri skin names for males.

'Japaljarri,' she enthused as I spoke out the familiar-sounding name. 'Yes, that's what they called him, Japaljarri.'

I smiled. She did not know what I had just worked out in my head; my brain, unlike hers, was infused with a Warlpiri way of viewing the world through the schema of kinship relations.

'What does that mean?' she asked.

I explained to her the Warlpiri skin system, and how the system determines who you call brother and sister, mother and uncle. 'Because your father is a Japaljarri, and you are his daughter, that makes you a Nungarrayi,' I told her.

I smiled again. She still had no idea what it all meant. I could feel the tension in the air, at least the Warlpiri part of me felt it. My heart beat just that little bit faster, my senses became slightly more heightened.

'And I am a Jangala,' I continued. For a moment I had to hold my breath and bite my tongue. I could not believe my luck, this impressive girl was my right skin!

Recovering my composure, I added diplomatically, 'That means you are my sister-in-law.'

Imelda was keen to visit Yuendumu and see the country where her father had played such an important role. Several months later, she phoned me to say that she and four of her girlfriends were going to come up for a trip. I advised them to contact the Central Land Council and apply for a permit to enter Aboriginal land.

'I hope I haven't put you in the shit,' Mick Jessop said. I had just walked into the Council building where `Mick worked as Council Clerk.

'We got a permit application from five women who stated they are coming to stay with you. I rang your house to confirm before approving the permit, and I spoke to your wife about it. I hope you weren't planning on having a good time on the sly.'

'No Mick, it isn't like that at all,' I replied.

Imelda drove up with her friends in the old Land Rover. When they arrived at our house, the local Warlpiri kids converged on our place eager to ply these new, weird-looking whitefellas (who wore dreadlocks and funny-looking clothes) with questions. Naturally the Yuendumu kids asked the visitors what their skin names were. Imelda answered that she was a Nungarrayi.

'What about them other girls?' the kids asked. 'Is that your sister?'

Being forest greenies, the idea of tribal sisterhood really appealed to these dreadlocked women from down south.

'Yes we're all sisters,' they answered.

Now they all had skin names, they were all Nungarrayis. Of course the rumours flew around Yuendumu and I was teased. 'Hey, Yakajirri!' the old men called out to me. 'We hear you've got a lot of new wives. A lot of Nungarrayi are camped at your place.'

'Yes,' I would answer, enjoying the joke and being the envy of the old tribal men who might only have one or two wives.

'Now I am even richer than Jungarrayi [the old man who had the most wives in Yuendumu],' I would boast. 'He has only four wives, but I have six!'

During their visit, the five white Nungarrayis drove out with Vesna, our daughter Deua and me to Mt Theo for a weekend camp. Old Agie Napurrula, my 'grandmother', came too. I had especially wanted Napurrula to accompany us on this trip, as I hoped to go visit Yumurrpa, a place for which she was the traditional owner.

Yumurrpa was a place that Imelda's father had described to her. He had told her about a cave in the Warlpiri lands which you could climb through to access an underground stream. He had worked helping the Warlpiri get that place back and he hoped Imelda would visit it.

After camping at Mt Theo and having the Nungarrayis entertain the sniffers with their greenie guitar songs of the southern forests, we headed out to Yumurrpa the next day. There, old Napurrula repaid the entertainment favour by telling the girls *Jukurrpa* stories of her country and singing creation songs.

There is a windmill and a large open water tank at Yumurrpa. It was really hot by the time we got there and the water tank looked as inviting as a regular swimming pool. I was happy to have a swim in my shorts, but the Nungarrayis, being liberated forest-protesting hippies, were happy to jump in naked.

For many years afterwards, Napurrula took great delight in reciting the tale of one Jangala swimming in the tank with the five naked Nungarrayis.

'And there was his real wife, *wiyarrpa* [poor thing],' she would say. 'Holding that little Nampijimpa [the skin name of our baby, Deua] and calling out over and over again, "Yakajirri, Jangala, come out of that *ngapa* [water]".'

Each time Napurrula told the story, she would laugh and the telling would become more animated. At one telling she even began singing the story. Usually the story would be told while sitting around the fire at Ned's house, to an audience that was nearly all Yapa, so most of the time it was told entirely in Warlpiri. Napurrula told that story so many times that I would not be surprised if at some stage in the future the story of the one Jangala and the five Nungarrayis is recorded in some anthropologists notebook and mistaken for real *Jukurrpa*.

Warlpiri Swiss Army knife

Even though my friendships with Aboriginal people in Yuendumu had grown strong through the program, I still had a longing to go deeper into the country. I wanted to really connect, to get to know it more deeply. Part of me still wanted to shed my skin like a snake and live with the nomads. Some part of me knew and hoped that they were still out there. Peggy and Hooker Creek said that nomads had visited Mt Theo that February.

'Really bush people out there, Myall (having never met whitefellas) bush fella,' Peggy enthused.

'*Junga mai? Pintubi*?' I asked. (Is that true? Are they from the Pintubi tribe? [the last group of people to walk in from the desert])

'*Lawa, lawa* (No, no). Might be Warlpiri fella, really bush one those ones,' she answered.

'Like *milipa mai*?' I asked, still sceptical. (Are they like the spirit beings who live near Mt Theo?)

'*Lawa. Yapa junga*. Really, really Yapa,' she responded.

Peggy and Hooker Creek had gone to Mt Theo on a mission that was destined to fail. It had rained very hard that February. Roads all around were flooded. The road to Alice Springs had been 'officially' closed, meaning that the police would fine you at the rate of $2000 per axle if they found you driving on the road. That's if they ever caught you.

The police had enough troubles of their own. The Aboriginal police aide's vehicle was bogged on the Papunya road. The whitefella police Toyota had got bogged on the Nyirripi road, while trying to rescue another bogged car. The last police Toyota they had they were keeping safe and not letting out of Yuendumu.

But no, Peggy and Hooker Creek and Shilling (Peggy's son-in-law) had to go to Mt Theo. They were worried about their dogs. But they didn't go in a four-wheel drive, they went in a Commodore. They called me from the Mt Theo pay phone to say they had made it and that they would be coming home on Wednesday.

By Friday they still hadn't returned. The rain hadn't stopped and we were worried, but the roads were all too muddy to launch a rescue mission. All we would achieve would be more bogged vehicles.

On the Friday night I met with the police and the Council Clerk to discuss getting a plane to do an aerial search. We intended to scour the roads from Yuendumu to Mt Theo, to locate the missing party and air-drop food and first-aid supplies. The plane was due to arrive in Yuendumu at nine o'clock the following morning.

At eight o'clock on Saturday morning I was up and had already begun to organise the air-drop supply package. Just to be sure, I decided to check Peggy's humpy at North Camp before meeting up with the police. She was sitting outside her humpy by the fire, still weary from sleep.

'We been walk a long way, Jangala,' Peggy told me. 'We been walking three days. Even that old man Japangardi and that little girl Rosina. We been walking, walking, walking.

'That car been bog down at Wampana (a swamp 70 kilometres out of Yuendumu). And we been walking from there. We been find 'em flour at Banana Bore (an outstation 40 kilometres out of Yuendumu) and made damper. We got bush tucker too, *manakitji* (bush grapes) and *yuparli* (bush banana).

'We been get really tired. And that little girl, Rosina, she been talk to us: "Come on *ja ja* (grandmother), come on *ta ta ta* (grandfather)." And we been walking right up to Wakurlpa (an outstation twenty kilometres north of Yuendumu). At Wakurlpa, Rex Granites pick us up.'

Rosina was six years old.

Peggy had arrived back in Yuendumu at about ten o'clock on Friday night. Rex had had a hunch to head out as far as he could without getting bogged to look for them. I had to rush around to the police station to cancel the plane.

After they had rested, Peggy and Hooker Creek told me the story. They had seen evidence of bush people visiting Mt Theo. There were strange human foot prints, food was missing and Hooker Creek even thought he saw some naked brown figures in the distance.

My yearning to connect was still there. I wanted to hang out in the bush with people who knew the old bush ways. I was still working at the school at this stage and the term break was coming up soon. There was no other place I wanted to go and visit so I decided to holiday at Mt Theo. Vesna couldn't understand it, so I went alone.

Johnny Hooker Creek hunting at Mt Theo 1994

I asked Peggy and Old Japangardi to only speak to me in Warlpiri while I was out there. I wanted to immerse myself in a Warlpiri world. I was going to spend two weeks living at Mt Theo.

I had been reading Neil Murray's book, *Sing for Me, Countryman*, where he had described learning how to make a spear thrower. He had to make it the traditional way, chewing raw kangaroo sinew in his mouth until he dry-retched and the sinew was soft enough to be used as string. The string was used to bind the spear hook onto the end of the spear thrower. As the sinew dried it would shrink, adding to the strength of the binding. I wanted to be taught how to make a spear thrower in the traditional way, too.

Neil Murray's stories and songs have been a great inspiration for me. Long before I visited Yuendumu, my friend Dave and I would be hooning through the streets of Melbourne in my grandfather's 1959 Vanguard, with Warumpi Band music blasting out of the stereo. We thought we were so cool, as most of our urban friends had not even heard of the Warumpi Band. The songs Neil and the other Warumpi members had written lifted us out of our shallow urban existence and inspired us with images of life in a 'desert paradise', filled with adventure, excitement and meaning. A place where you could get by 'living on the breadline', a place ideally suited to young men like us who had 'restless yearning hearts'.*

I had seen spear throwers before and I knew that they combined several bush technologies. You might say Stone Age technologies, but they are technologies that today very few people have the skills to create. Warlpiri call spear throwers *pikirri*.

The basic part of the *pikirri* is made of ironwood that is carved to make a shallow dish about 50 centimetres long and ten centimetres wide in the middle. The wood is carved very carefully so the thickness of the dish is between three and five millimetres all over. The edges of the dish are honed sharp. One end of the dish narrows to a point about one centimetre wide. The spear hook is secured with kangaroo sinew to this point. The hook is made from a small straight pointed stick about three centimetres long and four millimetres thick. It is positioned so that it overhangs the dish forming a hook at the end. This is the end where the butt of

---

* 'desert paradise' words from the Warumpi Band song 'Mulga and Spinifex Plain'; 'living on the breadline' words from the Warumpi Band song 'Breadline'; 'restless yearning heart' words from the Neil Murray song 'He Was Born'.

the spear shaft (which has a small hole for the hook) connects. The other end of the *pikirri* is the handle which is made out of spinifex resin. The resin is extracted out of bundles of spinifex grass by using the heat from a fire; while it is warm it is malleable. It is moulded to create a ball-like shape at the end of the *pikirri*, which hardens when cooled.

Old Japangardi took Hooker Creek, some of the teenage sniffers and me on an expedition to find just the right ironwood tree. A stand of ironwood was located far from any track, 30 kilometres from Mt Theo. After driving to this stand, we walked on foot while Japangardi inspected each tree to find the right one to make a *pikirri* out of. He cut out one side of the tree's trunk with his axe, a half-cylinder of wood about 70 centimetres long, leaving the rest of the tree still standing and able to live.

We then had to find a kangaroo which involved a further expedition.

'*Marlu, marlu, marlu. Yinya kakarrara* (Kangaroo, kangaroo, kangaroo. Over there to the east).'

The kangaroo cooking

The collective voices of teenagers shrilled as we drove slowly through the countryside. I pulled the Toyota to a stop while Hooker Creek got out, then crouching down, he stalked the kangaroo. Everyone in the Toyota was still and silent.

Hooker Creek made a long soft whistle through his teeth while he steadied the rifle on his shoulder. The kangaroo rose from its grazing and cocked its ears, holding itself still, listening for the whistle. Hooker Creek whistled again. The raised head of the kangaroo was now in his sights.

Everyone was happy as we sat around the fire that night, feasting on *marlu*. Old Japangardi made sure I got the tendons out of the hind leg of the kangaroo before it was cooked. These were to be chewed up to make the sinew string for my *pikirri*. He made sure I chewed the sinew too.

It took most of the next two days to carve the wood. Old Japangardi instructed me by taking turns at working the adze and tomahawk. He began a task and then it was my turn. As we worked, he sang traditional songs elders had taught him in his hunter-gatherer youth, in the days when *pikirris* were not artefacts but essential tools for survival. The *pikirri* had other uses apart from being an efficient spear launcher. Its dish could be used to winnow seed or collect water. Its hard sharp edges could be used to create fire when sawed against tinder softwood like *yinirnti* (bean tree) to create friction.

But Old Japangardi had not finished the *pikirri* yet. He took me for another walk. We walked into the hills of Mt Theo to a quartz midden. There were the remnants of quartz shaped by his ancestors making stone axes thousands of years ago. Japangardi struck one stone against another to break off a small flint about as wide as my thumb. It was razor sharp. This stone knife was fitted into the resin handle of the *pikirri*.

'You use him to cut that *marlu*, to get his guts out after you spear him,' Japangardi explained.

He had just made me the Warlpiri version of the Swiss Army knife. A true multi tool: spear launcher, winnow dish, water carrier, hunting knife and fire lighter.

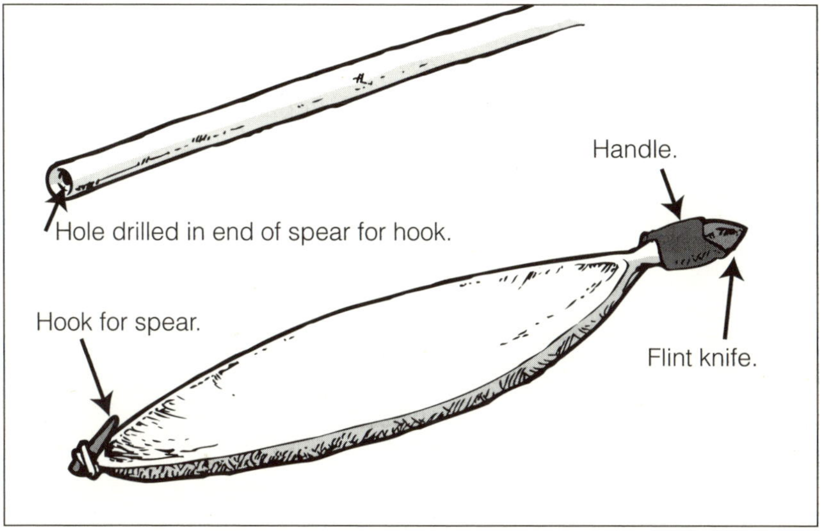

5: We'll Fund You, but You'll Starve

As my third year in Yuendumu drew to a close, our funding situation looked better than it ever had. During the year we borrowed everything except food to run the program. Anne Mosey, a white woman I had met when she was living in a humpy in Yuendumu, now lived in Alice Springs and worked for the Drug and Alcohol Services Association (DASA).With Anne's support, DASA provided some funding for food during the year.

Previously Anne had been the coordinator of the Yuendumu Women's Centre when night patrol started. She taught me a great lesson about Aboriginal self-determination and the role of whitefellas.

'I'll let you in on a secret, Yakajirri,' she told me. 'When the women suggested starting a night patrol, I thought it was a silly idea. I thought: yes, this will last about five minutes. But because I was employed to organise what the women asked for, I felt it was important to support the project.'

The night patrol became hugely successful at dealing with grog issues in the community and developed into a model that was copied throughout Australia. Anne and those women travelled everywhere as night patrol consultants. None of that would have happened if Anne had let her cynicism cloud her work.

The DASA money ran out. Despite this, the Mt Theo Program

kept going and consequently ran up a huge food bill at the store. Lindsay Japangardi Williams and I then spent months holding fundraising barbecues at the disco to repay the debt.

But now the program was going to be properly funded. Peter Toyne, the person who had organised the original 'petrol sniffer outstation' meeting that had started the program, told us his grant application had been successful. (Peter had helped set up the Tanami Network, an Aboriginal-owned videoconferencing network, and used this as the auspicing organisation to apply for the funds.)

Commonwealth Health agreed to give Mt Theo 'pilot' funding for one year. There was money for two part-time wages, to lease vehicles and for administration – but there was no money for food. It was a critical shortcoming. How were we going to feed the kids?

We had several meetings with Commonwealth Health who said they couldn't provide money for food or alter the budget. I felt so frustrated. What was the point of providing the grant if we could not feed the sniffers we took to Mt Theo? We simply could not run the program without food. Vehicles could be borrowed and people could work voluntarily, but food was our primary need.

Late in November, we had a breakthrough when Paul Ashe from the Office of Aboriginal Development organised a last minute meeting with Territory Health. He had managed to embarrass the Northern Territory government into providing us with funding for food. Paul convinced the local manager of Territory Health that, since the Commonwealth was supporting Mt Theo, the Territory would look bad if it didn't support the program as well.

He rang me at lunchtime one Friday and suggested that we get to town as soon as possible to meet with Territory Health. He said the local manager, who he had just spoken with, was going away on holidays that afternoon and wouldn't be back until the New Year. Now was our only chance.

Paul and many other people like him in Alice Springs (Anne Mosey, Blair McFarland, Craig San Roque, Kenny Lechlietner and Bob Durnam) have been a great help to the program. They were wise to the ways of government and how to hunt for funds which I knew nothing about. They did many behind the scenes manoeuvres to get support for Mt Theo.

Ned and I jumped in my Subaru and hooned to Alice Springs. We made it to the four o'clock meeting and successfully negotiated a grant for food money. It was only after we had left the meeting that we realised we did not have a spare tyre with us. It is crazy to travel those roads without a spare. Punctures are so common that most people routinely carry two spare tyres.

'Don't think about it, Yakajirri,' Ned warned. 'If you don't think about it you won't get another flat.'

We headed back to Yuendumu with our fingers crossed.

Hooker Creek's Toyota

The week after Ned and I had successfully resolved the issues around food funding, various Yapa came excitedly to tell me some more good news: 'Yakajirri, we've got GMAAAC money for Mt Theo Program …'

GMAAAC stands for the Granites Mine Affected Area Aboriginal Corporation. It was set up to provide mining royalties for the benefit of the community. Corporation meetings where funds are distributed are usually held twice a year. Yapa had told me they were going to ask for money for the program at the upcoming GMAAAC meeting. They instructed me to write a list of things we needed to take to the meeting. I wrote down things like funds for food, to employ a teacher and for an emergency vehicle and fuel.

The lack of an emergency vehicle at Mt Theo often played on my mind. What if a kid got bitten by a snake? Without a vehicle stationed at Mt Theo, an ambulance would have to be dispatched from Yuendumu, meaning a four-hour return trip in an emergency before the kid would reach the nearest available medical help at Yuendumu Clinic. An emergency vehicle based at Mt Theo would halve this time.

Yapa reckoned the situation was acceptable. Hadn't Hooker Creek and his ancestors all lived at Mt Theo in the past without an emergency vehicle? The hunter-gatherer past was not so long ago. Pintubi out west were still nomadic, living totally independently of whitefellas. All the program was doing was facilitating a return to country, to a traditional Warlpiri homeland.

'Don't worry, Yakajirri,' Yapa would tell me. 'Mt Theo is our home.'

Was my concern about an emergency vehicle simply a symptom of my own dependence on the security crutches of white culture? Didn't Yapa know best in their own country, with their own kids? Isn't that what self-determination was all about? Still, I didn't feel comfortable.

'Yakajirri, we've got GMAAAC money for Mt Theo Program,' the conversation continued. 'And Peggy's gone to town to get a vehicle for Mt Theo.'

The next day Peggy came over to visit me, proudly driving a four-wheel drive single cab Hilux ute. A single cab ute? How useless is that as an emergency vehicle at an outstation? It can only legally carry three passengers! At least it was a diesel; we all agreed that only diesel cars, not petrol vehicles, should stay at Mt Theo.

Mt Theo was closed at that stage. We had run out of funding for food and we were still holding barbecues outside the disco to raise funds to repay the last food bill at the store. Mt Theo was closed but the controversy had just opened. Within three days of the ute arriving in Yuendumu, various people involved with the program came to me to complain: 'Such and such is using that ute in the wrong way,' one person said.

'That's a program vehicle, but one family is using it all the time. What about my family? I help sniffers too,' argued another.

'That Mt Theo ute is being used to run grog … I should be boss for that ute, not that other person,' complained a third one.

I tried to address the situation by calling up the GMAAAC office in Alice Springs and asking them what the grant conditions were for the vehicle. I was told there were no grant conditions or rules governing use of the vehicle.

'The vehicle is threatening the cohesion of our program,' I pleaded. 'Everyone's arguing about it. People who used to work together are fighting, making accusations against each other and it is creating jealousies. Surely you can't just give us a vehicle without rules?'

'Look mate, we're about Aboriginal empowerment,' the whitefella on the end of the phone told me. 'That's what GMAAAC is about, letting the Aboriginal people decide.'

I hung up. Meanwhile the accusations, jealousies and tensions grew stronger in the community. People talked with me and then I tried to talk with Peggy about people's concerns. That didn't help at all.

A day later two whitefella friends of mine approached me with her complaints: 'Peggy's really upset with you,' they warned. 'She told us that Yakajirri was getting jealous for that vehicle.'

One of these blokes, Warwick Hummerston, who worked at Council, tried to help by brokering a meeting between all the various parties involved with Mt Theo. Some of the Council members along with Peggy, Ned and I sat down and established some vehicle rules to put a stop to the arguments. We came up with a set of rules that people seemed happy with and which looked good on paper. But within hours the rules were being broken. Not because people were unprincipled, but because the rules were overridden by a higher law.

The ancient Warlpiri obligation to fulfil requests made by

certain kin overrode any rule that could be made in the contemporary whitefella ceremony called a meeting. If a family member asked to use the Hilux, even though it might be for a purpose outside the rules, it was sometimes culturally impossible for a Warlpiri to deny that request.

Rules are always getting written and rewritten at whitefella meetings. Kinship obligations are enduring and are the unchanging Warlpiri law from the *Jukurrpa*. It was a great relief to me when the Hilux stopped working completely two weeks later. Once it was no longer a going concern, I hoped that the jealousy and arguments that threatened to tear our program apart would also stop. I remembered reading in my university research into petrol sniffing, how so many initially successful outstation programs had collapsed due to jealousy and arguments over vehicles. Now I had witnessed it firsthand.

Things started to look up for the program in the new year, my fourth year in Yuendumu. For the first time ever we had grants from the Commonwealth and Northern Territory governments. We had even found a person to coordinate the program, Liam Campbell.

Liam had been studying an outdoor education degree in Victoria and had a long history of relationship with Yuendumu. Previously he had spent a year running the youth program. He was a young whitefella with uni student dreadlocks who had grown up in a Christian community of mud brick churches on the outskirts of Melbourne. As a teenager, Liam had studied the Warlpiri language at school before he left home on an overloaded motorcycle to make a pilgrimage to the desert.

He seemed like the perfect candidate for the job. He even had an 'in' with the Mt Theo families. Two years earlier Liam had swapped his Toyota with Hooker Creek for a Subaru which established a relationship of obligation and mutual trust between them. Now they could humbug each other for anything.

I had only been back in Yuendumu a day or two when the complaints started: 'Yakajirri, why are Peggy and Shilling (Peggy's son-in-law) getting paid for working at Mt Theo when there are no sniffers out there?'

'What?' I asked.

'Peggy and Shilling got those two government wages for Mt Theo.'

I learnt that while I was away on Christmas holidays, an office worker in the Tanami Network (the organisation that was administering the government grants for us) had begun spending the Mt Theo grant by paying wages to Peggy and Shilling for looking after sniffers at Mt Theo. Mt Theo wasn't even open. No one was living there. Peggy and Shilling were living quietly at North Camp in Yuendumu and playing cards.

Perhaps the office worker shared the attitude of administration that sometimes pervades funded organisations: we've got this grant, we better spend it.

The administrator of the Tanami Network had gone away on a month's holidays so I couldn't discuss with him how to address the situation. Meanwhile, infighting and jealousy among Yapa over the grant was growing to a level similar to the one before the Hilux had broken down.

Peggy and Shilling quite logically felt they had already earned the wages on account of all the volunteer work they had done for the program over the years. They had worked for Mt Theo in the past and they intended to work for Mt Theo in the future. To them it was pure semantics, that they were not working now during the time when they were receiving the wages.

However, the problem was that many other people had also done volunteer work for the program over the years. These people felt an equal level of entitlement to claim wages, now that the government money had arrived and was being handed out, hence the jealousy.

'Why should Peggy and Shilling get paid when we've done work too?' they argued.

Meanwhile poor Liam, who had deferred his university studies to work for the program, was told his wage had been given away. It was falling apart again.

Liam Campbell

The jealousy meant Yapa were no longer working together and old rivalries re-emerged that I had hoped had died with the Hilux. It would take another four months before Mt Theo would open again. But before then we had to deal with Hooker Creek.

'No more sniffers at that Mt Theo,' Hooker Creek told me, effectively banishing the program from operating there. 'They been do wrong thing by me, Yakajirri. I'm the boss for that country and I'm the traditional owner. They been do wrong thing for me with that Hilux. With that GMAAAC money and with that government wages. Well, I say *no more.* Are you with me? (Meaning: do you understand how I feel?). I been say *no more.* No more sniffers at Mt Theo.

'I'm gonna live there quiet by myself. They all been do wrong thing by me, that program mob,' he declared.

Oh hell. We finally got the government money and the whole thing breaks down due to jealously. Hooker Creek, the senior traditional owner, had just closed the program down. If ever there was an example that reinforced all those hippy, Christian and Buddhist theories of mine that money and greed screw things up, this was it.

I wanted to cry. I felt this big knot in my stomach. I was so angry. Why didn't anyone else get it? How could the administrator start paying wages without thinking of the consequences? How could the GMAAAC people give out money for Toyotas with no rules? Didn't anyone know anything? If there was a formula on how to stuff up an anti-petrol sniffing program, these people were following it to the letter.

Kids were going to die. They were dying all over the desert – in South Australia, Western Australia, the Top End and Papunya (one of our closest neighbouring communities). Now they were going to die in Yuendumu too because of jealousy and greed brought about by dumb stupid whitefella things like money and Toyotas. There had to be a way to fix this. Thankfully Hooker Creek provided it.

'Is there anything we can do?' I begged.' Anything that would make you change your mind?'

'No,' he answered. 'They been do wrong thing by me.'

'Please, Hooker Creek, I'm your friend. Please, I'm begging you now. If we don't open Mt Theo, I'm really worried for those sniffers. I'm really worried some of them are going to die,' I pleaded.

'You could get me that Toyota,' he said.

The Toyota he had in mind was the Hilux. It was broken beyond repair but we managed to get some sort of a refund from the car dealer who'd sold it to Peggy. The money was combined with the next lot of GMAAAC funds which were distributed in April.

After the GMAAAC meeting, Liam drove Hooker Creek into Alice Springs to buy a Toyota Troop Carrier. As agreed to by the Yapa on the GMAAAC committee, the Toyota was put in Hooker Creek's name. Hooker Creek was happy and Mt Theo was going to open again.

Visit to a soakage

The first weekend after the Toyota was bought, Shilling and Hooker Creek's brother, Old Japangardi (Peggy's husband) borrowed it to visit Mt Theo. Shilling was Japangardi's son-in-law; he was married to Japangardi's daughter Jean. Liam and I went along too, with the intention of checking out the bore and telephone at Mt Theo. We left on Friday at sundown. The Toyota was mightily packed with swags, dogs and drums of flour as well as family members. Travelling in it became pretty uncomfortable, so Liam and I took turns to stand on the running boards and hold onto the side of the car, where we could feel the fresh air on our faces. Shilling drove carefully (after we yelled at him to slow down) while we wound our way through the desert night on the dusty bumpy road to Mt Theo.

Solar-powered phone box at Mt Theo

Mt Theo checked out well the following morning. The bore was good and not only was the public pay phone working but it was giving free phone calls.

Liam, Shilling, Jean, Japangardi and I sat around

the breakfast fire, drinking tea and brainstorming ideas for the program.

'We should have more things for those young people to do,' Jean advocated, 'more activities.'

Various ideas were suggested: having a pool table; making use of Liam's skills and introducing young people to challenges like rock climbing and abseiling (thereby encouraging young people to face danger in a positive way, rather than flirting with death through sniffing); and organising bushwalks such as a major hike back to Yuendumu as a way of finishing the program.

'We should visit more country, teach them more *Jukurrpa*,' said Shilling. 'And that old man [Japangardi] can teach them a lot of things like making spear and boomerang.'

We were all getting excited. It was a fantastic feeling, making plans for the future. One point we all strongly agreed upon was that the program at Mt Theo would be a Yapa-run program. Liam could teach some things he knew and work to provide support, but Yapa were to be boss for the program. Part of the preparation for the program meant planning trips and reconnaissance, a task we all looked forward to.

Shilling wanted to visit Mt Patricia, a small mountain twenty kilometres to the south-east of Mt Theo. There was no road going there, only a faint hunting trail that petered out after five kilometres. Old Japangardi was our guide.

It was easy to scrub bash in the general direction of Mt Patricia, but once we got there it was Old Japangardi who guided us to the erosion gully in the gravelled hillside that contained the soakage, a place where groundwater was close to the surface. The soak was hidden in a gully half a metre deep that was similar to hundreds of other cracks and ruts in the ground – nothing to distinguish it at first glance, just another shallow rut in the hill. But Japangardi knew this country. As a child, before his family ever knew white people, he grew up in an era when the knowledge of watering places was as important as life itself. Watering places are always sacred sites, with stories from the *Jukurrpa* containing information about their location and giving instruction on how to access the water and to care for its source.

Jukurrpa was like a map and a guidebook for Old Japangardi. It contained the essential information that people needed to know if they were to survive in the desert: where to find food and water, the particulars of each site and what time of year it would have water, all recorded in accurate detail.

One time, after my family had moved away from Yuendumu, I could see how these desert values had imprinted themselves on my own daughter. She had only just turned six and we were camping out in the forests of the Great Dividing Range. In the morning we went to gather water from a nearby river where it cascaded over the escarpment. It looked beautiful in the sunrise.

'Daddy, is this a Dreaming place?' my little girl asked me.

For all of her life growing up in the desert, every water place she had ever visited was sacred. The second thing she said to me was: 'Have we asked the old people if we can come here?' She knew that under Aboriginal law, one should always seek permission from the traditional owners before visiting a sacred site.

Japangardi looked at the gully and instructed us three young fellows to dig. Taking turns, two whitefellas (Liam and I) and one blackfella (Shilling) dug with crow bar, shovel and billycan. We found the water from Mt Patricia, water Japangardi had not drunk for many years.

'This place belong Japaljarri *Jukurrpa*,' he said.

Japaljarri was Japangardi's grandson. He instructed us to fill an empty Coke bottle with the oxidised water from this place and take it back to Yuendumu to give to his grandson so he could drink water from his own country.

On the way back from that soakage we got three flat tyres. Maybe we had got one or two flats on the way to Mt Patricia, it's hard to remember. But by the time we reached Mt Theo we had three flat tyres. We had run out of spares and were driving on the rim of a wheel.

'No worries,' Shilling reassured Liam and me. 'Yapa do this all the time.'

I had seen Yapa 'do this all the time'. On one occasion, Ned turned up at my place in a borrowed car he had driven from Alice Springs. It was riding on the rims of two flat tyres. As a result of the vibrations of bare metal rims on the corrugated road, nearly every nut and bolt in the car had vibrated loose. Not even the doors would open.

I called Frank at the Yuendumu Mining Company from the Mt Theo phone box to ask him for help. We were in luck. An exploration team was heading out past Mt Theo the following day and could drop off some spare tyres for us.

Liam and I quickly realised we had a rare opportunity. We were bored and stranded at Mt Theo with a public phone that gave unlimited free phone calls. It was time to catch up with all our far-flung friends. After ringing as many people in Australia as we could, Liam suggested calling his father in America. We wondered if the phone box would do international calls. It did. Liam had a great chat to his dad but afterwards, we were still bored and our spare tyres hadn't arrived.

'Well, we've got the country code for America,' said one of us.' Why don't we just call random numbers over there and see who we get?'

'G'day mate, we're calling from Australia,' we announced to a surprised American on the other end of the line. 'Just thought we'd ring up and say hello.'

It didn't take long after the reconnaissance trip to get Mt Theo up and running properly. Peggy and her family moved back and started to look after sniffers. Liam had bought a pool table that we wanted to deliver to Mt Theo, and Hooker Creek, the

Pool table at Mt Theo

proud owner of the new 'Mt Theo Toyota', had taken the Toyota as far away from Mt Theo as he could on a trip to visit his family at Wave Hill (about 700 kilometres south of Darwin) and Lajamanu.

Late on a drizzly May afternoon, Liam and I borrowed the Council's tipper truck to take the pool table to Mt Theo. Because we were dependent on borrowing vehicles to run the program, most of our trips to Mt Theo had to be conducted late in the afternoon or on weekends when the organisations that owned the vehicles didn't need them. We had packed the truck up with rations and were loading on the pool table, about to head out of Yuendumu when we got the message: 'Yakajirri, Liam, you gotta help Hooker Creek. His Toyota is broken down up near Mt Doreen.'

'What's wrong with it?' we asked.

'Dunno, might be fuel problem or something.'

Liam and I hastily put together a vehicle recovery kit: spare battery, jerry can of diesel, motor oil, jumper leads, tow rope and a jerry can of water. As we drove west on the Tanami Road, other Warlpiri who were travelling back from Lajamanu waved us down: 'Hooker Creek is waiting for you. He's broken down back there, just past Mt Doreen.'

Then along came another car. This one had Hooker Creek and his wife Nampijimpa travelling as passengers. Hooker Creek was really drunk.

'Yakajirri and Japanangka,' he slurred affectionately, calling us by our Warlpiri names as he patted our shoulders. 'My boys, my workers. You two work for me, hey. You gotta do right thing for me. You gotta go get my Toyota,' he said.

Another 40 kilometres on, there on the side of the road was Hooker Creek's Toyota. It was tilted at an angle where it had been sloppily parked in the ditch of a culvert drain. The once straight bull bar was a perfect 'v' shape and a shattered glass silhouette of Nampijimpa's face was imprinted in the windshield on the passenger side. They must have hit something pretty hard.

We checked the motor. The oil was fine but the radiator was empty. As we poured new water into the radiator, a puddle formed directly below it on the ground.

'Looks like the radiator's stuffed,' Liam said.

A broken-down car by the side of the road in the desert is considered fair game by all and sundry. Warlpiri tell stories of people getting a flat tyre and leaving the car to go and fetch a spare, only to return to find their whole car has been stripped. It can happen in a matter of hours. Contrary to racist belief, it's not just Aboriginal folk who steal parts. Oxyacetylene cuts in the chassis with whole gearboxes removed from vehicles, give an indication of the fast work of enterprising Alice Springs whitefellas who prey on the broken-down cars of the Tanami. Sometimes Warlpiri will become so enraged by this practice that if their car breaks down, they will set fire to it themselves as an act of subversion and revenge on the car parts raiders.

'They're not going to steal my parts!' they say as they leave their burning vehicle.

We were not ready to burn Hooker Creek's car, so we towed it off the road and hid it behind a stand of mulga scrub to prevent anyone from fleecing parts off it, and continued to Mt Theo. Soon afterwards, the heavens opened and the rain began to pour down. Desert rain is always big rain. Roads turn into rivers and creeks swell in a matter of hours. The falling rain slowed us down as the dusty road turned to mush. Wheels spun and the truck fishtailed while we fed in the revs to prevent being bogged in muddy corners of the snaking Mt Theo road. After unloading the pool table to the collective cheers of the young people, we shared supper with Peggy and her husband Japangardi, before heading back for more mud-sliding adventures on the way home.

By the time we reached Mt Doreen and the hidden Toyota, it was eleven o'clock. We flirted with the idea of putting the Toyota on the back of the truck, if we could find a loading ramp. But after measuring the dimensions with cubits and hand spans, we decided it wouldn't fit.

'Guess we'll have to tow it back,' one of us said.

Eighty kilometres on a muddy road, with flooded creeks, at night, towing a Toyota – what a mission! It wasn't safe for us to travel any faster than 30 kilometres an hour. The big brown bullocks that wander the road and can only be seen by the red shine of their eyes, added to our challenge. No good hitting one of them. And no good using the brakes to stop hitting one, as you risk being hit up the rear end by the Toyota: the Toyota whose windscreen is level with the back tray of the truck, the perfect height to decapitate whichever of us was brave (or stupid) enough to have volunteered to steer it. No good swerving to miss one of those bullocks either, as that would certainly cause the truck to fishtail in the mud and possibly roll, not to mention the effect it might have on the trailing Toyota that was still attached by rope to the rear of the truck.

It was a very long trip. Every time we crossed one of the creeks, the slowing down and acceleration caused the tow rope to snap. The ten-metre rope broke so many times during the night that it was progressively reduced to a two-metre rope by the time we reached Yuendumu. To add to it all, Liam was sick and got worse as the night wore on, and on several occasions we had to pull the truck over so he could throw up.

What are we going to do with this car? I thought. If those other Yapa saw it back in Yuendumu, if they saw how a drunken Hooker Creek has wrecked the 'Mt Theo Toyota', the trouble would start again. All the fighting, arguments, jealousy and accusations of vehicle misuse would start up all over again. We had only just settled the last fight. If we had another fight, who knows which traditional owner would decide to close down Mt Theo until they got a Toyota payoff? Or what if Peggy got sick of all the trouble and walked away and gave up? Somehow we had to stop people from seeing the smashed-up Toyota.

Liam and I vowed to keep this story quiet. We talked about towing the Toyota all the way to Alice Springs, under the cover of night. We couldn't risk the alternative. But driving at 30 kilometres an hour to Alice Springs was at least a ten-hour journey and we had to give the truck back to the Council in the morning. We simply didn't have enough time.

We arrived at Yuendumu at four-thirty in the morning and hid the Toyota behind my house in the backyard. We covered the damaged front end with a tarpaulin. We were both exhausted. To wind down after our big adventure, I climbed up on the roof of my house to sip a cup of tea and watch the sunrise. It was finally five o'clock, the end of the night. I had a meeting to attend in Alice Springs at nine o'clock. My day was only just beginning.

A week later we snuck the Toyota into town on the back of a truck, 'to get mechanical repairs'. When I got back from Alice a few days later, Liam and I sat down for a long cup of tea.

'There's got to be a better way,' we agreed. 'We've got to find a better way.'

Whitefella obligations

How does 'Aboriginal Empowerment' work? If you (the government/whitefellas) truly give Aboriginal people control over a resource, why would you expect them to manage it like whitefellas? Why would you expect them to deny relationships and obligations set down by *Jukurrpa* law? Any whitefella who has joined a tribe and gone through Aboriginal law will tell you of the huge conflict of obligations that weigh on a person who tries to live truly according to both whitefella and Warlpiri values of resource management.

How do we have a program vehicle that is not subject to humbug? How can we create a cultural obligation to make that vehicle do a 'job' and stick to 'rules' so that the vehicle is always available for 'work' purposes, instead of being lent to some relative, who can't be denied, who then takes it to Lajamanu? How do we keep an emergency vehicle at Mt Theo which Aboriginal people 'control', but can't lend out?

There are probably a few answers to these questions. We didn't come up with the definitive answer, but Liam and I decided to work within the Warlpiri system. We created obligations of our own.

As a whitefella with diplomatic immunity from the kinship obligation system who owns his own car, I am in a special position. In the Warlpiri obligation network, I am neutral. I haven't been through the law and no one can tell me what to do with my car. Theoretically, I can refuse all requests to borrow my car, which is something that is very hard, and in many cases impossible, for Warlpiri to do; to refuse requests for a resource they 'own'. But as a whitefella, I'm not bound by humbug.

So I could lend my car to Hooker Creek to keep at Mt Theo and give him strict instructions: 'This is my car and I want it to only sit at Mt Theo. I want only you and Shilling to be the drivers. I don't want this car to go to any other place or to be lent to anyone else. It is only for work at Mt Theo with sniffers.'

What happens when Hooker Creek who is the driver or manager of that car, is humbugged by some relative who he is obliged to? Well, Hooker Creek might be obliged to the humbug, but the car is not. The car belongs to a whitefella. So Hooker Creek can say: 'No, sorry, I can't lend out this car, I'm not the owner. It's owned by a whitefella who's cheeky and has put down strong rules. I'm only the driver.'

He can explain that, because I (Yakajirri) am a cheeky whitefella, I might just call the police if someone else takes off with my car! I'm the whitefella 'owner' with humbug immunity so under Warlpiri law Hooker Creek is absolved from his obligations to lend the car to kin.

Owners and managers

Under Warlpiri law, in any *Jukurrpa* story and at any ceremony or sacred site, there are two separate groups of people. They are called *kirda* and *kurdungurlu*. *Kirda* are referred to as the owners of a ceremony. They are the living embodiment of the *Jukurrpa* itself. For example, in a ceremony about an emu, the *kirda* who are the *Jukurrpa* owners will dress up as the emu and re-enact the role of the emu in the ceremony.

On the other hand, *kurdungurlu* are referred to as the 'managers' of the ceremony. Their role is to supervise, coach and encourage the *kirda* as they perform the ceremony, making sure all traditions are properly adhered to. Warlpiri sometimes refer to *kurdungurlu* as the 'policeman' for the ceremony; they are keepers of the law.

So with my private car, I am *kirda*, the owner, and Hooker Creek becomes *kurdungurlu*, the manager of the vehicle.

Liam and I both bought Toyotas with our own money, for the express purpose of using them for the program. Liam bought a Hilux that he used as his 'work' car for taking rations and people to and from Mt Theo. I bought a short wheel base Land Cruiser that was permanently loaned to Hooker Creek and stationed at Mt Theo as the emergency vehicle.

This strategy solved the vehicle problem. The program had work vehicles, which Yapa and Kardiya used but which were outside the humbug system. This strategy also strengthened the bond Liam and I (as two whitefellas) had with the Mt Theo families. Through lending our cars to people, using them to give people lifts, and do favours such as fetching firewood and sharing hunting trips, both Liam and I became deeply entwined in the Warlpiri network of kinship. At one level we were both still white and had diplomatic immunity to humbug, but at another level, possibly a deeper level, we were family. We were part of the Mt Theo family group, cared for and related to as son and nephew, brother and cousin.

The process of becoming family created the glue, the most important characteristic of the Mt Theo Program. This bond enabled Liam and me, together with Peggy, Jean, Shilling and Hooker

The short wheel base Toyota loaned to Hooker Creek

Creek, to bridge the gap between our cultures and work together for a common cause.

We all changed and merged our cultural worlds to come to new ways of working together. At times when I first worked with Peggy I felt frustrated. I was trying to enforce a community agreement about holding every sniffer at Mt Theo for four weeks to break the sniffing cycle. Peggy was frustrated with me because she sent sniffers back to Yuendumu if they were disrespectful or cheeky, or if they were lonely for their family. Neither of us was wrong, we just had different perspectives due to our different cultural worlds. For a long time there was tension, like a stretched elastic band, between Peggy and me: 'creative tension'.

Over the years, new Warlpiri and whitefellas who joined the program were also 'adopted' into the family. The Mt Theo family was more than a family name or a single clan; it included us all. Our relations were strengthened and renewed through the sharing of experiences, through our mutual support for one another, our interdependence and our sharing of everything: cars, blankets, swags and clothing.

My anthropology lecturers taught me how traditional Aboriginal people strengthened relations between clans and tribes through exchanges of resources and sharing, through establishing and deepening ties of generous obligation. Without realising it at the time, that's what happened to Liam and me. We were incorporated into the kinship network. Our obligations and our relations were continually strengthened and renewed. It might be by Liam buying someone a pie and cool drink at the shop, or by Hooker Creek feeding us bush turkey at Mt Theo. I think that incorporation is what happened with the whole program and with subsequent whitefellas like Morgan and Karissa, and subsequent Warlpiri like Rex Forrest, who joined our cause and became our family.

Yinirnti Warrku Warrku (Lake Mackay)

When spring time came, Liam decided to go on a trip. He had a friend, Dave, visiting from Melbourne who he wanted to take right out bush. Liam had recently got hold of a Global Positioning Satellite (GPS) receiver, which was very new technology at the time.

Frank Baarda, the boss of Yuendumu Mining Company, was the owner of the GPS. Frank gave Liam instructions for following some new mining exploration trails that headed out towards Lake Mackay.

'We're going on an adventure,' Liam announced to our two petrol sniffer mates, Shaun and Jerrod. 'We're going way out west to Lake MacKay. We'll be travelling for three or four days. Do you want to come?'

That was the way of it. Shaun and Jerrod were our mates. They might've been petrol sniffers who we took to Mt Theo, but we had spent a lot of time with them.

Jerrod was living at the Williams/Robertson house. His family told us to pick up their grandfather, Paddy Japanangka, at Nyirripi as he was a traditional owner for the country we planned to visit.

The five of us climbed in Liam's Hilux and headed west to Nyirripi to pick up the grandfather. Paddy Japanangka was an old man I had met before at ceremonies and when he visited family in Yuendumu. He was a traditional man: he had a piercing through his nose between his two nostrils which was probably made with a bone during the old hunter-gatherer days. Nowadays he would entertain his great grandchildren by sticking a paint brush or flower stem through the hole. They would break into raucous laughter.

'*Mulyu-rrupa, yakarra*! (Nose hole!),' they would exclaim, pointing at him.

I felt an easy rapport with Japanangka. Whenever we met he called me *jamirdi* (grandson) and rubbed my upper arm as a gesture of affection. I'm not sure why he liked me; it could've been through petrol Dreaming or ceremony stuff.

We pulled the Hilux into his place in Nyirripi. He was sitting on the veranda playing cards with his wife and daughter.

'*Nganimpa karnarlu yani Lake Mackay kirra* (We're all going to Lake Mackay),' I said to him in broken Warlpiri. '*Nyuntuurlangu yantarni mayi*?' (You can come too?)

He looked interested but didn't reply. Then his wife broke into fast speed Warlpiri that I didn't quite understand.

'*Yuwa, ngajurlangu karna yanirni, nyurrurla wana, Yinirnti Warrku Warrku kurra* (Yes, I'll come with you fellas to Yinirnti Warrku Warrku),' he replied. His face was beaming.

'*Yinirnti Warrku Warrku*?' I enquired.

'That's the Yapa name for Lake Mackay,' Jerrod informed me.

Japanangka finished playing his next round of cards and grabbed some blankets, a quilt, mattress, pillow and two boomerangs from inside his bedroom. There was an old swag canvas on the ground next to the rubbish bin at the entrance to his yard. We dusted it off and rolled his swag.

We jammed old Japanangka into the Hilux and drove north for 100 kilometres, past Nginyirripalangu Outstation to Kunjarri, the place of three rock holes. This was my 'father' Ned Jampijimpa's traditional country. We filled up an empty Coke bottle with water from the rock hole to take home to Ned so he could drink water from his own Dreaming.

Next to Kunjarri was Kunyalpa, another rock hole, a puppy dog Dreaming site. I filled my notebook with copious pages of maps and stories told by Japanangka at each site we visited.

As we approached a site he would begin singing, singing the story for that land. Then we would sit down on the ground, in the earth, and he would tell us the *Jukurrpa*, the Dreaming for that place. Mostly he told the stories in Warlpiri, while I noted down the sounds and pronunciations verbatim. (Ten years later with my weak Warlpiri language skills I have no idea what they mean.)

At night by the fire, I asked him to tell the stories again while I drew maps in the sand to clarify each place he referred to. Sometimes he rubbed out my drawings and completely redid the map for me. Each map was copied carefully into my diary. This is what 'real anthropologists' do, I thought, feeling jealous of people like Nic Peterson who must have done countless trips like this. I loved every minute of it.

All the while when we were driving, Japanangka would keep one eye peeled for goannas. Every time he spotted one, he interrupted whatever story or song he was telling and called out '*Wardapi* (goanna)!' The car would pull to a halt and the chase would be on. He was so quick, that old man, digging goannas out of the sand with his boomerang.

While Liam and I barbecued mutton chops for lunch, Japanangka feasted on goanna. We shared our dishes, each of us enjoying the variety of meats.

The next day we continued west on one of the Mining Company's roads, the El Alamein track. It was so rough that the Hilux could only travel at 20 kilometres an hour. It was really cramped in that car with six people on a bumpy slow track, so I got out of the car and started to walk – then I got smart and sat on the bonnet. We crossed the sand dunes and then travelled through a forest of desert oaks. Japanangka told us a travelling Dreaming story, a story of two groups of people from Mala and Mina Mina, the place nearby. He said the desert oaks were those people, people from the *Jukurrpa*, travelling east.

We ran out of road when the El Alamein track headed north. Japanangka wanted to head south to Yarlala where there was no road. Liam and I were worried about rescuers not knowing where to find us if we got stuck out there. We tied a bottle to a tree on the corner of the track and left a message inside it.

Yarlala is a sacred place with lots of history. Japanangka showed us where the old soakage was and where as a young man he had met a whitefella on a camel. He described how the whitefella had put timber around the soakage hole to make it look like a well and how that Kardiya drew water out with buckets for his camels. Japanangka said that there was a *Warnayarra*, a rainbow serpent, who had lived at that waterhole. He said the man with camels had killed that *Warnayarra* and chopped him into pieces which he then cooked in some 44-gallon drums.

'No good killing a *Warnayarra*,' he said.

The *Jukurrpa* for Yarlala is goanna Dreaming. Japanangka showed us where the goannas had danced in the dreamtime. You can still see them standing there – they had metamorphosed into stone. He acted out the dance for us, shaking his body all around, and told us the story. Then he went to the increase site*, a rock set apart from all the others that was smooth and white from being rubbed by humans. Japanangka sang and rubbed the sacred rock as people had for thousands of years; he sang the goannas into being. He sang them fat.

Yapa are custodians of the land, not just owners; they are spirit people. Each person inherits a sacred responsibility through their parents and grandparents, a ritual obligation to renew the Dreaming of their totems, to perform increase ceremonies. Like priests and priestess, through ceremony they reach into the sacred realm and bring its spiritual essence into the everyday, to breathe life into all living beings, plants and animals.

---

* An increase site is a place where increase ceremonies are performed, to increase/stimulate the fertility of the totems whose dreaming is connected with that place.

Japananagka performed an increase ritual, to stimulate the spiritual essence (left behind from the ancestral beings in the Dreamtime) at this site, to create more goannas and make them fat.

That is the essence of traditional life; it is the people's very reason for being, to bring forth life into the land.

Jerrod looked at Japanangka in sacred awe. He brought some tobacco over to his grandfather, like bringing an offering to an altar or like a payment for the story. His grandfather was giving us so much and we all felt compelled to give something back.

The magic must have worked. We caught two very fat goannas that day. One goanna was deep in its hole and we couldn't pull it out. We tried really hard but its tail broke off so we had to dig deeply until we caught it.

I had packed an emergency beacon in the back of the ute in case we got into trouble. One goanna wasn't dead. He climbed into the emergency beacon box. Liam and I heard the 'beep beep beep' sound from the back of the car. We were really worried when we found that goanna in the box. I suppose for the goanna it was a life-threatening emergency. Maybe he was a smart one.

From Yarlala we travelled west to Yinirnti Warrku Warrku. When we got close, Japanangka told us to stop. We all got out of the car and sneaked up a sand dune. There was a *Warnayarra* at Lake Mackay. Japanangka made us all be really quiet so that the *Warnayarra* would not hear us. We sneaked back down the sand dune and cooked goanna for lunch, being careful with our campfire smoke, for fear that the *Warnayarra* might smell it.

'Proper dangerous one, that *Warnayarra*,' said Japanangka.

After lunch Japanangka taught us young fellas how to extract spinifex resin using a fire. I never saw that *Warnayarra*, but Japanangka assured us he was there.

That night as we camped on our way home, Japanangka drew a map in the sand. South of Yarlala were his relatives.

'Bush people,' he told us.

He described the soakages that they would be living at, his mind a map of the network of waterholes that people could use in the desert. Sceptical, we compared his ground drawings with our

GPS and whitefella topographical maps. There were no roads or settlements anywhere in the area he described. But it was possible. Bush people who no one knew existed had been discovered before. That was in this area only thirteen years ago and we knew at least one of them had walked back.

Nic Peterson had told me there had to be another relative of that mob who walked into 'civilisation' in 1984. The young men had ceremony scars which only certain relatives can make, distant relatives, not one of the mob who walked in. There had to be a person or people who were still out there.

'We have to travel west,' said Japanangka. 'We have to make a fire and they will see it.'

He was inviting us to go with him on another trip. I couldn't believe it. Here was a man who regarded me with affection, a man who had been a nomadic hunter-gatherer in his youth and he was inviting me to journey with him, to meet his relatives who were still somewhere out there.

Two weekends later I camped at Mt Theo, which is another goanna Dreaming site. I had a dream that night. I had been hunting with whitefellas and trying to impress them with all I had learnt from the Warlpiri. I had amassed a sizeable catch of game: goannas and young kangaroos. I was about to smash a goanna on the head, to make sure he was properly dead. I didn't want a repeat of that 'come back to life' goanna who nearly set off the emergency beacon. I was going to smash his head, pop his eyes out.

I lifted my boomerang. At the moment of impact the goanna metamorphosed into a human child. I looked around at the other goannas and young kangaroos. They had all metamorphosed into human children too.

'Don't kill us!' they screamed at me as my boomerang smashed through the first skull.

I told Ned about my dream. He looked at me very seriously and said: 'Oh, Yakajirri, you've been here a long time. Now that land's really starting to speak to you.'

Ned guarding a sacred place

6: The Big Bad Wolf (and Other Bureaucrats)

I was so relieved.

I was finally going to work full-time on the Mt Theo Program. Warwick, the Council's project officer, had been talking with me for months about offering me a full-time job at the Council to work on the youth program and the Mt Theo Program. Liam thought it was a great idea.

When I changed jobs, Vesna described it as seeing a weight lifted off my shoulders. I would no longer have to struggle with the School Principal over putting my energies into the Mt Theo and the youth program. It was such a relief to move away from the school to a job where the campaign to stop sniffing would be my legitimate focus.

One of the first tasks I set myself in my new job was to clean out the kitchen in the youth centre. One of the big industrial sinks had been used as a rubbish bin for years and had ten centimetres of hamburger fat and grime covering its base. I started at seven o'clock in the morning and it took six hours, just to clean that end of the kitchen. But I was happy. I had the disco sound system playing music and I loved my new job.

At eleven in the morning some teenagers who heard the music stopped by the mesh window at the sink.

'Can we come in, Yakajirri?' they said.

'Only if you grab a broom and mop and work,' I told them.

Pretty soon we had a working bee happening. At lunchtime we raided the disco supplies of soft drinks and hamburgers and I cooked lunch for my new volunteers.

'Can we do cleaning again tomorrow?' one of them asked, in between burger bites. I smiled. I loved this job and I loved the music and the groovy youthful energy of teenagers. It reminded me of a song in the film 'Mary Poppins':

'In every job that must be done
There is an element of fun,
Find the fun and – snap!
The job's a game!'

I was now working 70 hours a week, but I was filled with enthusiasm and passion. And I had more good news in my life. On my last day of working for the school, during the end of term concert, Vesna gave birth to our second daughter.

Vesna had meant to go into Alice to have the baby, but the obstetricians gave her conflicting information about when the baby was due. Jessie was born in Yuendumu Clinic. Our friend the nurse, Judith Hummerston, delivered the baby. It was almost like a home birth, having a baby delivered by friends in your own local clinic: gum leaves on the floor of the birthing room, Liam and I sitting on the clinic veranda, smoking cigars.

'That Nampijimpa really *Yurrampi* (Yuendumu – honey ant Dreaming) baby,' Old Lucky told me. 'She's born here, just like Yapa. She's traditional owner for Yuendumu. Really Warlpiri, that one.'

I felt proud. Vesna and I really were raising little white Warlpiris.

Things were looking up. I was still on a high from our Yiniti Warrku Warrku trip, my new daughter had been born and I had the job I had always wanted. Liam and I were about to host a big funding meeting so we could get Mt Theo properly funded for the following year. Everything was going to be fine – and that's when the big bad wolf arrived …

Roland was the policeman who stood next to me shoulder-to-shoulder during the big community meetings in back when the program had started. He was solid. He was a good cop who had married one of the nurses from the clinic. Yapa praised me at those meetings when we had returned from the Maningrida trip and Roland was standing next to me.

'That Yakajirri, he really cares for them sniffers … he's doing really good job,' one old lady had called out.

I had been working for Council for less than two months when Roland became my new boss. I was happy when I found out Roland would be the new Council Clerk. Here was a boss who would really understand. He might even help us get a by-law on sniffing, too.

One evening just before Christmas, Roland and I stood outside the Council offices, looking west to the sunset. He had been my boss for about three weeks. I was happy to stand with him. I liked spending some of my working day in the office and we had both worked late that day. I offered to make him a coffee. Then he told me he didn't think my position was very effective at stopping petrol sniffing. I flew home to Canberra for Christmas with tears in my eyes.

'How can he say that?' I asked Vesna. 'Doesn't he realise how bad petrol sniffing would be if it wasn't for the Mt Theo Program?'

It hurt. When Roland had been in Yuendumu four years before, there had been 70 kids sniffing petrol. Now there were only sixteen sniffers. How could he say that I wasn't doing a good job?

I tried reading the Bible, praying and meditating. I wanted to be a better man. I wanted to act like Gandhi would have, with humility, but with conscience. I didn't want to feel this hurt.

When I arrived back from the Christmas break, Roland pulled

me into his office. 'We need to renegotiate your contract,' he said.

'Why?' I asked.

'It's too costly. It's an unfunded position that Council can't afford … It's a bullshit contract,' he replied.

Again I walked away fighting back the pain. I talked with my friend, Warwick. He said I wasn't the only one who had had this sort of discussion with Roland. It turned out that Roland had similar discussions with most of the Council's employees. He told the staff and Council members at the meeting that the Council was undergoing an operational review. All positions and operations would be examined and changes made accordingly.

Council meeting minutes were now being written by Roland, which was a change from the previous arrangements where the Council administration worker did it. With Roland controlling the only written record of meetings, no dissenting views were recorded. Everyone started to feel the heat. Most employees felt that their jobs were being threatened.

We were sitting in Warwick's backyard sharing an evening conversation. 'He's onto everyone, Yakajirri,' Warwick said.

'He won't honour my employment contract. I've got no housing for my family to move into and I think he's trying to sack me,' I said glumly.

'It's not just you,' Warwick continued. 'It's everyone: the Essential Services Officer, the postmistress, the mechanic, the plumber, the childcare coordinator. I don't think I'll have a job for much longer. We're all under threat. And you know the consultancy firm, LWC (Long Way Consulting) he's hired to do the review? Well, Roland is an owner of that firm. He created that firm with his friends. Last year that firm got a 4.2 million dollar contract to do capital works in Yuendumu. Don't don't be surprised if that firm gets a lot of other contracts from Council,' Warwick told me.

'But I've been hunting a lot of funding for the Mt Theo Program to go to Council,' I complained, 'and now he's trying to shut down the program. The other day he asked me what should be cut, the Mt Theo Program or the youth program? I told him it was like asking me if I wanted to live without my right brain or my left brain. We need both those programs to stop sniffing. At that Council meeting I asked him if he'd continue to employ Peggy and Liam in their jobs with the Mt Theo grant. He said he wouldn't guarantee it. He's got no idea! Peggy's central to the whole thing. I just don't want to see it fall apart,' I said.

'You've got to worry about your own job,' said Warwick. 'Have you been in touch with your union yet?'

'The union was useless,' I replied. 'They said he could make us all redundant. But I'm worried for Peggy and Liam, they're my employees. I've written submissions to get the funding for their jobs moved to Council. It's my responsibility to protect their jobs.'

I walked home that night worried. How was I going to protect this program?

Three weeks later as I walked into Roland's office, he demanded to know why he had received a flood of letters protesting against the threats to cut back the Mt Theo Program. There were letters from the Department of Corrections, Department of Health, the school, the clinic, and night patrol.

'You said you wouldn't guarantee Peggy and Liam's jobs … you called my employment agreement a bullshit contract. You've talked about cutting the program. I'm concerned, Roland. And I work with all these organisations. I talk to them. They're concerned too.'

'I'm telling you now not to discuss this with outside agencies,' he ordered.

'It's part of my job, Roland. I need to communicate with Corrections and night patrol and the clinic about the sniffers. It's my job to support the Mt Theo Program and to work for it. I've worked for it for five years and I'm going to keep working for it,' I replied.

'Like I said, there'll be lots of cuts at Council. There's going to be a lot of unhappiness. It's slash and burn, Andrew. I suggest you look at your options,' he declared.

I looked him straight in the eye.

'Are you playing hardball with me, Roland?' I asked.

'Yes,' he said, staring back at me.

'Well, batter up then.'

I was angry. I wasn't going to let him wreck the program. He wasn't as scary as some of the petrol sniffers I'd dealt with. And I had support. Every member of Council had given me a letter stating that the program would be protected and I wouldn't be sacked. We had letters of support from at least a dozen different organisations.

Two weeks later Warwick and I were having another late night conversation after I had closed up the disco.

'I think you've pretty much got this fellow licked, Yakajirri,' he said.

'What do you mean, Warwick?'

'Well, you've made Mt Theo such a political hot potato, he's not going to touch it.'

'Thank God,' I sighed. 'You know, a lot of Yapa are supporting us, Warwick,' I went on. 'A lot of those Council members who I approached for letters of support are really unhappy with what's going on. They say they should sack him. They told me it's no good having a whitefella like that making trouble for all of our community.'

'You know what Eddie [past Council President] said to me the other night?' Warwick asked. 'He said, why is every whitefella who works for Council coming to see him, worried they're going to get sacked. He said Yapa Council workers are unhappy too. Their conditions have changed from full-time Council staff to being on CDEP [work for the dole]. They want to sack Roland but they can't. They're worried if they sack him he will sue them.

And now he's trying to buy off Council members by promising them Toyotas.'

'Yeah, I've heard about that in other places, how a bad Council Clerk will buy off council members before a meeting, like promising them free fuel on the Council account if they vote the right way,' I said.

'Anyway, you're all right, Yakajirri, your program is safe. You've stirred things up too much.'

I had done my best and it seemed to have worked. At the Council meeting, Ned gave a speech about the importance of the Mt Theo Program and the youth program, and all the Council members moved a motion to protect it from the review. Roland was angry.

Warwick said, 'He'll probably back off for a while. It's a pity for the community, though. He's really bad news and people feel powerless to get rid of him.'

We sat in silence for a while. I thought back over the past few months. About all the effort it had taken. I thought about the new contract designed by Roland's firm LWC that he had tried to get me to sign.

'Hey, Warwick, you were around when Roland became Council Clerk. Did he go on the old Council employees' contract, or did he insist on one of those new LWC contracts?' I asked.

'I'm pretty sure he got one of those new contracts, why?'

'Do you have a copy of one of those LWC contracts here?'

'Yeah, I've got the one he tried to force me to sign. What are you going on about, Yakajirri?'

'I remember one of the things I was unhappy about in the contract was a clause that makes the contract null and void if your Land Council permit is revoked. I thought it was a bit hard, compared to the job I had at the school, where even if your permit is revoked they will give you a job in another area.'

'Are you thinking about how to sack Roland?'

'Well, everyone wants to sack him, but they're scared he'll sue them. The Council doesn't have to sack him – the traditional owners of Yuendumu can revoke his Land Council permit, which will make his contract null and void, right? Then he has to leave Yuendumu.'

'Geez, you should think about studying a law degree, Yakajirri.'

'Naw, mate, I've just read too many John Grisham books,' I joked.

The next day Warwick and I visited Ned at his house. Old Agie Napurrula was cooking damper on the fire outside, and dogs were running around.

'Hello, hello,' Ned welcomed. 'Good early morning to you. What's up, mate?'

'I think we've found a way to get rid of the big bad wolf, Ned,' I said and I told him about the contract.

Ned spent the day driving around and speaking to the other Council members and then spoke with me again: 'We're going to have a meeting, Yakajirri. Not in the Council rooms but at business camp where only *wati* (initiated Warlpiri men) can go: all us Council members, men ones and the traditional owners. That Land Council lawyer is going to drive out. Can you help me send him a fax? The lawyer wants to look at the contract before he comes out.'

He went on: 'We want you at the meeting, Yakajirri. We want you to support us. We need to get rid of this mongrel. We supported you and Mt Theo Program, now we need you to support us,' he said.

The lawyer came out and another secret meeting was planned at business camp for a fortnight's time. At this stage the Council President, Mook Mook, was sick in Alice Springs Hospital, so he wasn't involved in any of the meetings. The lawyer took the paperwork into town to show Mook Mook and keep him in the loop. One of the nurses working at the hospital was Roland's wife.

Meanwhile I was living out at Mt Theo. Peggy and Hooker

Creek had to go away on sorry business so I had to look after the sniffers.

Life at Mt Theo was kind of peaceful compared to the politics and machinations going on at Yuendumu. My major problem out there was that the suspension bracket had broken on the Toyota, so I had spent the day scrounging old leaf springs from a broken down Holden left out there.

That evening after supper I worked one of the leaf springs into a Toyota bracket. I placed the spring in the camp fire and then worked methodically to shape the red hot metal with an axe for a hammer and a rock for an anvil. I was in the process of creating a loop on the end so it could bolt back onto the chassis.

Josie, a fourteen-year-old girl, was watching me. She had a beautiful smile and over the last year I had watched her blossom from a shy yet aggressive sniffer into a confident happy teenager. During the past twelve months she came to know us well at the program. She still sniffed occasionally in Yuendumu but nowadays she was more often than not an enthusiastic participant at the youth centre. Some nights at Mt Theo she and her friend Sandra would lead the group in singing gospel songs to the stars. 'We're one big happy family,' they would chorus.

'What are you doing, Yakajirri?' she asked, looking intently at my blacksmithing efforts.

'I'm making a piece for the car. I'm making this piece of metal round so I can fix the suspension.'

'Who learned you for doing that?'

'My grandfather taught me, my mother's father. He used to work in a blacksmith shop in Melbourne a long time ago, before motor cars, when he was a boy. He told me stories of doing this work.'

I looked at Josie. Her grandfather was still alive. He was the one who sat down at the soakage near Mt Theo and laughed as he told me stories of his family walking around in the hunter-gatherer days with no trousers. And now I was telling Josie about my grandfather and his stories and our whitefella traditional skills.

The next day with the car fixed, Osmond and Austin came up to me.

'We want to go hunting, Yakajirri. We are hungry for *kuka* (meat). Take us hunting so we can get some kangaroo.'

I had a short wheel base Toyota which only had seven seats and I had sixteen teenagers to look after. I had a duty of care to all of them. I couldn't just take Osmond and Austin hunting and leave the others behind. If something happened at Mt Theo and I'd left the others unsupervised, there would be trouble. What if someone tried to hang themselves while I was away? What if there was a fight?

Osmond and Austin had grown into burly blokes, and joining them in their chorus were three other young men, Macca, Vasco, and Lister.

'We want to go fucking hunting, too fucking boring this place. We'll smash that fucking Toyota! We want to go hunting!' they demanded.

From the young blokes' perspective, my reluctance to take them hunting was completely unreasonable. Peggy and Hooker Creek would take them hunting most days. Leaving the other young people unsupervised wasn't a problem for Peggy because she always had a relative like her husband or a son who could look after the ones left behind. I had no one with tribal adult authority to leave behind to look after the sniffers.

The situation was escalating and I didn't want a riot on my hands. If these young blokes got too worked up, they could easily overpower me and steal the car. Then they could run away to Yuendumu to sniff petrol and set a dangerous new precedent on escaping from Mt Theo.

Many whitefellas reading this account would argue that I shouldn't have been out at Mt Theo on my own looking after sniffers anyway. But there were no Yapa available to go to Mt Theo because of sorry business. I did have a whitefella co-worker, Liam, but he was busy running youth activities in Yuendumu.

It didn't make sense for us to close Mt Theo down, because all the sniffers would return to Yuendumu and start sniffing again. Nor did it make sense for us to close the youth program down and have both Liam and me living at Mt Theo, as then the kids of Yuendumu would be bored and have no alternative youth scene to sniffing.

'We want to go fucking hunting!' Austin yelled at me.

'Okay, I'll take you hunting, but we all have to go,' I said. 'I'm not leaving anyone behind. If we go hunting, everyone has to come.'

It is pretty hard trying to fit seventeen people into a seven-seat short wheel base Toyota. But nothing is impossible for Yapa. At outstations, people frequently sit on the roofs and bonnets of vehicles. I had seen Yapa do it many times and I had transported people this way once myself when I came across a broken-down carload of people stranded in the desert when my car was already full.

But moving people this way is dangerous. I was uncomfortable doing it but I felt I had little choice. I needed to appear reasonable to these young Warlpiri men if I was going to manage the energy of the situation. I needed to think and operate from a Warlpiri perspective.

I resolved to travel slowly, no quicker than a fast-moving bicycle could travel. We jammed as many people into the Toyota as possible. There was no room inside for our billycans of food and tea or for our water bag. They hung outside the car on the side mirrors. Nor was there room for the rifle which we needed to hunt kangaroo.

Once the car was full, we still had seven people left over. Vasco put a big mattress on the roof rack and five young blokes climbed up on the roof. Osmond and another bloke then sat on the bonnet.

I put the rifle bolt and bullets in my pocket. The golden rule for rifles is you always keep the bullets and bolt separate from the gun itself. Osmond offered to nurse the disabled rifle across his lap.

We drove out to Ginty's Bore, which was the nearest swimming hole. Ginty's is a beautiful man-made waterhole next to a dry sandy riverbed lined with ancient ghost gums. Finches and *ngatijirri* (green budgerigars) darted in and around the reeds that lined this little oasis. A windmill creaked, drawing water up from underground.

We had swimming races, boiled the billy for tea and had tinned spaghetti sandwiches for lunch. The river bed was filled with the laughter of Warlpiri, alive in their own country; except technically, it wasn't the Warlpiri's country. Ginty's Bore lies on station land, a pastoral lease controlled by a whitefella called Braitling. The lease is the last bit of Warlpiri land that they had been unable to claim under the Land Rights Act.

None of that bothered us. Warlpiri knew they had a right to be there, to hunt on that land and swim in its water. You just weren't allowed to kill that white man's bullocks, that's all. We were going to hunt kangaroo, not bullock. I was going to make sure of that. The rifle bolt and bullets were still in my pocket.

On the way back to Mt Theo we had an accident. Ten kilometres north of Ginty's Bore was a section where the road had been washed out and it needed careful driving. I slowed the car down to less than ten kilometres an hour and slipped it into first gear. I had successfully negotiated the ruts on the way out to Ginty's. They were about 20 centimetres deep.

The car jolted as it slipped down one of the ruts and everyone panicked. Osmond jumped off the bonnet, flinging the rifle away. As the car shuddered to a halt, Vasco jumped off the roof. I flung the driver's door open. Osmond was reeling on the ground, holding his thigh and crying out in pain. Vasco was holding his arm, blood pouring out of it. He had gashed it on a bolt on the side of the car when he jumped off the roof.

I looked at both of them. A bandage would fix Vasco, but I was worried about Osmond. Had he broken his leg? If it was broken he would need medical treatment, not bush first aid.

The VHF radio sandwich box was unloaded and the antenna wire slung over a tree.

'This is Victor Zulu Eight Charlie X-Ray, calling VJD for a medical emergency. Over.'

The radio was patched through to Yuendumu Clinic where I spoke to Judith the nurse and asked her to send out an ambulance, and also bring out Eddie Jampijimpa Robertson and Hooker Creek.

The good thing about VHF radio is that everyone who has their VHF radio on can hear you. My mate Darren who was a liaison officer with Yirara College in Alice Springs heard my call while he was driving and got on air to give me some words of support. The bad thing about VHF radio is that everyone can hear you and you never know who is listening in.

'They're going to sack you, Yakajirri. Then you can't stop us sniffing,' Lister teased from inside the car.

'Yeah. You'll be in big trouble for this one, Yakajirri. They gonna kick you out of Yuendumu. Maybe even give you payback,' chorused Macca.

It was almost like a victory for them. Finally these guys would be rid of me, the bane of their sniffing lives. They were right; I had already thought about that, which is why I wanted Hooker Creek and Eddie to come out. Maybe my work with the program was going to end right there.

By the time the ambulance arrived, Osmond was walking around. Much to my relief he had only corked his leg when he had jumped. Eddie and Hooker Creek spoke to everyone about the accident. I asked them if they wanted me to leave the Mt Theo Program.

'No, Yakajirri, we know this road, you're all right. We want you to keep working for us. Take these sniffers back to Mt Theo,' they said.

Back at Mt Theo I thought long into the night. I knew Osmond and Vasco's families would be upset. I was worried that, despite all the support people had given me over the last few months, I might still be sacked or kicked out of the community by Yapa for injuring their kids.

Liam, Vesna, Peggy and Hooker Creek came out to see me the next night. I could not stop shaking.

'Braitling (the pastoralist leaseholder) heard you on the radio,' Liam told me. 'He rang the police. He's going to issue you with a trespass notice. The police have told Roland. He wants you charged.'

Roland didn't have many friends in Yuendumu. His closest friend was the police sergeant who was a gruff sort of man. There was a rumour he might be one of those cops who got sent to Yuendumu for punishment. He seemed angry and cynical about being there.

I had always had good relations with the police, working together side by side. Some of them used to visit my house for tea and cakes. The policewoman used to call me 'sweetheart'. Roland's arrival seemed to have changed all that.

Peggy and Hooker Creek looked at me sitting there, shaking. Liam was brewing up espresso on the campfire.

'Don't worry, Jangala,' Peggy said. 'We been together long time. We always together.'

Hooker Creek moved closer to me and rubbed my back. 'Don't worry for all those whitefellas,' he said. 'You Yapa now, you with us. You can stay here at Mt Theo.'

I was still worried. I had never been charged with anything. I had always tried to live within the law. My stomach was knotted. I didn't want to lose my job. Vesna would never be content to live at Mt Theo.

I wrote a letter of apology that I asked Liam to read out at the council meeting that week:

> Dear Councillors,
>
> I am sorry for having the accident. I am sorry those boys were injured. If you want me to stop working for Mt Theo or to leave Yuendumu, I will go. If you need me to go through payback in order to stay working for the program I am prepared to do that.

I had seen someone get speared in the leg for payback. I knew it would hurt but I also knew it was a survivable experience. It was something I was prepared to go through if that's what it took to keep working for the program.

Liam later told me that when he read the letter, everyone in the council room laughed. Everyone except Roland.

'We know that road. We know those sniffers and how they are always humbugging to go hunting,' they said. 'We can't spear Yakajirri just for Vasco getting a cut arm. It was an accident. Yakajirri is trying to save those young people's lives. He is saving them from petrol.'

Ned spoke up for me: 'He's really Yapa, that Yakajirri. He's not like other Kardiya. He lives out at Mt Theo just like Yapa with those sniffers.'

Roland said he wanted me sacked. He produced a photocopy of the fax cover sheet Ned had got me to write when I helped him fax the contract off to the Land Council lawyer. Roland was fuming, but the Council refused to sack me.

One week later, Ned showed me a letter sent by the Department of Local Government. The letter threatened to suspend the Council. It cited various reasons for this, but basically the problem was that the Council members refused to cooperate with the Council Clerk. Under the Yuendumu Community Government Council's constitution, if the Department suspended the Council, then the Council Clerk took over all the decision-making power on the Council's behalf. It meant Roland would have total control.

Roland had succeeded in getting rid of the child care coordinator, the plumber and my friend Warwick. I told Liam we had to protect the program. Liam and I spoke with Ned and Peggy and all the other elders involved with the Mt Theo Program. We decided to move the program and all its funding back to the Tanami Network. By moving it away from Council, we could protect it from Roland.

It was our big year for funding, too. Finally all our submissions had paid off. The Commonwealth Government was going to grant us over half a million dollars. They had asked us for our wish list. We asked for a solar power system at Mt Theo, a satellite phone, a house in Yuendumu for Liam and me to live in, and wages and food for the team. And that half a million dollars was no longer going through Council. The Commonwealth had agreed to move it to the sanctuary of the Tanami Network.

We all breathed a sigh of relief. A little song was going around in my head: 'Who's afraid of the big bad wolf?'

Two weeks after we shifted the funding, Ned came round to my place one morning in an ecstatic mood. 'Guess what Yakajirri – the big bad wolf's going. He's resigned.'

'Bullshit, Ned, I don't believe it.'

'No, it's true. He handed in his letter of resignation today.'

'Show me a copy of the letter and I'll believe it.'

Ned jumped in his car and drove to the Council office. He returned ten minutes later, proudly showing me the letter.

'Well do you want some breakfast, my father?' I asked him.

'You betcha, mate,' he answered.

We shared a morning feast of bacon and eggs washed down with orange juice. We couldn't stop grinning at each other.

School time

Two months after the wolf left, we had managed to get a teacher at Mt Theo. Michael Morgan, who had been a teacher in Yuendumu in the early nineties, returned to help us set up the Mt Theo School. The Commonwealth Disadvantaged Schools (CDS) Program funded a teacher's wage at Mt Theo for four months. Nationally the CDS Program was dismantled by the Howard Government at the end of that year so it was the one and only time we had a teacher at Mt Theo for a substantial length of time.

Morgan was a charismatic 'live wire' Catholic, who could emotionally connect with young people. When he was a teacher at Yuendumu School, kids tried to transfer out of other teachers' classes to join his class – he was fun and popular. He once told me that his strategy for managing behaviour in the classroom was to have all the kids really like him, so they would want to do the right thing to please him. He was a hit at Mt Theo, teaching in a one-room school four days a week.

Education at Mt Theo

School at Mt Theo meant that in addition to traditional activities, such as hunting and artefact making there was much more for the young people who were sent out there to do.

Yuendumu

Tanami Road near Yuendumu

Yakajirri and Vesna at home in Yuendumu

Young people at Mt Theo (photo by Frances Mocnik)

Yakajirri delivering the rations
(photo by Frances Mocnik)

Corroboree boys

Growing up in Yuendumu (photo by Frances Mocnik)

Life after sniffing

Hooker Creek and Yakajirri at the Mt Theo turnoff

Janice's first trip

Janice Klar was a government lady. There have been many government officers who Mt Theo had dealt with over the years, but Janice was special. She was a slightly built blonde woman who wore floral dresses and seemed to be someone who would probably enjoy listening to Carole King records. She had trained as a social worker and had lived on the Pitjantjatjara Lands in South Australia, where she had seen the destructive effects of petrol sniffing first hand. Janice had a heart of gold; she had taken in foster kids and raised them as her own.wh

The Mt Theo mob first got to know her when she was working for Northern Territory Correctional Services. Many of the young people we dealt with had also been involved with sniffing-related crime. Correctional Services and Mt Theo worked closely to both keep these young people off petrol, and provide a positive way of keeping them out of prison.

Janice's fiancé at the time, Bryan Clarke, was the first journalist to publish a newspaper article about us. He made Mt Theo the lead story in the *Alice Springs Star*. When Janice changed jobs to work for Commonwealth Health, our major funding body, we thought all our Christmases had come at once. Here was a government lady who really understood what the program was about. That is not to say other government people were unhelpful, it was just that there were so many of them. Commonwealth Health and other government bodies seemed to have an incredibly high rate of staff turnover. It almost became a pasttime for me to recite the long list of names of government officers whom we had told our story to, before they moved on from that job and we were back to square one again with the new person.

Janice helped us a lot, particularly when we had to deal with the big bad wolf. She was a person who was very serious about the work Mt Theo was doing. We had worked with Janice for over a year before she undertook her first field trip to Mt Theo itself.

Usually when we had government visitors, we would do a straightforward trip to Mt Theo: drive out to the outstation in the shiny government Toyota; show them some of the landmarks and wildlife on the way, while entertaining them with program anecdotes and some serious discussion about the issues we dealt with. But Janice was different, she had dealt with problem kids and she had lived in the Pitjantjatjara Lands; so we decided to allow her to ride shotgun in the cage truck, while we did a sniffer round-up and then ran the sniffers to Mt Theo. No sanitised version for this lady – she was going to see the real thing.

The cage truck was what an African refugee truck would look like if it had to comply with Northern Territory road rules. The Yuendumu Council had acquired the truck years before. It was purpose built for transporting Warlpiri passengers and swags. In many ways it was an ideal desert vehicle. People could pack in whatever they wanted: swags, flour drums, ochre, camp dogs and the carcasses of any game they might shoot along the way. At the end of a trip it could be hosed out. This truck was most frequently used at ceremony time, when the Warlpiris would travel far and wide, to the Top End, to the Pitjantjatjara Lands and Western Australia on blackfellas' business.

There was a set of twin doors at the rear of the truck and a small single door on the side of the cargo space near the cab. Above the cabin was a mesh window that provided air flow into the cargo space.

I collected Janice from the Council guesthouse early in the morning. We drove to the police station and together with the police went around to the homes of the young people who had been sniffing recently. At each home the usual debate would go on. 'I'm not fucking going to Mt Theo,' the young person would yell.

After being badgered by their family and seeing the sight of the local policeman, they would eventually concede and get in the truck. Family members would then hastily assemble swag and blankets and throw that swag in the truck as well as thrust some dollars in the young person's hand. As the morning wore on and we assembled more young people on the truck, our task became easier. The young person would see their peers were already on the truck and the idea of getting on it became less repulsive.

Finally we stopped at the shop where I bought soft drinks and pies for the sniffers to eat on the road. Normally I'd also chuck in a packet of cigarettes bought with private cash. But now I had the 'government lady' from the Health Department on board and I couldn't be seen to do that. This change in behaviour didn't go unnoticed.

Tobacco has a traditional place in Warlpiri society. Long before whitefellas came, Warlpiri harvested *pituri* (bush tobacco), which they claim has medicinal properties. It is a specialty item that is potent yet small enough to be easily carried by hunter-gatherers. *Pituri* was traditionally used in trade and ritual exchange, and even today, it is used as a way of paying for ceremonial knowledge; people still give the 'teacher' tobacco.

In contemporary Warlpiri society tobacco remains a highly prized gift. Nowadays tinned tobacco and cigarettes often take the place of *pituri*, both as a matter of convenience and preference. In the Mt Theo Program, tobacco is the most frequently requested gift by Peggy and Hooker Creek. It is contemporary currency and its giving carries with it a message of generosity, respect and honouring of relationship.

Tobacco is also a tool of modern-day youth workers. In cities across Australia, where youth workers meet up with street kids, offering a cigarette is frequently used as an icebreaker or as a tool to de-escalate conflict. Offering a cigarette to a young person carries street credibility. As a gift of indulgence and respect, a cigarette carries the message: I treat you as an adult.

As a tool of calming and engagement, tobacco is frequently used to reach out to alienated young people who have serious drug and mental health issues. Many times in my career I have witnessed the power of the gift of a cigarette and its effectiveness in defusing dangerously violent situations.

Some people reading this account may argue that giving tobacco to young people is evil; that tobacco is a drug that kills. I don't dispute that, but in contrast to petrol sniffing and alcohol, tobacco is a lesser drug. It doesn't cause violence or social chaos. Sniffing kills people in their teens and twenties. If we can help sniffers to live long enough so that tobacco (which kills people in their fifties and sixties) becomes a health issue, then we are doing really well.

Of course, the Warlpiri sniffers didn't understand why I hadn't bought them any smokes. They were initiated young men and were considered by the community to be adults, to have the right to smoke. They had given me money at the shop to buy them cigarettes and I had given it back, refusing to buy them smokes. They must have asked themselves why Yakajirri was being such an arsehole.

They knew I would normally have tobacco on me, and my refusal to provide them with any simply didn't make sense. As we drove further along the Tanami Road they became more and more pissed off.

'Yakajirri, give us a fucking smoke,' they yelled.

I ignored them, conscious that I couldn't let this Health Department lady see me give my 'under age' clients cigarettes. The sniffers were fed up. To deny a direct request in their culture is tantamount to denying the relationship, or shouting out loud: 'I don't care about you.'

Dion opened the side door of the cage truck. We were travelling at about 80 kilometres an hour. I pulled the truck up to a stop.

Dion leapt out of the truck and headed bush before I had a chance to get round to his side of the truck.

For safety reasons it was normal practice not to padlock the doors of the cage truck. But with this behaviour, it was safer to lock the doors. I used some fencing wire to secure the door shut, so that it could only be opened from the outside.

We now had six of our original party of seven sniffers, but those six were still pissed off. As we drove further along the road some of the young men climbed up on the wall behind the cabin and managed to pull open the mesh window above the cab. The truck was not a new truck. The roof of the cab had dents and cracks in it. I did not know that the roof leaked but Janice and I were about to find out.

The bottles of soft drink I had given to the young people were poured out on the cabin roof. The truck continued to rattle along the road and slowly but surely the sugary sticky soft drink liquid leaked down through the cabin roof and began to drip on us. I drove on, trying to ignore the chaos and make light of it in front of the government lady.

'Oh, don't worry Andrew,' she reassured me. 'I've worked with juvenile offenders, mate, and I've seen it all before.'

Well, I hadn't. I thought, this is one of the most embarrassing trips I've done. My humiliation was only to get worse. The young men, having now run out of soft drink, were urinating into the empty soft drink bottles. One of them then climbed onto the cabin roof, with the truck still travelling at 80 kilometres an hour, and threw a urine-filled bottle through the side window of the cab. Janice and I were soaked in piss.

Oh God, I thought, a kid on the truck roof, now that's really unsafe. I had to stop. When I pulled the truck to a stop, Patch, Osmond and Esau climbed out through the window on top of the cab and took off into the bush. It was pointless to chase them as I still had three sniffers left in the truck who would also run off the moment I left them alone. I got out the satellite phone and called the Yuendumu police to alert them about our four runaway sniffers. Janice and I continued on to Mt Theo.

We arrived at around two o'clock. Michael Morgan, the teacher at Mt Theo, appeared very stressed and was eager to hightail it out of there. It was a Thursday, the last day of his four-day week at the outstation. Morgan had a brief conversation with Janice before heading home via the shortcut road. Janice looked around the outstation and met Hooker Creek and Peggy and the young people in their care. The school looked superb. There were desks and books and a blackboard. Everywhere was clear evidence that the Mt Theo Program was working.

As we drove back to Yuendumu it started to rain. I dropped Janice back at the guesthouse and then went round to see Morgan.

'What's that back road like?' I asked him, aware that it had been raining on his trip back.

'Pretty good,' he said.

'Any problem with rain, any boggy places?'

'No mate, it's as good as gold.'

I picked up the short wheel base Toyota from him and went out to find Snowy, Patch's father. Patch was one of the sniffers who had run away. Snowy was home having supper with his wife Krista and their kids. Patch was also there.

'He ran away from the cage truck,' I explained. 'I've got my Toyota here. Do you want to help me take him to Mt Theo?'

Snowy was a helpful parent and I was glad to have his company. Together with Patch, we drove around to collect the other runaway sniffers. We managed to find two more.

Three out of the four runaways was not bad. We felt pretty good and headed out on the back road to Mt Theo – the road Morgan had said was 'good as gold'. Going the back way would save us 80 kilometres on a round trip.

The road might have been good four hours ago when Morgan had travelled it, but that night, after hours of rain, it was more like a shallow river. We drove through fifteen-centimetre deep water for 40 kilometres, our headlights reflecting off its dark shiny surface. To maintain traction, we had to travel in low range four-wheel drive. It took us hours to get to Mt Theo. After dropping off the sniffers, we headed back to Yuendumu via the main road, where conditions were only slightly better.

We had left with a full tank of fuel, but travelling in low range four-wheel drive chews up the juice. We travelled about 290 kilometres that night before the car ran out of diesel. Its usual range was 400 kilometres.

It was midnight and Snowy and I were both exhausted. We had no swags, the ground was wet and we were still a fair way from Yuendumu. We lit a fire for warmth and I offered Snowy the inside of the car to sleep in, while I slept on the patch of ground that had been dried out by the fire. I didn't sleep well.

I had arranged to meet Janice at eight o'clock the next morning in Yuendumu. My problem was not only how to get back to Yuendumu, but how to make it to that meeting in time.

What a fool I would look.

I had taken this nice government lady who had done so much to support the program, and I had showed her how dodgy it was to be carrying sniffers in the cage truck. I had placed her in a position where she had been practically urinated on by the sniffers and now I had run out of fuel on a run to Mt Theo. I really did look like a completely dodgy bloke, and I was the program's manager!

At sunrise I got up and started jogging towards Yuendumu. I passed the 'Y-20' road sign; I had twenty kilometres to go. Could I jog that in two hours? Could I meet with Janice and then return with fuel and rescue Snowy? Could I make it all look good?

I had only jogged about one kilometre when I saw a Britz rental campervan tucked away in the bush. I recognised its Toyota

Land Cruiser shape immediately. It had to be a diesel. Maybe these people could help me.

Those poor tourists, they probably thought they were in the middle of nowhere; they had finally got away from it all. I knocked on the windows of the van.

'Hello. Hello. Can you help me?' I called.

'*Vas is das*?' answered a sleepy German voice.

'Hello mate,' I called. 'Please, please, can you help me?'

'Vot is ze problem?' the man asked in heavily accented English.

'Thank you mate, I have broken down, I have run out of fuel and I was wondering if you could please give me five litres of diesel, my car is only one kilometre down the road.'

'No, no, dis ve cannot do. Ve carry only enough fuel vor ourselves.'

'Well, can you give me a ride please, mate – which way are you heading?'

'Ve are going to Alice Springs today.'

'Mate, can you give me a ride to Yuendumu? It's only twenty kilometres down the road on the way to Alice Springs.'

'Ya, dis ve can do. But first ve have our breakfast.'

The German woke his sleeping wife and had breakfast with her while I waited impatiently outside their van. I needed help.

As they drove me into Yuendumu, I explained to them how I had run out of fuel and how I had two spare jerry cans of diesel stored in a shed in Yuendumu.

'If you could please give me a lift back to my car with a jerry can,' I asked, 'I would be more than happy to pay you money for your trouble.'

'No, no,' the man replied. 'Ve have helped you enough.'

It was six-thirty and I was stuck in Yuendumu with no way to get back to my car. No one else is awake in Yuendumu at six-thirty in the morning. Who could I humbug first?

I went around to Peggy's son's house. Scotty will help me,

I thought. Scotty was a bloke around my age. He was one of Yuendumu's most consistent musicians and a bit of a legend guitar player among young people. I woke him up.

'Please, please, Scotty can you help me,' I pleaded. 'My Toyota has run out of fuel up near the Mt Doreen boundary. I have a jerry can of diesel, but I need to get a ride to my car.'

'Ah, Yakajirri, I would help you,' Scotty explained still half asleep. 'But my car is no good. The wheels are different. I got fourteen inch on one side and narrow tyre on the other side. I don't want to drive it.'

'Please, Scotty,' I begged. 'We can drive really slow, so it doesn't hurt your car, I really need your help. I've never asked for your help before, but I have always helped you.'

I then proceeded to recite a list of all the cars he had owned that I had helped him rescue when they had broken down. I also listed all the other favours I had done for him.

'Remember that time my wife and I helped you rescue that old Holden ute of yours that had no windscreen and no bonnet?'

At this point, Scotty's wife Audrey, getting sick of my monologue, chimed in and told him to help me. Scotty drove me out in his 'no good' car with no problem at all.

I made it back to Yuendumu with my Toyota and enough time to have a shower and prepare for my eight o'clock meeting with Janice. At the meeting I proudly informed her we had caught three of the four runaway sniffers last night.

'Whatever it takes, we are determined to save these kids from sniffing,' I said, articulating the commitment all of us felt to the 'cause'.

Janice was travelling back to Alice at lunchtime and, being a Friday, Vesna and I were planning to go to town for the weekend. Janice agreed to give us a lift, as our family Subaru was in Alice with the mechanic.

On the way, Janice stopped her government car at Tilmouth

Well, the roadhouse halfway between Yuendumu and Alice. We sat down for coffee and while we were relaxing on the veranda, I noticed the Britz van parked nearby. The German couple recognised me and walked up smiling: 'You made it back okay,' he said.

'Yes, and how did you go?' I bluffed. 'Did you make it back okay?'

'Ya, ya. Ve are fine,' he replied and they walked away.

'How do you know them?' Janice asked.

Aware that whatever I said might go in a government report on Mt Theo, I decided to put a bit of spin on my explanation: 'Oh, they were some tourists we met on the road last night. We helped each other out.'

vehicle rules

That weekend, while I was in Alice with my family, Andrew Cowen rang me and asked me to pick up a white girl from town. Morgan, the school teacher at Mt Theo jokingly said, 'Only bring her out here if she's good-looking.'

I met this 20-year-old student from the Australian National University in Canberra. She was staying in a room at the end of a carport attached to a house in Alice Springs. We sat on the concrete of the driveway. She had bare feet and was wearing a white cotton blouse.

Karissa Preuss came to Yuendumu with me and my family (our car broke down on the way, near Tilmouth Well) and stayed in Cowen's house. Morgan took her out to Mt Theo.

'She took to life out there like a duck to water,' he said.

A few weeks later I had a meeting with the Tanami Network Manager, Stan Morrow and Janice Klar as well as the manager from Commonwealth Health. We talked about an emergency vehicle for Mt Theo. At the time, Mt Theo had two vehicles, a second-hand Troop Carrier and a short wheel base Toyota which were private vehicles bought by me and loaned to the program. The head gasket on the Toyota had recently blown and been repaired at considerable expense.

Stan Morrow was arguing that if the government provided us with new vehicles, then our repair costs would be lower than with old second-hand vehicles. They were considering funding the program to purchase a new vehicle.

I pointed out that if they provided us with a vehicle, then they should also provide us with rules to go with the vehicle, otherwise there could be no guarantee that the relatives of Yapa involved with the program would not humbug the vehicle to be used for non-program purposes. We needed government-imposed rules to counterbalance the Warlpiri obligation system. Without such rules, I warned that the vehicle would most likely follow the pattern of so many other community-owned vehicles, where they ended up running all over the countryside to the Top End, Western Australia and South Australia. If this happened, we would have no emergency vehicle stationed at Mt Theo.

I also pointed out that jealousies over GMAAAC vehicles had almost destroyed the program before, with traditional owners threatening to close the program down. I spoke about how the documented history of other petrol sniffing outstation programs had shown that many programs had collapsed due to infighting over vehicles.

The Commonwealth Health manager responded by saying it wasn't up to the government to create vehicle rules for organisations. He said that if infighting over vehicles would threaten the very existence of the program, then the community didn't really value the program, and if it collapsed, so be it.

'But if it collapses and these kids keep on sniffing we might not have another chance,' I pleaded. 'We might not find another outstation or another group of people to look after these kids. This is a rare chance to stop these kids sniffing. If we lose it, it may never come again.'

The government officers wouldn't change their position so I refused their offer of a brand-new Toyota and kept using my two old bombs. The program was too important to put at risk for the sake of a car.

I felt so frustrated, I went around to Cowen's place to find someone to talk to, Morgan, or Liam or someone. Karissa was the only one home.

I was crying and I poured my heart out to Karissa. This thing was so precious, and these government people just did not understand the reality of the power of humbug and obligations in the Warlpiri world. They did not understand any of it. As I described to Karissa the depth of relationships and obligations that tie the program together, she looked at me and said, 'It's like a marriage, isn't it?'

Nine months later, after the head of the Office for Aboriginal and Torres Strait Islander Health had visited Mt Theo, and I explained directly to her our dilemma about the vehicle, the government agreed to provide us with rules, and we accepted their grant of a Toyota.

Holding it together

Liam and I were driving back from Mt Theo in the cage truck, rattling down that corrugated road.

'You know, I'm amazed at how this thing holds together,' he said.

'Yeah, it's a pretty solid old truck,' I replied.

'No, not the truck, I'm amazed how this whole program holds together. Like, what makes it all stick? There just seems to be so much chaos going on all the time. Closing down for sorry business, reopening, vehicles breaking down.'

'Yeah,' I said, 'It's almost like one of those video games – as soon as you think you've worked things out, like how everything fits together culturally, mechanically and logistically, when you think you're finally getting a handle on things, bang, something will come in from left field, and just ups the level of complexity. Like getting to a whole new level in a game.'

'So what do you think holds it all together, Yakajirri?'

'I think it's love. I think it's us as a team, all of us – Gordon, Lindsay, Ned, Peggy and Hooker Creek, you and me. It's that we'll do anything for each other – that's what holds it all together.'

I recalled this conversation the following year when Hooker Creek and I went off to deliver a paper about Mt Theo at the Australasian Drug Strategy Conference in Adelaide. People had been saying to me, 'Mt Theo is at the cutting edge of substance abuse programs for remote Aboriginal communities' and 'My department has been trying to set something like Mt Theo up for twenty years, how do you do it?'

I thought a lot about why we had succeeded where others had not; about the pressure points and stresses involved in the program and what holds it together.

One of the key factors seemed to be the relationship between Yapa and Kardiya in the program – the cross-cultural relationships of mutual obligation. Kardiya involved in the program respected that Yapa did things differently. We recognised that Yapa had made huge personal sacrifices to do the work of caring for sniffers.

In working on the program, Peggy and Hooker Creek missed out on many of the normal aspects of contemporary Yapa social life because they were living at Mt Theo non-stop. They missed out on the freedom to travel when they felt like it, participating in sorry business and ceremonies, and the extended family and social life of living in a settlement: all aspects of life that Yapa living in Yuendumu valued highly and considered a normal part of life.

Most Yapa people in Yuendumu did not have jobs that required them to work seven days a week, being on duty 24 hours a day, whereas the workers at Mt Theo carried that level of responsibility. It was the love and support they received from other people in the program that sustained the workers at Mt Theo.

As Peggy put it, 'We look after all the petrol sniffers, even though they're not our family. You have got to help us too, family way, sorry way, tucker way, dollar way.'

This meant that as Kardiya staff, Liam and I had cultural obligations to fulfil, and by doing so we helped nurture relationships of mutual duty that in turn sustained the Yapa staff.

Examples of those obligations were:

- letting co-workers use the phone to contact distant relatives to discuss ceremonial and sorry business
- giving co-workers food if they were hungry
- lending co-workers money
- giving co-workers lifts or lending them a car so that they could attend ceremonies and fulfil cultural obligations
- picking up co-workers when they were stranded in town or out bush to get them back to work.

A lot of the whitefellas who live on communities reject such obligations as humbug. They say they are not in the 'duty statement'. But as someone with anthropological training, I knew that in Warlpiri culture, these obligations were important. I could only expect my Yapa co-workers to continue to feel obliged to work on the program if the program (or Liam and I personally) assisted them to catch up with aspects of their cultural life that they missed out on through their work at Mt Theo.

While people liked getting paid wages, wages did not carry the same weight and meaning as personal relationships. Wages were not what kept the program going through the difficult times. Emotional support and relationships of mutual obligation did.

7: Sniffer Bait

When someone sniffed petrol in Yuendumu, chances were we'd find out and take them to Mt Theo. There was always conflict and negotiation around how long someone would stay out there, but generally it was for four weeks at a time. Most of the sniffers resisted going to and staying there. In contrast, young people who were not sniffing were happy to go to Mt Theo.

Mt Theo has been described as a cross between a prison farm and a holiday camp. It depended on whether a young person was compelled to be there or not. Young people who never sniffed and

At Mt Theo

ex-sniffers would often volunteer to go out to Mt Theo to keep their sniffer friends company. These young people would laugh and sing out from the Toyota as it wound its way around Yuendumu before heading out to the mountain. Their sniffer mates were shamed and hid their heads under blankets in the very same Toyota. It was a dynamic we often worked into our strategy to get sniffers to Mt Theo. It's easier to convince a young person to go somewhere when their mates are already in the car.

Sometimes after the disco, Morgan and I unwound for an hour and then did a sniffer patrol. After midnight on a cold April night, we smelled petrol on the wind. Kids were sniffing. It was school holidays and we had borrowed the school bus to run excursions as part of the youth program. Time to do a night excursion to Mt Theo, we thought. We had some 'bait', in terms of drinks and chips left over from disco, but we did not have enough fuel.

There are no 24-hour petrol stations in Yuendumu. The only way to get diesel for the bus was to borrow it, but that involved waking someone in the middle of the night, which we didn't want to do. The other option was to steal some fuel and replace it later.

'Well, we work with sniffers,' one of us encouraged the other. 'Might as well put some of them old sniffer skills to good use.'

This was in the days of mandatory sentencing for property offences in the Northern Territory, so we were taking a bit of a risk. We could have gone to jail for stealing and the policeman already didn't like me.

Under the cover of darkness we snuck into the Mining Company yard carrying a short length of garden hose and a jerry can. The Women's Centre Toyota was on the mechanics hoist so it looked like an obvious target. That Toyota wasn't going anywhere and the Women's Centre were our friends – at least they would not send us to jail. As we siphoned a load of diesel with the garden hose, we promised each other that we would replace the fuel in the morning.

After filling up the bus with the stolen diesel, we cranked up the stereo and began a midnight cruise of Yuendumu. Outside the Council building, standing around a fire for warmth, was a group of non-sniffing teenagers. Among them was a charismatic sixteen-year-old from Willowra. Lorin had a husky voice, perfect teeth and a lean sprinter's figure. There was something really strong about her, some energy. All the young men had crushes on her. She was way cool.

Morgan and I invited Lorin and her friends to come with us for a midnight hoon to Mt Theo. They were bored and we offered some excitement for the evening. We reassured them that we wouldn't leave them there and that we'd bring them straight back. We just wanted them to convince the sniffers to get on the bus. We told them it would be the midnight party bus and offered them chips, cool drinks and smokes.

A bus loaded with teenagers, high on music and sugary soft drinks is a party that's hard to resist. It is more fun than sniffing petrol. Especially when you are a teenage bloke and the spunkiest girl in the desert is calling your name.

We took three sniffers to Mt Theo that night. Lorin and her non-sniffer friends slept in the bus on the drive back. We dropped them off at their homes in Yuendumu just after sunrise.

Morgan and I were both exhausted, but we knew that we were winning: sniffing was going to end in Yuendumu very soon. Meanwhile our poor hapless sniffers were waking up at Mt Theo, feeling hung-over and trying to remember how they got there. There was no petrol at Mt Theo and, while it could be a fun place to hang out, kids got bored and tried to run away.

Running away

Our first group of runaways struck out when the program had only just begun all those years ago. The old people took them to

Road to Mt Theo

Jurlpungu to gather bush tucker. Jurlpungu is the happy hunting ground of the Warlpiri. It has a dry creek bed where you can reliably dig for water. Sometimes Peggy would dig out a water hole in the creek bed big enough for her to have a bath. Jurlpungu is plentiful with bush fruits and kangaroos and the Tanami Road is only twenty kilometres away.

'That main road is pretty close up here,' Flint said to Brando and Lenin. 'Can't be too far to walk, hey?'

They snuck away from the group and made a run for it. Hooker Creek and Old Japangardi tracked them. Search parties were launched from Yuendumu. The Mining Company, clinic, Council and school sent out vehicles and staff.

'Can't have too many motor cars out there,' said Roy Jupurrula, the police aide. 'They'll drive everywhere and cover up all them boys' tracks.'

With so many vehicles hunting for them, the young blokes went into hiding. They were missing for two nights before Peter

Toyne found them, early one morning, trying to hitch down the Tanami Road. They were hungry and exhausted. They accepted defeat and returned to Mt Theo.

One of the critical elements in Mt Theo's success was the 'tyranny of distance'. The outstation is 50 kilometres from the nearest road so it's hard to run away. In comparison, Mala Bore, the other outstation where we used to send female sniffers, was relatively easy to run away from, being only twenty kilometres from the Tanami Road. Frequently the female sniffers we sent there walked to the Tanami Road and hitch-hiked back to Yuendumu. Young people tried to run away from Mt Theo, too, but they never made it further than about 25 kilometres. This tyranny of distance was one of the reasons why Mt Theo became the preferred outstation compared to Mala, and it ended up looking after both male and female sniffers.

In the days before we had a vehicle permanently stationed at Mt Theo, running away was a big hassle. When kids ran away, Peggy or Hooker Creek called us in Yuendumu and we borrowed a vehicle to search for the kids. When we found them four or five hours later they were tired and thirsty. They happily jumped in the car and we dropped them back at Mt Theo.

I would teasingly berate them for not carrying enough water. 'If you are going to run away, you've got to do it properly. You've got to take enough tucker and lots of water.'

However, it was a real concern. So much so that we decided to place water drums every ten kilometres along the road from Mt Theo towards Yuendumu so our runaways wouldn't go thirsty.

Once we had a vehicle permanently stationed at Mt Theo, the kids seemed to stop running away. It may have been that before a vehicle was out there, the kids were so bored that they ran away as a way to pass the time. Having a vehicle enabled the elders to broaden Mt Theo's range of activities with regular excursions. It helped overcome any 'cabin fever' the sniffers might have felt.

However, having a vehicle brought its own problems. It gave the sniffers another means of escape. Young people stole the emergency vehicle twice in the history of the Mt Theo Program. Generally there was a level of respect.

One young man did not share that respect. Mason was different. He was a social misfit in the Warlpiri world and seemed to act in a manner that suggested a disregard and lack of compassion for others. Compassion is the defining characteristic of Warlpiri culture.

Mason was highly intelligent and, although he didn't read or write much, he could solve puzzles in 'find a word' and 'code breaker' activity books that others had long given up on. He won at checkers every time. On several occasions he sabotaged the Mt Theo Toyota by loosening the wheel nuts, causing the wheel to come off while driving. He would sneakily turn off the bore, so Mt Theo ran out of water. He had the insight to know how to stuff up the program and appeared to have little conscience about carrying out acts of sabotage where other sniffers would draw the line. Some of his more dangerous acts of sabotage became a safety concern.

Mason's intelligence, together with his poor social skills and his compulsive repetitious behaviour, suggested to us he may have been autistic. We tried to get him assessed by a psychologist in Alice Springs but, without sharing a common language or culture, the whitefella psychologist was unable do a proper assessment. Mason needed help. He was a sniffer but he also had more complex problems. Mt Theo seemed to be the only service willing to help him. His parents and brother cared for him deeply but they were doubly burdened, both by his psychological condition and his sniffing.

When Mason ran away from Mt Theo he did it in grand style. I thought that we were winning, we were finally beating petrol sniffing: most young people had given it up. Mason and Fiddle were the only two sniffers left at Mt Theo and they were being looked after by Johnny Hooker Creek.

It was winter and the three of them were camped inside a tin house. A Mt Theo tin house is like a single car garage without a roller door. It is more like a shed than a house. Tin houses like this proliferated throughout the desert as a standard design of the 1980s outstation movement. There were no door handles on the doors, only pad bolts on either side to lock it shut.

Johnny awoke one morning to find Mason was gone and the door was locked from the outside. He and Fiddle were trapped inside. The metal louvre windows offered no escape. Johnny unscrewed a leg from the bed he had slept on and used it to punch a hole in the wall. Once outside, he discovered that the Toyota was missing. Mason had stolen the keys while he was asleep.

Johnny then tried to phone Yuendumu, only to find that Mason had stolen the telephone handset and put an axe through the back-up pay phone, severing its metal-encased cord. They still had the tractor, but Mason had stolen the keys to that, too!

Fiddle hotwired the little Kubota tractor and he and Hooker Creek drove 52 kilometres to the Tanami Road. The tractor didn't travel very fast and all the dogs from Mt Theo followed them. At the Tanami Road, they tried to flag down tourists for a lift. But no tourist travelling the 'wilds' of the desert was prepared to risk stopping to help out a couple of rough-looking blackfellas with a posse of dogs.

Johnny and Fiddle were stuck there all day and all night with only a small fire, one blanket and some dogs for warmth. It was the middle of winter, and in the Tanami that can mean frosts. They had no water as Mason had drained the water tank and switched off the bore.

Meanwhile back in Yuendumu, I hadn't had phone contact with Mt Theo for 24 hours. I was worried as they were meant to call me every day and they weren't answering my calls. Time to kick in the backup procedures, which meant sending out a party to Mt Theo to investigate why there had been no phone contact. Early the next morning as I was packing my Toyota the police rang me.

'We found a note on the police car stuck under the windscreen wiper this morning,' Libby the policewoman told me. 'A tourist must have left it. It said two men were stuck at the Mt Theo turn-off with a tractor and a lot of dogs.'

I bought pies, iced coffee and smokes from the store to take to my friends. When I arrived at the Mt Theo turn-off, 125 kilometres from Yuendumu, Hooker Creek and Fiddle told me the story. We then set off to find Mason and the Toyota. Hooker Creek looked carefully at the Toyota's tyre tracks, noting tread patterns and the position of various tread styles – the right-hand tyre was a Kuhmo instead of a Dunlop.

Hooker Creek tracked the Toyota over 200 kilometres to Papunya. It had broken down 30 kilometres north of that community in the sand dunes. From the tracks, it appeared that Mason had walked and later hitched to Papunya. We towed our broken-down Toyota into Papunya for repairs but we didn't find Mason.

What happened to him was very sad. He was probably sniffing when he stole another car in Alice Springs. He was probably high on petrol fumes when that car collided with a road train.

The Mt Theo mob and I went to his funeral. Peggy was so angry that someone she had cared for, for so long, had died. But caring for him was not enough. I saw his mother not long afterwards, this poor Pintubi woman walking in a shopping mall in Alice Springs. She held my hand and thanked me for looking after her son. Tears streamed down both our faces. She asked me to visit his grave. He was the first one to die directly from sniffing. *Wiyarrpa*. A bunch of flowers marks the spot where he died on the Tanami Road.

Jedda and the big needle

Jedda always faked sickness to get out of being at Mt Theo. Morgan used to describe how she displayed an array of symptoms from vomiting and nausea to throwing fits.

The elders at Mt Theo were very concerned if any young person was unwell. If the sickness could not be cured by Old Japangardi who was a *ngangkiri* (traditional healer/witch doctor), they insisted on sending the sick young person to Yuendumu clinic for some whitefella medicine.

Jedda knew this and played it to the hilt. Morgan described occasions when Jedda appeared so sick that she would have to be carried to the car, as she was too 'unwell' to walk. As they drove to Yuendumu Jedda progressively got better. Morgan's favourite yarn from this era was the occasion when halfway back to Yuendumu they came across a big mob of kangaroos at Jurlpungu. Hooker Creek was with them (he had a rifle handy) and had to go 'a-hunting'. He shot a kangaroo, injuring its leg, but didn't completely bring it down. As the kangaroo hopped away, the Warlpiri gave chase.

'And there was Jedda,' Morgan described, 'who was apparently so sick we had to take her the clinic right away. She recovered instantaneously; she leapt out of the Toyota and bounded through the bush after that kangaroo, as fast as Cathy Freeman. She wasn't sick at all.'

It was good for old Hooker Creek to see how Jedda had duped him once again. Faking sickness sometimes caused tension between the Warlpiri and the whitefellas on the program. Morgan and I didn't want kids who were more than likely to sniff again brought back to Yuendumu unnecessarily, simply because they were good at acting sick. On the other hand, Hooker Creek and Peggy didn't want to ignore medical symptoms when they were responsible for the lives of young people and were 180 kilometres from the clinic.

The solution for Jedda's fits came in the form of a needle.

Hooker Creek rang me up from Mt Theo, extremely concerned that Jedda was fitting and vomiting: 'We don't want her to go unconscious out here,' he pleaded. 'You gotta come right away.'

I asked Hooker Creek to put Jedda on the phone and told him to let her know I would be writing down her symptoms so I could tell them to the clinic. As I listened to Jedda articulate a range of contradictory symptoms, I could tell from her voice that she was not that sick after all.

I went to the clinic and explained that our 'Oscar-winning actress' from Mt Theo was 'sick' again. As I gathered together some first aid supplies I asked the nurse if she could give me a really big syringe. I didn't need a needle on the end. I just needed it for a prop.

When I got to Mt Theo, I told Hooker Creek and the gathered group of young people that I had spoken to the clinic about Jedda's symptoms and that they had given me a big needle to make her better.

'This needle will fix her,' I explained as I withdrew the huge syringe from the first aid supplies. 'She should stay here and I'll give her the needle, that's what the clinic said.'

'*Yakarra*! Needle *wirijarlu*! (Oh, my gosh! What a huge needle!)' the kids exclaimed.

They rushed into the tin shed where Jedda was waiting on her sick bed.

'Needle *wirijarlu*!' they told her and they retold all I had said.

Jedda was obviously disappointed that her 'sickness' hadn't won her a ride back to Yuendumu. But she was more frightened of getting a big needle stuck in her, and she made a miraculous recovery. A few minutes later she came out of the shed and told me she felt much better.

'Oh, we're really worried about you,' I told her. 'I'm going to stay here for all of tomorrow to make sure you don't have a relapse. We don't want you to get sick again. The nurse told me if you start to get sick or have a fit, I have to give you this big needle. The nurse said you should stay here at Mt Theo, though, no coming back to Yuendumu, too much bad trouble with petrol.'

Jedda was at the peak of fitness from then on. I took Hooker Creek aside and explained the ruse to him. When I left Mt Theo I made a big show of handing the syringe to Hooker Creek who then locked it in his tucker box.

'I'm leaving the needle with Hooker Creek,' I announced. 'And I've instructed him to give it to Jedda if she gets sick again.'

Jedda didn't get 'sick' at Mt Theo again. Most of the kids hardly ever got sick – the outstation life tends to be healthy. If a young person did get sick, we preferred to bring the nurse out to Mt Theo, rather than the patient going into Yuendumu. This avoided part of the attraction of sickness, being a ride into Yuendumu and escape from Mt Theo. On nearly all of the clinic visits the nurse reported that our sniffers were in good health.

Jedda's last episode of sniffing occurred during the last wave of sniffing during early 2002. She's now a member of the Jaru Pirrjirdi 'Strong Voices' team and regularly volunteers to stay at Mt Theo to 'look after those young people'.

You've got to leave

If Mt Theo was a prison and not a school, how did we expel someone? It was a very tricky business. It was unsafe to have certain kinds of behaviour out there 180 kilometres away from the clinic and the police. We simply couldn't afford to have a young person staying there who presented a serious risk of harm to themselves or other people. It was unsafe for us to have residents who were uncontrollably violent, who self-mutilated or who were suicidal.

On the other hand, we couldn't be seen by the petrol sniffers in Yuendumu and the young people at Mt Theo as caving in to violence. If young people thought the way to avoid being forced to stay at Mt Theo was to act violently or suicidal, then many of them would have copied this behaviour and we would have had a completely ineffective program.

For the most part, our dealing with such behaviour was discreet. Serious suicide attempts were dealt with by transporting the client to the mental health ward in Alice Springs. This served as a disincentive to 'fake' suicidal behaviour. Teenagers were happy to say 'if you send me to Mt Theo I will kill myself' but they weren't happy to be sent to the mental health ward.

Violence was also tricky to deal with. Sometimes it was straightforward and we threatened the young person with assault charges and jail time if they didn't settle down. In most cases that curbed violent behaviour. However, some young people appeared uncontrollably violent and warnings about jail time had no effect. That was when the young person had to leave. Decisions about these matters largely rested with the elders who monitored and managed behaviour at Mt Theo. Expulsions from Mt Theo were rare but they did happen.

At about two-thirty one winter afternoon I arrived at Mt Theo in Hooker Creek's little Subaru. After unloading the rations, Hooker Creek and I sat beneath the shade of a ghost gum sharing his old tobacco pipe. As we smoked, Hooker Creek told me of his concerns about one of the young men, Brad: 'He's been fighting again, really bad trouble that one. He been punch one of the girls and running around with iron bar, trying to smash people. He been bust up that telephone.'

All the usual threats about police and jail were made but Brad just relished that sort of conflict. The last time the police tried to arrest him in Yuendumu he threw petrol on the policeman and then threatened to throw lighted matches at him. We didn't want to send Brad to prison, as one of our goals was to prevent young people from getting locked up. But we didn't want to send him back to Yuendumu either, as we knew he would go straight back to sniffing and his violence would have been rewarded. Originally Brad had arrived in Yuendumu from Hermannsburg and he was keen to return to Hermannsburg.

'My grandfather's on the Council there. I can stay with him,' he told us.

We rang Ntaria Council at Hermannsburg to speak with the grandfather.

'That Brad Simmons has been banned from our community for a year,' said the serious Arrernte voice on the end of the phone. 'He's been causing too much trouble here.'

We were back to exploring other options. Brad said he had an uncle in Lajamanu he could stay with who was a policeman. We tried to phone the uncle and got no answer. We had to take the chance.

The Subaru only had enough fuel to get back to Yuendumu and Lajamanu was over 600 kilometres away. It was a Tuesday which meant that the roadhouse at Rabbit Flat was closed. Rabbit Flat only opens between Fridays and Mondays. But we didn't have much choice. There was too much tension between Brad and the other young people at Mt Theo. He had a short fuse and the others seemed to enjoy setting him off. It was unsafe to leave him there.

We rang Rabbit Flat and spoke to the proprietor, Bruce Farrands, to let him know that we were coming and wanted to buy fuel. Bruce is a wild character straight out of a classic picture book of outback legends. He has a big bushy beard and is married to a landscape artist from Paris, who he somehow romanced with the idea of building a roadhouse at Rabbit Flat. When Bruce and his bride arrived in the 1970s there was nothing, except for maybe a rabbit, to give the place its name. Nowadays the huge cedar trees they planted serve as a beacon for the outback traveller in an otherwise flat and desolate landscape. The roadhouse itself is a besser brick fortress. Trade is done through a small window that is less than 60 centimetres (two foot) square and even that is protected with heavy-grade security mesh. Bruce has to unlock a door in the mesh to conduct a purchase and the door is just big enough to slide through a carton of beer.

Locals say if you arrive at the roadhouse when it's closed, Bruce will confront you with a gun and tell you to get lost. If this all sounds a bit paranoid, then there is good reason for it. Rabbit Flat is 80 kilometres from the West Australian border and 300 kilometres from the nearest police station. It is Australia's most remote roadhouse. Bruce stocks all the things that are prized in the desert: fuel, cigarettes, beer and cash. What sort of self-respecting bandit wouldn't be tempted to rob the place before fleeing to Western Australia? The legend of Bruce and his gun-toting habits helps keep people honest.

Our other problem was that Hooker Creek and I didn't have any money on us. I had planned to go straight back to Yuendumu from Mt Theo so I wasn't carrying any cash. When we arrived at Rabbit Flat we confessed our cashless situation to Bruce. We had already explained to him over the phone our problem with having to relocate Brad.

'No worries,' said Bruce. 'You guys are regular customers, you can book up.' I was so grateful. Bruce must have a pretty broad definition of 'regular customers' as I had only been to Rabbit Flat three times in the preceding six years. But we knew of each other. The bush telegraph told me all his gun-toting stories and he must have heard about that crazy young whitefella from Mt Theo.

After having a meal and buying fuel we continued to Lajamanu. When we arrived at midnight, we found Brad's uncle. Sure enough there was a police Toyota parked outside his house; he really was a policeman.

While Brad went inside to catch up with his cousins, Hooker Creek and I explained the situation to the uncle.

'I'll keep a sharp eye on him,' the uncle assured us. 'No one sniffs in Lajamanu, we don't let them.'

The uncle spoke the truth; sniffing is very rare in Lajamanu. Kids who sniff all day in Yuendumu and other places simply don't sniff in Lajamanu. While this perplexes whitefella experts who believe in the 'addictive' qualities of sniffing, it makes complete sense to Warlpiri. Sniffing is just not the done thing in Lajamanu. It is too shameful for anyone to sniff there.

Before we left, the uncle showed us the certificate of commendation he had recently been awarded by the Northern Territory police. Things were going to be all right for Brad.

Hooker Creek and I drove back to Yuendumu through the night. We took shifts and made it home just after sunrise. The poor little Subaru had taken a hammering on that road; half its muffler had broken off.

'We're running out of sniffers,' I said to Hooker Creek, above the roar of the exhaust. 'Those girls are due to go back to Yuendumu next week and they had only sniffed for one night

Stuart Pope, with young people at Mt Theo 1994

before. They probably won't sniff again. Then we'll only have two sniffers left.'

Hooker Creek grinned and looked at me with his milky old drover's eyes. 'We're doing a good job, hey. Good stockmen, you and me. We been catch a lot of wild sniffers and muster 'em up to Mt Theo, give them good country, good tucker and make them quiet ones.'

'Yeah,' I agreed. 'But we've got those government bigwigs coming out in two weeks and we've got no sniffers to show them.'

The head of the Office of Aboriginal and Torres Strait Islander Health and the chairperson of the Prime Minister's Council on Drugs were due to visit us, but our program was so effective at stopping sniffing in Yuendumu that we were running out of clients.

'We should get that runaway one,' Hooker Creek suggested.

I knew the boy he was talking about. He was on a court bond to be at Mt Theo but he had run away when he went to Papunya for a relative's funeral and was now sniffing at another community, 250 kilometres away.

We got Francis Jupurrula Kelly of the TV series *Bush Mechanics* fame, to weld up the broken muffler. He fixed it with a piece of old galvanised pipe that had once been part of the school fence. Morgan joined us as the third 'stockman' and we headed off, driving south over the sand dunes. When we arrived at that distant community, our runaway sniffer was easy to find. He was sitting in the bedroom of his family's home, sniffing petrol from an old milk tin.

'You gotta go now,' his family said and he calmly came with us in the Subaru.

As we drove out of town we could see sniffing was rife in that place. Young people were openly walking down the street in broad daylight, soft drink cans filled with petrol held under their noses. It was a shame we could only take one. But we had a right to come and gather him. We had no right to round up all the other sniffers we saw that day. They were not our tribe, and culturally it was inappropriate to have them at Mt Theo.

The Pintubi-Luritja people need a homeland of their own, a place where their sniffers can get well again. And they need good people, blackfellas and whitefellas to save those young people's lives. I'm sad when I think of that day in that place, knowing that some of those young people we saw are now dead from sniffing, and knowing that stopping sniffing is not impossible.

It just takes people who care enough. It may only take eight years to save a generation of young people in a community, but what an honourable way to spend eight years of your life, to do something that really counts, something that makes a difference.

8: The End of Sniffing

When we first began tackling petrol sniffing we thought we could fix the problem in a few months. We had no idea back then that five years later sniffing would still be pervasive in our community. I came to the conclusion that sniffing would never really be extinguished. I likened our work to bailing water out of a leaking boat. If we were consistent and we worked hard enough, we could deal pretty much with the problem, but petrol sniffing was always going to be there. Then came the summer that changed everything: my fifth summer in Yuendumu.

Government funding was really important here and so were people. Despite our troubles with the big bad wolf, we were well funded that year. I had quit working at the school was now able to work for Mt Theo full-time. So in addition to having Liam, who had been doing most of the whitefella support for the program (running rations and supplies to Mt Theo and putting on the disco), another whitefella was able to be devoted full-time to the cause. The biggest difference this made was that Mt Theo no longer had to close down when the elders had to go away on sorry business. In the past, the sniffers were sent back to their families in Yuendumu whenever the elders had to go away. The young people always promised not to sniff again, but inevitably some kids sniffed and encouraged their friends to join them.

Having a 'spare' whitefella changed all that. When the elders went away, I lived at Mt Theo and looked after the sniffers. The consistency of keeping young people at Mt Theo and away from petrol meant we were able to more effectively stop sniffing in Yuendumu.

Morgan running the Mt Theo school four days a week was making a difference too. A consistent program of activities centred around the school had a positive impact on those young people – six months later they were no longer sniffing.

The most significant person responsible for the change that brought the end to petrol sniffing was Johnny Hooker Creek. Over that summer, when Peggy and everyone else went off on ceremony business, Hooker Creek stayed at Mt Theo and for the first time, it stayed open over summer.

Summer had always been the worst time for petrol sniffing in Yuendumu. It was when sniffing numbers escalated and when Mt Theo was usually closed. The kids were often bored during the long school holidays and sniffing flourished among the restless youth. Often Mt Theo would be closed for three or four months as elders were tied up in cultural business that would take them travelling to join in corroborees all across the Western Desert stretching from Katherine to Kalgoorlie.

This summer Mt Theo stayed open. Sniffers were kept there all summer long. They were not sent home, unless they promised not to sniff. If anyone was found sniffing in Yuendumu, they were sent straight out to Mt Theo for four weeks. By January sniffing was nearly gone – it was amazing. I could not remember a petrol-free summer before.

Another person who had an impact was Karissa Preuss, the young university student who spent that summer at Mt Theo. Karissa had been volunteering at Yuendumu School, and when Morgan went on school holidays we asked her if she would like to be the 'teacher' at Mt Theo and support Hooker Creek. She packed a box full of books, pencils and paper and continued the 'Mt Theo School' that summer.

At twenty years old, she wasn't much older than most of the young people who were living out there. It was like a cultural exchange of youthful energy: for part of the day Karissa would help the sniffers to read or fill in workbooks in the little school shed or outside on swags. For the rest of the day, the Warlpiri would teach Karissa language and skin names, how to collect bush food, and the Dreaming stories of Mt Theo.

Hooker Creek and Karissa Preuss at Mt Theo 1998

Images from that summer are of barefoot young people, white and Warlpiri, sharing a feast of bush turkey, having barrel races on 44-gallon drums, swimming in water tanks, collecting bush tomatoes, and hunting goannas with crow bars and digging sticks. We celebrated New Year's Eve by rigging up a wire in a tree as an aerial and tuning in the AM radio on a broken cassette player, so we could listen to rock 'n' roll (broadcast from country Victoria as it was the only station we could pick up), while 'getting drunk' on red cordial and dancing in the New Year.

Like many young white people, Karissa liked spending time with friends engaged in D&Ms (deep and meaningful conversations). No one had told Karissa you could not do that with Warlpiri teenagers. Counsellors, psychologists and youth workers had tried but no one reported success. Maybe it was because Karissa was more of a peer than an authority figure that made the difference. Or maybe it was her youthful naivety which meant she related to the young people at Mt Theo just like she did with her friends back home.

The magic of it was that Karissa engaged the sniffers in deep and meaningful conversations about life, their families, and their hopes and dreams. Her curiosity about wanting to get to know her new group of friends acted as a catalyst. Almost accidentally, she engaged the young people in conversations that reflected on the very issues that underlie petrol sniffing. No one had done that before.

As the warmer months wound up, more and more sniffers moved back to Yuendumu and didn't sniff again. There was a change in the air; you could walk round Yuendumu on any night and the air was different – you couldn't smell petrol. By June we had run out of sniffers.

When the chairperson of the Australian National Council on Drugs, Brian Watters, and the head of the Office of Aboriginal and Torres Strait Islander Health came out to Mt Theo to visit our program, we only had two sniffers from Yuendumu left, Fenella and Esau, who were nearly at the end of their stay. We actually asked Esau to stay a few days longer to keep Fenella company and to look like we had clients. We also had the other sniffer we collected from beyond Papunya, the one we brought back, so we could show these government bigwigs our program actually did have some clients.

It was unbelievable … I had given up hope that this situation was possible, that sniffing would stop in Yuendumu, and Mt Theo would run out of clients. It had been six years since those first desperate attempts to stop sniffing. But it had finally stopped.

An outreach program is born

We worried that the government would stop funding the Mt Theo Program if we were no longer seen to be 'treating' any clients. A large part of the program's effectiveness was the deterrent factor. As long as Mt Theo remained open, there was a deterrent against sniffing for young people in Yuendumu. Mt Theo also gave

Members of the Ngaanyatjarra Pitjantjatjara Yankunytjatjara Women's Council visiting Mt Theo in 1999 to learn about how to set up similar anti-petrol sniffing progams in the Pitjantjatjara lands.

Yuendumu a mechanism to deal with sniffing if it arose in the future. The stories I had read about sniffing campaigns in other communities revealed a pattern of sniffing starting up again a few years after an anti-petrol sniffing campaign ended. Maggie Brady, the social anthropologist, said it is cyclical. It's like a kids' craze that returns every few years – like yoyos and hula hoops. We needed to keep Mt Theo open, to maintain the focus and energy.

Over the years, we had been approached by people in other Aboriginal communities to look after their petrol sniffers at Mt Theo. We were reluctant for many reasons – the main one being that the elders at Mt Theo were concerned about any fallout if something went wrong while they were looking after a kid from another community. If a kid became sick or injured, there was the threat of payback escalating into intertribal and intercommunity fighting. We were also concerned that a non-Warlpiri kid wouldn't respect the *Jukurrpa* of Mt Theo or the authority of the Warlpiri elders.

But now we had run out of sniffers and people were still asking us for help. Hooker Creek, Peggy and I sat around the campfire at Mt Theo and talked about taking on kids from the other Warlpiri communities – Lajamanu, Nyirripi and Willowra. We thought we could offer these communities Mt Theo as a place to send their petrol sniffers.

When we discussed this with elders and Council members in Yuendumu, we were overwhelmed by their praise. They said, 'We're really proud of you. We're proud of what you have done saving these petrol sniffers' lives and we're proud of Mt Theo. Other Yapa are talking about Mt Theo across the desert, in Papunya, Lajamanu, Kintore, Balgo and in the Pitjantjatjara lands. Yapa are happy for us.'

Headline

The big bad wolf was not finished with me yet. I'm not sure what forced him to leave in the end, whether he had been exposed for his links to the firm that had conducted the review, or if the Department of Local Government had pressured him to leave because of all the trouble. I don't like having to pick up a light sabre to defend the program – I hate conflict, but I believe in standing up for what's important.

The police sergeant might have hated me too. The wolf was his mate and I had clashed swords with his mate. Despite many protests from the community to the police, I was still being charged for the accident at Ginty's Bore. One of his drinking mates told me the sergeant said I was going down. I was up on three charges: Committing a Dangerous Act; Driving in a Manner Dangerous; and Driving without Due Care.

The criminal charge of Committing a Dangerous Act worried me. It carried a maximum seven-year prison term. My lawyers advised me to plea bargain because they couldn't assure me that I wouldn't be stuck with a criminal conviction if I did not. I did not want to go to jail. I did not want a criminal record. I was one of the good guys, wasn't I?

I trudged around Yuendumu asking members of every family group to sign letters asking for the charges to be dropped. As I approached each household, I thought 'I've been here before'.

There wasn't one household in the community that hadn't been touched by sniffing. And there wasn't one household where the Mt Theo Program hadn't been there to help. Praise and support was heaped upon me at every home: 'Of course we'll sign it, Yakajirri, you helped our kids.'

I realised how deeply the program was embedded in the community; every family had been touched by it. Even the Justice of the Peace who had signed my charge sheet had written me a letter of support.

Johnny Hooker Creek at the Australasian Drugs Strategy Conference 1999

My court date was in Alice Springs. I had just flown back into Alice with Hooker Creek. We were guests of the South Australian police at the National Drugs Strategy Conference in Adelaide where we were lauded as heroes. They paid for our airfares and put us up in the Adelaide Hilton. Now, on the very next day, I was in court, a defendant and a guest of the Northern Territory police.

I was wearing the same suit I wore at the conference. I was shit scared. I didn't want to go to jail.

The conditions of the police prosecutor's offer of a plea bargain was that they would drop the criminal charge if I pleaded guilty to the lesser charge of Driving without Due Care, a charge that carried a mandatory six month licence suspension. My lawyer argued my case. He told the story leading up to the accident. He said I was remorseful, citing that I had used my own money to buy a bigger Toyota, a Troop Carrier for the program to use, to avoid any further repetition of people having to travel on the roof. He also mentioned the letter of apology that Liam had read out to the Council. He pointed out that people still wanted me in the community.

I felt I had no choice; I didn't want a criminal charge so I pleaded guilty to Driving without Due Care. The magistrate disagreed.

'But he was driving very slowly and carefully,' he argued with the prosecutor. 'Surely this charge is not appropriate.'

'But he's already pleaded guilty to the charge, your Honour,' countered the prosecutor. 'And we refuse to withdraw it.'

'I'm thinking about the impact it will have on the community if this man loses his licence. He's the lynch pin for Mt Theo,' the magistrate said.

The magistrate knew the Mt Theo Program well. He had seen me in Yuendumu Court many times, standing next to young petrol sniffers, offering them support. He knew what the Mt Theo Program was about and the good work we did. He was much better at defending me than my own lawyer. He adjourned the court for an hour so that he could research the legislation, looking for a loophole to avoid the mandatory licence suspension, but he couldn't find one.

The magistrate asked me about my plans. I said I was planning to move to Canberra at the end of the year with my family. He agreed to defer sentencing until then so my loss of licence wouldn't affect the community. When he finally sentenced me in December he recorded 'no conviction' and described my punishment as 'an injustice'.

Meanwhile the media had jumped on the case. Aboriginal Customary Law and tribal payback by spearing were hot issues. In huge letters splashed across the front page of the *Centralian Advocate* was the headline, 'Driver: Give me payback,' and an article describing my case. They had picked up on my letter of apology read out at Council, which my lawyer had referred to, indicating that I was prepared to go through payback for injuring Osmond and Vasco.

Fourteen months later the new Sergeant at Yuendumu Police Station rang me at home in Canberra: 'When you are coming back?' he asked. 'Things are pretty crook here and if you come back you'll be welcomed as a hero.'

It felt good that the police liked me again and that the last vestiges of the big bad wolf era had gone.

Two fires

When Morgan came back from his Christmas break at the start of the new year he took over Liam's position in the program. Liam figured that sniffing was nearly beaten, and had gone to work for Warlukurlangu, the Arts Centre. Morgan had bought himself an old 1970s Toyota Land Cruiser station wagon. It ran for six months taking rations to Mt Theo before it died.

My Warlpiri grandmother Agie Napurrula and I were driving to Mt Theo with Peggy's daughter-in-law Veronica and her two children. Veronica Nangala was 19 years old. She was a pretty Pitjantjatjara girl from Pipalyatjara. She had big brown eyes, framed by exquisitely long lashes. I had first met her at Mt Theo four years earlier when she had just married Peggy's son Japanangka. She was fifteen back then. They made a beautiful young couple, basking in the innocence of first love.

The Toyota was packed full of rations: 20 kilos of meat, 40 kilos of flour, milk powder, vegetables, oranges, cordial etc. We had just crossed over the big sand ridge that sits south of Mt Theo when smoke started pouring out from the engine. I pulled the Toyota up in the shade of a tree and popped the bonnet. Hot black oil was spewing everywhere from the head of the motor.

'What's wrong, Yakajirri?' Veronica asked me.

'Looks like we've blown a head gasket, Nangala. We can't drive this car anymore or we will wreck Morgan's motor.'

It was time to sit down, have a cup of tea and a smoke and think. The backup plan was that if we couldn't get home that night, Morgan would worry for us and organise a search party. He would also be worried for his Toyota. That is one of the beautiful things about borrowing other people's cars. If you break down in someone else's car, they will nearly always organise a rescue party for you, simply because they want their car back.

But getting rescued in the middle of the night is embarrassing and, besides, I could see Mt Theo from where we broke down, with its big dome-shaped hills on the horizon. I told Napurrula and Nangala that I was going to walk to Mt Theo and ask Hooker Creek to get them.

The road between Mt Theo and us did a bit of a dog-leg, turning north-west for twenty kilometres before sharply heading east for three kilometres.

'Yakajirri,' Veronica said, 'When that road goes *karlarra* (west) and Purturlu (Mt Theo) is *yatijarra* (to the north), you should foot walk straight to Mt Theo through the bush.'

She drew a map on the sand indicating how I could cut across and head straight to Mt Theo, rather than following the longer route of the dog-legged road.

'Good idea, Nangala, I'll do that.'

She flashed me one of her smiles. I packed an empty flour bag with some water and oranges and headed off for my bushwalk to Mt Theo.

'Good luck, Yakajirri,' chorused Nangala and Napurrula.

'Good luck Yakaji,' echoed the kids.

I love bushwalking.

And I love Napurrula, my old grandmother who 'adopted' me and who makes me damper.

And I love big smiles that make me feel good all over.

And I love those little kids with echo voices, little Napaljarri, my niece, Veronica's daughter, for whom I had made a *parraja* (baby carrier) when she was a newborn.

And I love Hooker Creek, my old man friend who is waiting for me at Mt Theo.

I love this job, being part of this whole thing, being part of this family, of this community, of this network of relationships.

It's easy to feel like singing when you head out on a walk like that, striding through the desert. I felt strong and fit; I had nothing to worry about. Mt Theo looked less than twenty kilometres away, I had plenty of water and the afternoon sun was not too hot.

I strode out along that road, my boots kicking up little puffs of dust. I walked over the last little sand ridge, so that when I looked back I could no longer see my friends or the Toyota. When I got to the bend Veronica had told me about, where the road turns west, I left the track and made a beeline for Mt Theo. I sang Shane Howard and Neil Murray songs out loud, filling my lungs with joy and my mind with lyrical words about this red heart land.

It was an easy march and I was making good time but the sun was setting and there were a few small limestone ridges between me and Mt Theo. The ridges weren't difficult to climb but they obscured my view of the outstation itself which sits on the mountain's eastern flank. So I based my navigation by looking at the hilled domes at the top of the mountain, and plotting my path by them.

The setting sun was a problem. Once it was dark I would no longer be able to see the hills in the distance, and then how would I find my way to Mt Theo? There was no track to guide me.

I am no sailor. I do not know how to navigate by the stars, but I had lived with Warlpiri for six years and I knew the power of fire. So this was my plan: before the daylight was gone, I would start lighting little spinifex fires as I walked. That way, once it was dark, I would have left behind me a line of fires pointing to Mt Theo. By looking back at them, I would be able to work out which way to go.

Meanwhile, unbeknownst to me, Hooker Creek, sitting at Mt Theo, had seen my smoke. The smoke from my little fires. He knew fire means people and people usually light fires if they have broken down to signal to others for help.

In the old days before whitefellas, smoke from fires was used to announce one's presence when visiting the country of another tribe or clan. People would see the smoke and know that someone was coming. They would then light a fire of their own, to 'answer' the smoke.

Even today, Warlpiri talk about nomadic people who still live the bush life in the desert. They say that if you go west of Nyirripi and Lake Mackay and light a fire, the nomads will answer your smoke.

Hooker Creek was expecting us to arrive with rations so he drove out to look for us. He later described to me how he drove down the road twenty kilometres until he found my footprints near the bend, where my tracks had left the road and headed into the bush. He didn't see the broken-down Toyota with Napurrula and

Nangala and the two kids. Their position was obscured from view behind the sand ridge.

Hooker Creek looked north after my footprints and saw the smoke from my fires. He drove back to Mt Theo and took his Subaru on a rough hunting trail that headed south towards the limestone ridges. He drove until the trail ran out. Then he lit a fire of his own.

As I climbed to the top of a limestone ridge I saw the glow of a fire in the distance. It made me curious. It was a big fire and wasn't from Mt Theo. It was a little too far south. I thought they were burning some rubbish off at the tip.

But the fire made a good landmark at night, so I headed towards it. As I weaved through the maze of low limestone ridges, I would sometimes lose sight of this fire, but at least I had something to aim for. I rounded yet another ridge and the fire appeared to have moved. It seemed to be in a different place. Then I saw that there were two fires. More weaving and yet another fire appeared.

Straining my eyes to look at this third mysterious fire, I could barely make out the silhouette of a figure crouched over it, and then a small burst of flame as a clump of spinifex came alight.

I answered by lighting a fire of my own and kept walking on. A few minutes later another fire, this time closer, was lit by the distant silhouette. Again I answered with a fire of my own. And that was how we came to meet that night, Johnny Hooker Creek and I: two lines of fire across the desert.

Hooker Creek's carton of beer

After moving the Mt Theo Program back to the Tanami Network, we hoped our administrative problems were over. In fact, things had gone relatively smoothly for nearly a year since we had escaped the Council and the big bad wolf. The Tanami Network was a video-conferencing network set up by the same people who were the founders of our program: Peter Toyne, Ned, Robin Japanangka and Peggy. Previously, Peter Toyne had managed to get some funding for the Mt Theo Program through the network.

By the time we moved the program back to the Tanami Network, Peter Toyne had left Yuendumu and had moved into a career in politics.

Our problems started in winter after a new network manager was appointed. He attempted to administer the program using a methodology called 'line management'. Part of this methodology was to insist that staff get prior authorisation to travel between Yuendumu and Mt Theo.

The manager worked part time and lived 300 kilometres away in Alice Springs. The system didn't work because nearly all travel to Mt Theo was unplanned and in response to an incident or opportunity. For example, if we noticed young people sniffing at night while we were running the disco, we would try to collect the sniffers at one or two o'clock in the morning, and take them to Mt Theo. Sometimes the young people would agree to come with us and sometimes they would not. If young people were willing to go to Mt Theo it was important to run with that energy. It was an essential factor in the program's success that we were able to seize each opportunity to break kids out of the sniffing cycle.

So it was completely impractical to seek 'prior authorisation' for such trips.

The other problem was that the Tanami Network bookkeeper told us and the Commonwealth that the network was under investigation from the Securities Commission and was at risk of having its bank accounts frozen and assets seized. Mt Theo Program's funds and assets were also at risk.

The solution we proposed was that we incorporate the Mt Theo Program into an independent body. We were sick of having the program mucked around nearly every time a new whitefella took up a management position in whatever organisation we were administered under. We invited the regional manager of Commonwealth Health to a meeting with the program founders, staff and traditional owners at Mt Theo to discuss the proposal. One week before this meeting, Johnny Hooker Creek approached me:

'Yakajirri, I gotta take my brother Crocodile back to Lajamanu this weekend and I want you to come with me. I'm worried when I get up there all my brother and old stockman mates are going to take me drinking at Top Spring and I'll never get back to Mt Theo for work.'

Hooker Creek spoke the truth. I remember on previous occasions when he had gone to Lajamanu for a quick trip and then had disappeared for months at a time, drinking in Top Springs and then at Katherine. He was wise to ask me to accompany him on the trip.

We headed out of Yuendumu on a Saturday morning in Hooker Creek's little Subaru. After 300 kilometres of rattling down the Tanami Road we reached Rabbit Flat at about lunchtime and then continued up through Supplejack. About 100 kilometres north of Rabbit Flat, we saw a skinny blackfella broken down by the side of the road. He had a clapped-out Falcon, with no bonnet, no glass in any of the windows or windscreen and no tyres. He was driving the car on four metal wheel rims that had started off round but were looking more like squares. This bush mechanic was from deep in the desert; he had dreadlocks, not the stylish Bob Marley look, but stringy matted brown hair ropes, thick with desert dust and goanna fat. He waved us down. He didn't speak much English and probably hailed from one of those Madujarra or Pintubi tribes that are still rumoured to be living nomadically in the desert – Myall bush people, as the Warlpiri call them.

The metal fuel pipe that fed into his carburettor had cracked. We didn't have many tools – a shifter, a few screwdrivers, a pair of long nose pliers and a file for sharpening Hooker Creek's axe. We looked at the broken pipe and came up with a plan.

If we could cut the cracked bit of the pipe off, then we could create a new flange and stretch it to fit the carburettor. Using the file as our hacksaw, we cut the pipe and then heated the metal in the fire the bushman had lit to cook a goanna. Once the metal was soft from heat, we used the long nose pliers to create a new flange. Miraculously it fitted back on the carburettor.

The wild bush mechanic sprang into his car and kicked the starter over. The engine fired and coughed then sprang into life. And petrol pissed everywhere. The flange was good, but it was not a good seal, and consequently petrol sprayed out of it every time the engine turned. We needed a gasket.

Back to thinking.

Chewing over ideas I realised that I was chewing on a Mintie sweet. I chewed two more Minties and used them to create a seal for the fuel pipe. It worked like a charm. The bush mechanic told us he was going to Piccaninny Bore Outstation, about twenty kilometres away, to look for rounder wheel rims to put on his car. There was no way you could find tyres with air in them, so new round rims were the next best thing.

Hooker Creek, Crocodile and I continued north to Lajamanu and arrived by late afternoon. Hooker Creek introduced me to all his relatives as his nephew.

'This my *nguniaryi*,' he said. 'We been working together long time at Mt Theo together looking after all those sniffers. We been travelling all over together. We been go down to Adelaide to big conference (Australasian Drugs Strategy Conference) with all the police. We stayed in a big motel and went to a wine taste with all the police together.'

We stayed at the home of Hooker Creek's son, who had been a sniffer at Mt Theo when the program first started.

The next morning Hooker Creek and I headed back towards Yuendumu. When we arrived at Rabbit Flat, the desert roadhouse was like a party going off. Every man and his dog was there. There were people from Yuendumu who were returning from Western Australia. There were newly adopted relatives of mine from Lajamanu, who were calling me nephew and shouting me and Hooker Creek beers. One man even gave me his watch, to signify our eternal friendship. The travelling 'tax man' was there and even the wild Pintubi bush mechanic was there – his Falcon had made it, with its new round rims.

After a few hours, I decided it was time to leave and suggested to Hooker Creek that we got a six-pack of beer for the road, as I knew there was no way to convince him to leave such a great party without a bit of grog bait. Hooker Creek, who seemed to have no money, agreed. I bought the six-pack and then, as I was walking out, Hooker Creek (who I believed had no money) miraculously produced another $60 and bought an additional full carton of beer 'for the road'. We left the party and headed south towards Chilla Well.

As we were driving along I thought to myself – what are we going to do with that carton of beer? We were planning to go to Mt Theo that night and there was no way we could take the beer there. We passed Chilla Well and turned onto the Mt Theo road with only 50 k's to go. I had been enthusiastically feeding Hooker Creek the beer in the hope he would fall asleep and I could stash the full carton in the bush before we got to Mt Theo.

Mt Theo is a sacred place. It has a long established ethos that grog is not allowed. Luckily, 10 kilometres before Mt Theo, Hooker Creek fell asleep. I slipped the Subaru into neutral and let it gently roll to a stop. I checked the passenger seat. Hooker Creek was still asleep. I opened the door ever so gently and sneaked out the carton of beer. I walked about 50 metres off the road out into the scrub and hid the carton of beer under a bush, next to a big gum tree that I would recognise. I broke off a eucalypt branch and swept away my footprints as I walked to the car. Ever so gently again, I closed the door and then slowly released the clutch to ease the car into motion. Hooker Creek was still asleep. Two kilometres before Mt Theo as we rounded the sharp right-hand bend Hooker Creek woke up. He looked around the inside of the car and exclaimed: 'Where's my carton of beer?'

'I hid it in the bush back there between here and Chilla Well.'

'What did you do that for? It's my carton of beer.'

'Shh, Johnny,' I said. 'You know we're not supposed to bring grog into Mt Theo. You know how upset Peggy will be if we turn up here drunk with a full carton of beer.'

'It's not her fucking country, I want my fucking carton of beer. I'm the fucking traditional owner, it's my country and my beer.'

'Hooker Creek, it's cool, I know where the beer is, and we're going to drink it, I promise you, as your nephew, *ngamirni* (uncle). You and me, we're going to go and get that beer and we're going to drink it. But not now, we're going to drink it later. Right now we gotta go to Mt Theo.'

When we arrived at Mt Theo, Peggy berated Hooker Creek for being drunk.

The next morning, a Monday, Hooker Creek drove Peggy into Yuendumu for a meeting of Tanami Network directors to discuss the upcoming business with the Government about the independence of the Mt Theo Program. I stayed behind at Mt Theo to look after the young people.

I'm sure Hooker Creek drove along the road to Chilla Well very slowly, keeping a sharp eye out for any signs of where the car had stopped and where the beer was hidden. Hooker Creek is an expert tracker. He is able to track runaway sniffers at night through rocky country where a white man can find no trace of a track. One Christmas he even tracked me down, by following my steps on a bitumen road and locating my tracks in a thin strip of dirt where I left the road to enter a friend's driveway. So for the next week, this expert tracker drove up and down the road from

Mt Theo to Chilla Well, looking for the tracks that would lead him to the carton of beer. He never found that beer.

Meanwhile Morgan and I were gearing up for the big meeting with the Government at Mt Theo on Friday. Strategically it was probably the most important Government meeting in the history of Mt Theo. It was the meeting to decide the future of the program, whether we could be trusted to run our own show as an independent organisation.

On Thursday night I spoke with Morgan: 'Listen mate, I've got a carton of Hooker Creek's beer hidden out near Mt Theo that we've got to get rid of. I can't give it all to Hooker Creek 'cause he'll drink the whole lot in one sitting by himself. So how about you and me and Hooker Creek and Robin drink it tomorrow night after the Government meeting.'

'Good idea,' said Morgan. 'That way we can celebrate if things go well. We can grab some nibblies and ice at the store and get an esky to chill the beer in. Are you sure Hooker Creek hasn't found it already?'

'No way, mate, he rings me up every day from Mt Theo asking me where I've hidden it.'

The Government blokes arrived in Yuendumu at about ten o'clock the next morning. A convoy of seven cars headed out towards Mt Theo. Ned Jampijimpa jumped in with the government blokes as their guide. Program founders and traditional owners piled into old Falcons, Commodores and Toyotas for the trip to the mountain. Morgan and I were the last to leave. We got meeting supplies from the store: chops, salad and bread for the barbecue. We also remembered to get ice to chill the beer.

When we got to that spot on the road ten kilometres out of Mt Theo, we stopped the car. I noticed footprints leading to the bush where the carton of beer was hidden. Oh hell, I thought. But the beer was safe in the bush and I felt perplexed as to who was the owner of the footprints. I put the beer on ice in the esky and went back to the car. When we arrived at Mt Theo, Ned was laughing.

'We found your carton of beer, Yakajirri.'

Oh shit, I thought, we were trying so hard to impress the government blokes that we were responsible enough to administer the program on our own. And here on Aboriginal land, where it is illegal to have alcohol, and at the very outstation where we ran a rehabilitation program for petrol sniffers, the government blokes had found a hidden case of beer.

Ned was laughing at me: 'We found your carton of beer, Yakajirri. This government bloke here, he needed to stop and have a piss so he went off in the bush and found your carton of beer.'

What were the chances? There are 140 kilometres between Yuendumu and Mt Theo and, of all the places to take a piss, he chose to stop in the exact spot where I had stopped. And then he chose the same side of the road as where I had hidden the beer! The beer that Hooker Creek, the expert tracker and thirsty alcoholic, had been looking for all week. I had to think fast.

'Where was this carton of beer, Ned?' I inquired, acting dumb.

'About ten k's back there on the road.'

'Ah,' I said thoughtfully, pausing for effect and to give myself time to think up an explanation. I felt stressed and the government bloke was standing right next to Ned.

'A carton of beer ten k's out,' I said. 'Maybe it belongs to one of those traditional owners coming from Lajamanu. Everyone knows we're really strict about no grog at Mt Theo, so it's been left a respectful distance away, like leaving it at the boundary.'

Ned seemed satisfied with my explanation. It was common knowledge that Yapa travelling from Lajamanu to Yuendumu often stopped to buy beer at Rabbit Flat. It was also a well known practice for drinkers to stash their grog in the bush before entering a dry community, out of respect for the liquor laws. And sometimes that stashed grog was left behind and forgotten.

With the beer issue dealt with, the meeting went on to the

main business at hand. The government blokes listened carefully to our proposal and agreed to support us to create an independent organisation: at last Mt Theo Program would be free.

After the meeting, as everyone was heading home to Yuendumu, I asked Robin Japanangka to stay behind and get a ride with me and Morgan. That evening at sunset Morgan, Robin, Hooker Creek and I celebrated the success of the meeting with that chilled carton of beer, sitting under the gum tree ten kilometres out of Mt Theo.

'Geez, that was a close one when those government blokes found that carton of beer,' said Morgan. 'I thought we were goners. Bloody quick thinking, Yakajirri.'

'But truthfully correct,' said Robin. 'Hooker Creek is a traditional owner and he was travelling from Lajamanu.'

'I dunno,' I said. 'We were just lucky they were in the first car of the convoy and we were the last – the explanation wouldn't have worked if they had found the ice.'

9: Tightrope

Pama Jukurrpa – sweet Dreaming – grog theory

In the Warlpiri language the word *pama* is used to describe the food category for sweet fruits and bush honey – food that is rich in nutrients, vitamins and natural antibiotics, foods that make you feel good. Today, *pama* also includes sugar and grog; things that are sweet and make you feel good.

In traditional Australian desert culture there was no rationale for making the agriculturalist cultural distinction between wants and needs. European and other agriculture-based societies have created these distinctions as a way of surviving in their particular environments. In Europe, where the snow covers the ground for three months of the year, it made sense for human beings to create self-imposed restrictions on food intake, in order to ensure that their food supplies would last.

The Tanami Desert, the home of the Warlpiri, is not Europe. The environment is totally different and the ways of survival are different. Prior to the invention of four-wheel drives and air conditioners, very few whitefellas ever lived there.

The Warlpiri survived and thrived for thousands of years in the desert without water bottles or fridges. Just like those supreme adaptors to deserts, camels, desert people learnt to eat and drink when food and water were available, and stored liquid and energy in their bodies.

Camels drink and eat their fill when the opportunity arises so that they can traverse and survive in an arid environment. Likewise in the desert hunter-gatherer life of the Warlpiri, there was almost no rationale for restricting personal intake of food and water, apart from the obligation to share with others. If you wanted food and water, generally you needed it. If your body craved a particular food like meat containing iron or honey containing antibiotics or fruit containing vitamins, then it made sense to eat that food until the craving was satisfied.

Pama describes the 'health food' section of the traditional Warlpiri diet, the food rich in vitamins and nutrients. It made no sense to create a cultural restriction on the intake of such beneficial foods.

Out of the survivalist nature of hunter-gatherer culture comes the ethic which Maggie Brady describes as 'everyone has the right to indulgence and everyone has the obligation to indulge the other'. If a person wants food or drink, no other person has the right to tell them not to eat or drink; rather, people are obliged to help provide food and water for each other. It worked with bush foods, but what happens when you introduce refined sugars into the mix?

Soft drinks, cordial that makes pungent bore water palatable, biscuits, ice cream, chocolate – all of those feel-good foods that whitefellas put in the 'special reward' category of desserts and indulgences – are foods that European whitefella culture has developed a special place for and put restrictions around. 'No dessert until you finish your dinner,' has been the traditional refrain of generations of whitefella parents as they socialise their children.

Warlpiri culture never had a 'dessert' food category. Forty thousand years of desert survival had developed the ethic of responding to what foods your body wanted and eating them. When the first whitefellas arrived in the Northern Territory they didn't find a race of obese overweight Warlpiri; they found a lean and fit people who could survive and travel through country where whitefellas and their horses perished. Obviously the Warlpiri methods of survival and their accompanying ethics and values were working.

Introducing refined sugars, encouraging people into settlements and to live a sedentary lifestyle created a different outcome.

How did people come to live in settlements anyway – why are they not still hunting?

There is a bit of a story. Firstly you have to imagine that you are a Warlpiri hunter and gatherer, living one hundred years ago. It is not an easy way to make a living – the desert is a harsh environment. Sometimes during droughts you have to walk 80 kilometres between waterholes, only to find that the waterhole is dry when you arrive. To survive, you have to lick the dew off leaves or even drink your own urine. Then you and your spouse and the kids have to push on overnight, when it's cool enough to travel, hopefully with enough moonlight to guide your way, to make it to the backup waterhole, another 40 kilometres away.

You might try to sing that country up closer and sing to keep your spirits going. But it's hard. When you get to that waterhole, which is only really a dried up soakage, you have to dig for an hour, through the dried crust and then the thick mud before you finally find a kind of sludgy murky soup. If you wait another hour for the sediment to settle, you might be able to get a drink. The water is muddy and earthy and rank, but at least it is water. You can rest for a while.

Your chores aren't over yet. You still have to eat. Tomorrow when you have some strength back, you will go hunting. And you'll eat anything, sand lizards, witchetty grubs, and maybe get some grass or wattle seed that can be ground into flour. After a few more days of recovery you might get ambitious and hunt something big, like a kangaroo. But even after spearing the kangaroo you might have to track it for a day before you can catch it and eat it. A spear is not like a bullet; it generally does not kill on impact.

Digging for goannas (photo by Frances Mocnik)

To survive in the desert you have had to develop some commonsense practices. One is don't waste energy. It is summer time now. The rains have come which is good, but it's very hot. If you are camped in the shade beside a waterhole in a place rich with goannas and yams and bush sultanas, you don't go walking out in the 45-degree temperatures in the middle of the day 'for exercise'. Hard times will come again. Right now you need to replenish your body from the hard seasons of drought. In summer time the country is rich with bush fruit that follow the summer rains.

Because you are camped in a good spot with ample food and water, chances are that your family group is joined by other family groups who also want to share in the bounty of the season. It's a good life right now. Warlpiri paradise, as they call it.

It's good to have the company of other people. Stories are shared, *Jukurrpa* is talked about, you learn more from those old people, ceremonies are performed, boys are made into men and girls are promised and married.

But the good times can't last forever. With so many people at one waterhole the bush foods start to peter out and soon it is time for the big gathering to end. It's time for everyone to break off into their own small family groups and find other waterholes to camp by.

Imagine when you are living that hunter-gatherer life, how attractive is the prospect of keeping the party going?

Imagine if you could do that.

That's why ration stations set up by whitefellas were so attractive. They had a seemingly endless supply of food and water. Permanent water by way of a bore or windmill and rations (flour, sugar and tea) distributed daily or weekly, either in exchange for labour or by welfare. All of a sudden, you get to hang out with lots of people and lots of family who you miss. There are more opportunities to share stories and learn *Jukurrpa* and do ceremonies because so many people are able to camp together around the ration station.

Many first-contact Warlpiri, such as Johnny Hooker Creek, told me this was why they started to live at ration stations or missions such as Haasts Bluff. They went there originally to catch up with family. But missionaries being such great hosts, the food kept coming.

The story is not just about attraction; there was coercion, too. Pioneer pastoralists intentionally polluted and caved in some waterholes to keep the Warlpiri off the land, and then they hunted Yapa away from other waterholes using the threat of violence. Events such as the Coniston Massacre instilled such fear in Yapa, that when pastoralists told them to leave their land, they feared any sign of resistance would have similar consequences. In a desert where permanent water is critical to survival, these acts made hunter-gatherer life almost impossible, forcing people to seek refuge at the missions and ration stations.

In addition to the pastoralists, the Australian Government's assimilation policy in the 1950s and '60s established the Aboriginal settlements of Yuendumu and Papunya. These communities were set up with the objective to teach/force the people of the desert to take up a whitefella's style of life.

This is how Aboriginal people in the desert came to take up the sedentary life of living in a settlement. But I'm getting off the point – which is *pama* – sweet things that are good for you (or have been for the last forty thousand years).

Refined sugars introduced and distributed by whitefellas, mixed with an indigenous culture of 'indulgence' that categorises *pama* as nutritious, coupled with a sedentary lifestyle, and what have you got – widespread diabetes. In some communities the rate of diabetes among Aboriginal people can be up to ten times higher than the rate among non-Aboriginal Australians.

Diabetes is a simple problem compared to grog, but many of the issues are the same. In fact, *pama* is the contemporary Warlpiri word for alcohol. Warlpiri didn't have an indigenous word for alcohol because they had no indigenous alcoholic substances. Whitefellas brought in the grog and Warlpiri named it *pama* – a prized food (drink) that makes you feel good.

Now, us whitefellas, we like grog. We've been making it and drinking it for thousands of years. Two thousand years ago at a wedding in Galilee a woman, Mary, said to her son: 'They are out of wine.'

Jesus' first miracle was to change water into wine. According to the most dominant religion in the whitefella world, Jesus is the son of God. At his last supper before he was crucified he instructed his disciples to share wine as a way of remembering him.

Being whitefellas, we relate to alcohol with the same set of cultural values that we use to relate to other things in our cultural world. We bring to our relationship with grog all of our agricultural values of deferred gratification, rationing and self-imposed limitation. We even esteem people who have cellars full of bottled wine that just sits there and is not drunk for years. Vintage wine we call it, and praise the oldest wine the most. At dinner parties wine buffs proudly recite the various ages of their wines, while whisky drinkers cherish old whisky. 'Aged 15 years', the labels proudly read.

Alcohol fits into our cultural world alongside work, saving, investment and family. Ideally, when things work well, all parts are in balance. When things are out of balance and alcohol dominates the other parts, or when a person no longer brings to their relationship with alcohol those key whitefella values of deferred gratification, rationing and self-imposed limitation, then we label that person an 'alcoholic'.

So what happens to people who culturally never had the values of deferred gratification, rationing and self-imposed limitation, but rather have the two key cultural values of: 'everyone has the right to indulgence' and 'to survive in the desert don't waste energy'. What happens to these people when grog is introduced? You only have to go to Alice Springs to find out.

The Todd River that bisects the town of Alice Springs is a beautiful place. It's a dry river with a wide sandy bed, lined with magnificent and ancient shady ghost gums. Green and yellow tussock grass grows on the banks. In many places you can see the tracks where kangaroos have dug in the sand to find water. After rain the river floods and during the following weeks the local kids of Alice Springs enjoy swimming and frolicking in the remnant waterholes to escape the desert heat.

I always enjoy walking across that river, a sanctuary of bush in the middle of town. It's more fun than taking the concrete bridge.

One Saturday afternoon when I was walking across the river

to my mate Craig's house, a girl's voice sang out to me: 'Hey, Yakajirri!'

I turned around to see Ella, with her friends Doreen and Nadia, sitting in the shade of one of those gum trees. They were all smiling at me. I knew these girls well; years ago they had been sniffers and had spent time out at Mt Theo, and then at the youth centre in Yuendumu.

I walked over to their welcoming smiles and sat down with them. It felt good to be with some mates and escape the heat in the shade of the ghost gums. We small-talked a little bit and they offered me a glass of chilled white wine. It might have been a chardonnay.

It was really nice, just sitting there in the sand, talking story with old friends, reminiscing, enjoying the contrast of desert warmth and chilled wine. It was just like a picnic. Well, almost.

One difference was that the 'glasses' we used for our wine were not made of glass but were soft drink cans with their lids cut off, to form aluminium tumblers. Another was that our wine, instead of being poured from a chilled glass bottle, was served from a cardboard cask, and it was moselle, not chardonnay. But apart from that aesthetic, the atmosphere was pleasant and the company was good. And I was thinking to myself: I can really understand the attraction of spending time just chilling out with friends drinking wine by the river – it's really nice.

What a great way to spend an afternoon, why wouldn't I want to spend every day like this? I guess the answer is because I have other things I want to do in my life too. I'm an adrenaline junkie for a start – I like excitement and adventure – and you need all your senses turned on to enjoy those – alcohol actually numbs the experience. I also want to have a meaningful and purposeful life. I want to work, I've been socialised with a whitefella work ethic. I'm also materialistic; I feel an obligation to provide my wife and kids with a house that I pay the mortgage for with my wages. Personally I don't mind camping out, but Vesna is not prepared to raise our family in a humpy.

But what if I did not have those things? What if I had the desert survival ethic of 'don't waste energy' instead of a work ethic? What if, no matter how much money I earned in wages, the cultural obligation laws that required me to distribute money the instant it arrived meant that I could never save for a house or invest in a business? If that was the case, why not spend each day enjoying the view, talking story and drinking wine?

Why do people stop drinking? A whole other book could deal with that issue, but I think having a personal purpose in life is important. I see Yapa who drink all day in Alice Springs for weeks or months on end, but who will give up their drinking in town to go back out to Yuendumu, or Papunya, or Mt Theo to do something with purpose, like attend ceremonies, play in the community football competition, go on country visits or save the lives of petrol sniffing kids. Many, many Aboriginal people do not drink at all.

Yapa drink for lots of reasons. Robin Japanangka's tightrope theory (see next section) describes the sort of cross-cultural stress many Yapa who try to be 'two way' people deal with. For some people, drinking is a release from that pressure. People drink from sadness and pain. With the high mortality rate amongst the Aboriginal population, it seems that people attend the funeral of a friend or family member every couple of months. Nearly every Yapa has experienced deep grief over the loss of a loved one. There is so much sadness that alcohol seems like an appealing tranquiliser, an almost rational choice for self-medication.

People also drink for company. Many Warlpiri have told me that they drink because their family and friends are drinking. I'm not an expert on alcoholic behaviour, but recovering alcoholics have told me that one of the hardest things to deal with is the peer group pressure to drink.

A friend of mine described to me how her Aboriginal husband, who is a recovering alcoholic, had gone through many rehabilitation programs in both Melbourne and Alice Springs: 'And then he'll be sitting in the café, in Alice, waiting for CAAAPU (the rehab program) to pick him up and take him on an excursion, when his three drinking mates will sit down with him and ask him to go drinking with him. They will sit there patiently, and they won't leave him. The pressure is really on – they just sit with him until they get him to crack and he goes drinking with them at the hotel.

'He's a brain-damaged man, he's suffered so much from the grog, it's killing him … but they won't let up.'

—

'We have no *Jukurrpa* for grog,' said Andrew Japaljarri Spencer, in relation to how grog causes such havoc in the lives of Aboriginal people.

And havoc is exactly what it causes. In 2007 Alice Springs reputedly had the highest per capita murder rate in Australia and the highest per capita stabbing rate in the world. And nearly all those stabbings and murders were amongst the Aboriginal population and were alcohol related.

Some Warlpiri in Yuendumu regard Alice Springs as a dumping ground, the home of dysfunctional people who have given their lives up to grog. 'Why else would you live there?' they ask. The people who have their lives together generally don't live in Alice Springs; rather, they inhabit the bush communities hundreds of kilometres away from the nearest pub.

Tourists who go to Alice Springs are often confronted with street scenes of groups of drunk blackfellas, and that's often the only impression of Aboriginal people they get to take home. 'A bunch of drunken humbugs – that's what they are.'

But many Warlpiri people I know share the same perspective. I know Warlpiri who refuse to stay with other Aboriginal people in Alice Springs and who will pay for an expensive motel room to avoid having to deal with drunks when they visit town. You don't have to be a racist to dislike drunken behaviour.

While I was visiting Central Australia in 2007, there was a public meeting held in the centre of town to discuss a new Federal Government proposal to buy out the town camps. Town camps were owned by Aboriginal people, and provided much of their housing. Each week the local paper was filled with horror stories of violence and crime associated with town camps.

At the meeting an Arrernte* man got up and spoke: 'They shouldn't be talking about closing down the town camps,' he said. 'They should be talking about closing down the grog shops – they're the problem.'

That night as I walked into a bottle shop to buy some beer to take to a barbecue, I noticed some drunk Aboriginal people fighting in the middle of the road. Cars were driving around them; it was in the middle of the CBD. An angry man ripped the shirt off the woman he was arguing with, leaving her naked with her breasts exposed and dangling in the middle of town. She would have felt totally humiliated.

'They should be talking about closing down the grog shops.' The Arrernte man's words echoed in my mind.

What a different place Alice Springs would be without grog. Subtract 95 per cent of the violence, 95 per cent of the crime, 95 per cent of the murders.

The government, it was alleged, was trying to force the Aborigines off their land by stealth. These people have suffered so much already, their land invaded, waterholes poisoned and polluted, being massacred by bullets at places such as Coniston, they were never asked if they wanted this to happen. They never invited it. Did anyone ask permission to bring grog into this country?

---

* *Arrernte* are the tribe that are the traditional owners and inhabitants of the Alice Springs area.

I know that when a whitefella proposed to open up a grog shop only 100 kilometres east of Yuendumu, the Warlpiri said no.

In the 1990s, Tilmouth Well, the roadhouse between Yuendumu and Alice Springs, had applied for a licence to sell takeaway grog. It would have brought the grog problem 200 kilometres closer to Yuendumu. The application was staunchly opposed.

'That's why we have a dry community,' Ned Jampijimpa told me. 'We don't want those problems like they have in Alice Springs.'

Yuendumu is a dry community. That means it is illegal to bring grog into Yuendumu. If you do, you will face criminal charges and the vehicle bringing in the grog will be impounded and confiscated. People are happy with these laws. Keeping the grog shops 300 kilometres away in Alice Springs helps to make Yuendumu a relatively safe place and a relatively functional community.

There are legitimate ways to drink in Yuendumu. One can apply for a liquor permit, which allows a person to bring a small amount of alcohol into the community for personal consumption. But if you give the grog to lots of people, or if you cause any trouble or are seen drunk in the community, then your permit is revoked. Anyone can apply for a permit, white or black, and anyone can get their permit revoked for misbehaviour.

—

As whitefellas in Australia, we feel totally comfortable outlawing drugs that we have no *Jukurrpa* for, that are not part of our traditional culture, such as opium. We know that such drugs wreak havoc on our people.

We regularly blame immigrants for bringing trouble to our country. We blame Italians for bringing the Mafia, Muslims for bringing terrorism, and Asians for bringing triads. Well, in Alice Springs, I, as an immigrant in the Arrernte lands, was hearing an indigenous Australian man complaining about what my whitefella culture had brought to his country – grog.

'It will never work,' my mates in Alice Springs told me that night when I took the beer to their barbecue.

'Whitefellas will never agree to closing down all the grog shops in town.'

So whose problem is it? I don't know the solution, not yet, but it would be good to see all of the problems of grog come to an end. I'm not sure if I am part of the problem or part of the solution. It could be argued that, because I drank with those girls in the river and because I have beers with my work mates Robin and Hooker Creek, I am part of the alcohol problem. I think I held this view of drinking myself when I first arrived in Yuendumu as an almost innocent 'non-drinking, non-smoking virgin'. But over time I have changed.

I use grog primarily as a specialty item for bonding and exchange with whitefellas. I remember at one stage the store manager in Yuendumu was being particularly helpful and supportive of the Mt Theo Program. I wanted to thank him, to show my gratitude, and the gift of a home-made cake just wouldn't carry weight with this rough diamond of a man. I needed to give him a gift that was culturally appropriate to his white Australian macho culture so I gave him some beer. That was the first carton of beer I ever brought to Yuendumu.

In my culture, we whitefellas use drinking as a bonding ceremony, to create social relations: 'We should have a beer together,' we say to one another. This expression is often the Australian male way of inviting someone to a deeper level of friendship. It is also used as an offering of reconciliation after a conflict.

As I've got older I've learnt to drink. The 'Missing Person, Missing Soul' chapter in my life was actually a turning point for me when I changed my behaviour and consciously decided to drink alcohol as a way of managing stress.

So why do I, a substance abuse worker, drink with my Aboriginal colleagues? Well, one reason is a matter of practicality. I've often drunk with people as a practical way to stop them drinking.

Sounds crazy, doesn't it? However, drinking with someone creates a bond. So if I'm drinking with someone in town and we are hanging out together and want to keep hanging out together, I can suggest that we buy a carton of beer for the road and drive home to Yuendumu. More often than not the person will agree. We drive to Yuendumu, stop at the boundary, drink the beer (outside the 'no grog allowed' fence) and the next day we are sober and in a dry community. The person who I've brought with me might then stay sober for months, particularly if they go out to Mt Theo. Compare that with the alternative: if they had stayed in town they would continue drinking grog every day.

If I approached my alcoholic friend who is drinking in town and did not have a beer with them but just said, 'Let's go to Yuendumu,' nine times out of ten they would refuse to come with me, because drinking is important to them and it is hard to convince a drunk to leave the pub or party while the beer is flowing.

The process of me and my alcoholic friend drinking together and bonding, and developing that shared vision for the journey out to Yuendumu, changes the energy of the situation. With the promise of a fun journey and beers for the road, my alcoholic friend will come home to the desert where grog is absent and life is good.

I also drink with Aboriginal people because they are my friends and I treat them as equals. I would be accused of being a racist if I only drank with whites.

I admit that I enjoy sharing a beer with my friends. My inhibitions diminish and people say my Warlpiri improves.

So I don't know if I'm part of the problem or part of the solution. But I hope one day to be part of the solution. I hope one day the river of grog dries up in the desert; that we respect whose country it is. Maybe, like with petrol sniffing in Yuendumu, the problem will only be solved if the blackfellas and whitefellas of Alice Springs stop passing the buck and the whole community works together to deal with the grog problem.

Cross-cultural relations: Robin Japanangka's tightrope theory

After about three years of living in Yuendumu I was having a yarn with Robin Japanangka Granites. Robin is an amazing guy. He was the chairperson of the Yuendumu School Council when I first worked for the school. Following Marg Reilly's sage advice* of making myself accountable to the School Council instead of the Principal, I decided Robin, as the chairperson, was my boss. He was also a mentor to me. Robin was a bloke who could communicate with whitefellas and work in the whitefella world. Together with Peter Toyne, he set up the Tanami Network, a videoconferencing network between Yuendumu and three other desert communities. Robin was able to sit at a computer in Yuendumu, link up to a satellite and then show you live images of people walking down the street in Stockholm. And this was before the days of the internet. Robin had a broad nose and eyes that often had a milky yellow tinge road mapped with thin red blood vessels. He had a cloud of grey fuzzy hair on his head. This often made me feel that he looked like a koala. He was a beautiful man.

Robin was well travelled in both the Warlpiri world of Aboriginal ceremonial business, and the whitefella world of European and American cities. He was politically astute, an excellent chairperson of Council and committee meetings, an activist and a motivator. It was Robin's leadership by example of night patrolling the school until one o'clock every morning that helped kickstart the campaign to stop sniffing. Robin wasn't afraid to stand up to whitefellas when he thought things needed to change, but

* Marg Reilly shared the house with Vesna and me during our first year in Yuendumu. Previously she had been Yuendumu's youth worker in the 1980s.

he was always a diplomat at handling organisational and policy disputes.

Robin could do the 'Mandela' and put on a suit to look like a statesman; he could also be a travelling Warlpiri business man, covered in red ochre and white feathers. Often in the evening when I would visit Robin at home, I would find him sitting in just a pair of shorts on his veranda next to a small cooking fire. Across from him, his wife, Alma, a teacher at the school, would be cooking damper.

Robin did me the honour of giving me a Christmas card at the end of my first year, which he signed 'from your best friend'.

After I had been living in Yuendumu for three years, although I had many friends and people who had adopted me, such as my grandmother Naparrula, I still felt an incredible gulf of understanding between myself, as a whitefella, and the Warlpiri. I felt that, like most of the other whitefellas in Yuendumu, I stood at the edge of this huge chasm which we were looking across, with Aboriginal people standing on the other side.

I raised this idea with Robin: 'Robin, it seems to me that us whitefellas and blackfellas are standing on opposite sides of the Grand Canyon. We're looking at each other and waving at each other, but our cultural worlds are so different that we are not connecting at all; there is this huge gulf between us.'

Robin was quiet for a while, and looked into his evening fire. Then he answered: 'No, Yakajirri, I think you are wrong. I see tightropes across that canyon, and I see people like you and me walking those tightropes, connecting both sides.'

Years later, after Mt Theo Program had experienced many battles with various administrators, middle managers and council clerks who had attacked the program and turned many of the arguments into personal ones, Robin reminded me again of the tightrope theory.

It's pretty scary to think about going out on a limb, out on that tightrope, and lots of whitefellas I know are either too scared to do it, find it too difficult to get the right balance, or just do not even want to cross to the other side. From what I've seen and read, Yapa have similar feelings and experiences about the tightrope.

Robin said to me, 'You know that tightrope and canyon thing we talked about years ago. Well I've been thinking more about it lately, with what's happened to me with jealousy Yapa side, and what's been happening to you and the program with your trouble with those council clerks and managers. You know how I said that you and I were walking on those tightropes between our cultures … well, I reckon there are people on both sides, Yapa and Kardiya, shaking those tightropes. They don't want to see us walk that tightrope out of our own culture. Those whitefellas you have trouble with want you to be like them, not coming across the canyon to be with us Yapa. And some Yapa are the same with me, they are jealous, so they shake those tightropes because they want to see us fall.'

Robin wasn't a pure saint. He would drink sometimes, and when desert Warlpiri drink, they make camels look second-class at hump filling. Many wise whitefellas I know who were workmates with Robin in the 1980s say he drinks because the cross-cultural stress just gets too much. They say that there are huge expectations on him from both whitefellas who want him to be an impartial statesman, and Warlpiri kinsmen who demand that if he enters the whitefella world, then he should return to them the large levels of whitefella resources that he can hunt.

Pregnant and sniffing

When I first met Brianna she was ten years old. She was skinny with desert-blonde matted curly hair. Her face had a narrow chin which triangled up to a widely spaced pair of eyes that darted about wildly. And she had a temper. Her Year Five teacher described her as a 'hell bitch'. It was nothing to see Brianna standing outside the classroom, pelting rocks at the windows and the class occupants. Maybe it was inevitable that Brianna would find petrol, or that petrol would find her.

Maybe it was a stroke of luck that it took so long for petrol and her to hook up. By the time she was sixteen, she was sniffing petrol and she was pregnant. Being pregnant at sixteen is not unusual in Yuendumu. Many young people marry and start families at that age.

However, sniffing and being pregnant at the same time was unusual in Yuendumu – it wasn't the done thing. But this girl was different and her temper was wild. I remember being woken up by the policeman in the middle of the night: 'Brianna is sniffing and she is on the roof of the Council building, threatening to jump off.'

We went round and there she was, standing on the roof, with an amassed arsenal of rocks and stones, throwing them down on anyone who threatened to challenge her.

Another evening I was called to the clinic. Brianna was fitting as a result of overdosing on petrol. She was eight months pregnant. What could I do? If I took her to Mt Theo, I would place this heavily pregnant girl hours away from medical help. If I left her in Yuendumu, she was bound to continue poisoning herself and her child with petrol. The clinic staff recommended she go to Mt Theo. They said it was her only hope.

Two weeks later we got the emergency call from Mt Theo, late at night: 'You better come quick, Brianna's going to have a baby.'

I drove out in the Yuendumu four-wheel-drive ambulance with Darren, the on-call nurse from the clinic. Darren was a single bloke about my age. On the way, we talked about life and doing what you are passionate about.

'Do you know the way to check if you are doing what you really want to do in your life?' Darren asked me. 'Ask yourself if you would still be doing the same job, even if you weren't being paid for it. If the answer is yes, then you are really doing what you are passionate about.'

At Mt Theo, Darren examined Brianna then put her on a drip to delay labour. We phoned through to the Royal Flying Doctor Service, who arranged to meet us at Yuendumu airstrip. We then drove the 180 kilometres back to Yuendumu, dodging bullocks and 'roos as we thundered down the Tanami Road.

Yuendumu airstrip was lit up with green and yellow lights as the Flying Doctor plane landed. We were relieved to have made it without having to do an emergency delivery on the roadside. The Flying Doctor Service is great and is really appreciated by people in the bush. On night runs like this they sometimes deliver take-away pizzas from Alice Springs to the nursing staff in Yuendumu. Those gestures are a great morale booster for on-call nurses faced with 'combat conditions' in remote communities.

In Alice Springs, Brianna gave birth to a lovely baby boy and then came home to Yuendumu. Our fingers were crossed. Maybe this time she would give up petrol. No mother in Yuendumu had ever sniffed before. But Brianna broke the mould. She sniffed. She left her baby with his grandmothers and went with petrol. *Wiyarrpa, wiyarrpa, wiyarrpa* (poor thing).

There are sniffer girls in South Australia who sometimes soothe their babies to sleep with petrol-soaked rags. We never wanted to see that happen in Yuendumu. We had to take Brianna back to Mt Theo.

Brianna's breasts were full of milk and they were hurting with no baby to suckle them. *Wiyarrpa*. There were many times that summer when Brianna tried to kill herself. One time when the elders were away on sorry business and I was supervising at Mt Theo, she tried to strangle herself while everyone was asleep. The young people (all sniffers) and I took turns at holding a vigil throughout the night to watch over her.

Then she tried to run away to the hills and we had to track

her through the bush. She threw rocks and sticks at us, cursing and swearing, yelling at us to leave her alone. She held a knife to her throat and threatened to stab herself or anyone that came near her.

'I want to fucking kill myself!' she yelled.

Just keeping her from harming herself in that environment was exhausting. We contacted the mental health service in Alice Springs and took her to hospital there. They seemed to do nothing. 'We can't hold her against her will,' they said. So they sent her back to Yuendumu where she went straight back to sniffing.

It's hard to know why Brianna finally stopped sniffing. Her family did a lot of hard work, not just her mother and father, but her brothers and sisters too. A lot of love was poured into that girl.

She survived and so did her baby. She still had an edge to her but she mellowed with age. Her peers no longer sniffed. Her brother who was a sniffer eventually became a leading light in the Jaru Pirrjirdi 'Strong Voices' project, the group of young people who work to ensure that the next generation of Warlpiri kids never want to sniff. Three years later Brianna approached us and asked if she could join the Jaru Pirrjirdi team too. Youth culture in Yuendumu had changed.

Politically neutral

I'm an activist by nature. I have high ideals. People like Gandhi and Luther King are my heroes. While living down south I've gone to protests and stood up for what I believe in.

From reading this book you can probably tell that, although reluctant, I am prepared to pick up my light sabre on occasions to defend the program against a big bad wolf. When I moved to Canberra to join the public service, my mate Mike Harries, the Vice Principal at Yuendumu School, asked me, 'Did they ask you in the public service interview how many bosses you'd got sacked? I'm sure if they knew the truth they would never give you a job.'

From the granting of self-government in 1978 until 2001, the Country Liberal Party (CLP) was the only party to ever hold government in the Northern Territory. Some people described it as a 'one party state'.

There were rumours of people losing their jobs or organisations getting their funding cut if they vocally opposed the government. The wife of one of my friends was absolutely convinced that her husband had been forced out of his job in the Health Department, because he did letterbox drops supporting the opposition party on the weekend before an election. I'm not sure if any of this is true, but there was definitely a climate of fear.

For me, the most important thing was to stop sniffing. That was my *Jukurrpa*, my responsibility. I knew government support was important for the Mt Theo Program so I decided I did not want to piss the government off. I did not want the program to suffer just because of my political idealism.

I bit my tongue. While my friends, many of whom were a lot more conservative than I, went off to protests against the Jabiluka Uranium Mine, I, the teepee-dwelling greenie, stayed at home. I did not want Mt Theo to be tainted with that 'radical' brush. If I had any other job I would have gone to the protest.

It's good to have friends. Mick Jessop, the Council Clerk, who was so supportive of the program, was a dyed-in-the-wool CLP man. He once considered running for the Legislative Assembly as the member for Yuendumu. I remember going to the Alice Springs Show one year with my kids. Mick was at the CLP tent and proudly introduced me to the conservative politicians.

'This is Andrew from Mt Theo,' he said.

They shook my hand and patted me on the back and told me what a good job Mt Theo had done and how they were behind us all the way.

'Good job having those elders sort the young people out, the old tribal way,' a man said.

Somehow Mt Theo's philosophy suited the conservatives' outlook.

Continuing my walk through the showground I ran into Peter Toyne, whose leadership had helped start the program and who I have always admired. Peter was the local Australian Labor Party Member. He introduced me to all his Labor mates. I got a similar round of handshakes and back slaps. I knew Peter's heart was with us at Mt Theo.

I walked on, thinking this is what we want, bipartisan support. Respect from both sides, respect like the Red Cross has, like the Salvos have. Politically neutral, a good works bandwagon that everyone wants to get on and support. Over the years governments have changed. But both sides of politics continue to fund us and support us.

10: Destiny

After seven years in Yuendumu, Vesna and I and our kids moved to Canberra. I had promised Vesna I would try to make a new life in the city. Morgan was going to look after the Mt Theo Program and everything would be fine. After all, we were running out of sniffers.

I have often said that if apple picking was the biggest industry in Canberra then I would have become an apple picker. But the public service is the biggest industry there so I became a public servant. It was good to have a rest. I needed a break from the heat and small-town gossip among whitefellas in Yuendumu. Some of the big bad wolf's poison remained in those relationships, especially with the Council Clerk. It didn't matter who the Council Clerk was, they automatically did not like me. Maybe the stories had been passed on.

The public service is a great place to recuperate. They really look after their staff. It was like my mother-in-law (who cleaned government offices) had described: 'No very hard work, air conditioning, drink coffee whenever you want, and wear a nice suit.'

I looked at myself in the mirror each morning and tried to kid myself that I was just going to a different sort of cultural ceremony. Instead of being painted up with ochre and wearing feathers, I wore a suit. My mate Blair told me to develop Zen-like patience and practise the art of performing good works whilst remaining in a seated position behind a desk. Other days I would look at myself in the mirror wearing that suit and think: you're so full of shit.

I spent my weekends going bush and I built a hut in the forest. It was my very own outstation, a place I could camp with my family.

I'd been in Canberra for about four months before I heard whispers from the desert. Unlike the heart stirrings of my youth, the call now came in an electronic form. Down the telephone wire I heard Morgan and the program were having a hard time. Peggy, Hooker Creek and Morgan all hinted I should come back. From my hut, I wrote a letter to my mate, Mike Harries, who was still there.

'How bad are things?' I asked. The letter continued:

> ... It's actually good to be living a self-indulgent meaningless existence. I don't know how long I will be able to manage a life bereft of meaning for ... If I come back to Yuendumu, Vesna would hate me ... It's a hard row to hoe, being split between the call of the desert and family.
>
> It snowed in the forest, at my hut, just the lightest dusting, like icing sugar on the ferns.

Sorry business

Each Monday I donned the suit and rode my bicycle to the office. One June afternoon I got an email: Peggy's husband, Old Japangardi had passed away. Tears splashed down my face onto the computer keyboard. I told my supervisor my uncle had just died and I had to go away on sorry business.

I couldn't stop it now. I couldn't stay away any longer. I couldn't pretend any more. I had to go back. I had to be with Peggy, *wiyarrpa*, I had to comfort Hooker Creek for the loss of his brother. I had to go to sorry camp and sit down and wail and express all my grief for this beautiful old man. This man who had welcomed me to his country, country that had become my Dreaming.

The buses to Alice Springs were booked out. It was the start of school holidays and I would have to wait four days before I could get a bus seat. The airfare was over $1000 and I didn't have the money. So I walked. I walked and I prayed, still wearing my public service suit and tie, feeling myself swept up in a river of emotion.

Old Japangardi

I hadn't hitchhiked since my early twenties, when I could trade on the innocence of my youth. 'Oh God, please look after me and take me to Yuendumu,' I prayed. I was there less than 48 hours later. The lifts came from everywhere, sweeping me along like a river.

'Why are you hitchhiking in a suit?' my curious drivers asked. I told them I was going to a funeral.

I sat down at sorry camp in Yuendumu and wailed. Someone gave me a swag to sleep in. Rex Granites gave me his coat to keep me warm.

'Oh, Yakajirri,' people cried. 'We knew you would come.'

It felt so good to hear my Warlpiri name again. I felt as if I was immersed in an ocean of love and support. My kinsmen, my countrymen, united in our grief.

I couldn't speak at Japangardi's funeral. I was too overcome by emotion. But everyone else talked. They told his story, our story, the Mt Theo story. They told it like it was real and it really mattered. It was usually me who told that story, over and over again, to government bureaucrats, in submissions and in reports. Sometimes I told it so many times, I would wonder if it was true or if it was just me talking, making it all up. But it was real. Yapa and Kardiya were telling Japangardi's story, not my story. But it was the same story.

Dave Hodgkin, an amazing whitefella friend of mine who was working on the program, wrote a tribute for the funeral:

> Old Japangardi passed away last week.
>
> Peggy Brown's husband, a great man, I'm privileged to have met him. The owner of Mt Theo Country.
>
> At 78 he was a man who knew the time before the whitefellas came. He spent the last seven years looking after lost teenagers, nurturing petrol sniffers back to health. As he said to me when I first met him, 'We been saved a lot of lives 'ere, BIG mob.'
>
> Watching old Japangardi, rampant teenage blokes, some men, some boys, climbing on him, pulling his hair, teasing him. Young girls and women joking about being the 'right-skin' to be his wife then stealing his tobacco. Watching him smile, quietly sitting by his wife, looking after his country. Sacred spears in the roof battens of his house.
>
> Japangardi lying in his humpy with his family gathered round, paying 'proper' respect, worrying for him in his last few days. Taking him out bush, back to country, feeding him bush tucker, *yakajirri* (bush sultana) and bush potato, *marlu* (kangaroo) and bush turkey, making special ointments from their fat. Peggy stomping through the night, yelling at *Kutajis* and Bushmen (spirits), praying to *Warpirra* (God) for her husband.

—

Every speaker at the funeral said, 'We've got to continue that old man's work.'

Traditionally, after the death of a senior traditional owner such as Japangardi, an outstation would be abandoned for at least a year to let the spirits settle. Mt Theo had closed on his passing and no one was sure when it would open again.

Two weeks after the funeral, petrol struck back. Bored sniffers poured petrol out in snake-like trails on the pavement at night and then set fire to the snakes. A teenager was burnt, this time to 90 per cent of his body. Everyone was sure he would die. I visited him in hospital in Adelaide. I had to go through two sterile doors to get to him in a sealed room. The room smelled like death. He did not die, but he lost limbs as a result of the burns.

'It's like a bushfire, burning through our community,' Otto Sims, the chairman of Mt Theo Program said in *The Australian* newspaper.

I returned to my job in Canberra and petrol sniffing was in the media. The headlines screamed 'Babies soothed to sleep with petrol-soaked rags'. Warlpiri sidestepped the Mt Theo avoidance issue and reopened the outstation. Otto told me over the phone that saving young people's live was too important.

Peggy wasn't allowed back at Mt Theo and neither were her family. They had to maintain the cultural avoidance for a few years. But Hooker Creek went back to look after the sniffers and Rex Forrest stepped up to the plate. Rex is a Mt Theo traditional owner who normally lives at Willowra, but his son had been a sniffer, so he joined in the cause.

Heroes

[From my journal]

Charlie Perkins died on Wednesday, the papers are full of tributes. He's considered a 'hero'. He led freedom rides in the

1960s challenging racism in Western NSW. He was the first Aborigine to graduate from university. In Canberra I went to school with his son, Adam. We both struggled in the same maths class. Adam had blue hair, a leather jacket and earrings. He was the punk and I was the hippy wearing a mohair jumper and a land rights t-shirt. The papers say that Charlie was a 'National Living Treasure'.

I've lost three of my heroes in the last twelve months. Barry Cook who founded Injartnama, that outstation near Hermannsburg where Lloyd took me with the sniffers – Barry devoted his life to rescuing Arrernte and Luritja alcoholics from fringe camps of Alice Springs. 'A rough diamond saint' was what the newspaper said. The Alice Springs magistrate, Cathy Deland, wrote: 'He gave when there was nothing left to give. He gave hope to replace despair. A truly wonderful man. Even the heavens cried on his passing.' It rained that day in Alice.

So I'm thinking about my three heroes who have passed away: Barry Cook, Charlie Perkins and Old Japangardi. It makes me think hard, hard about whether my life will be as worthwhile as theirs, will I be able to die and look back on a life that made a difference? I really want to. My life in the public service is pretty meaningless. It's been a great rest, but now I've recovered from the hard work and hepatitis of Yuendumu, I'm hungering for a meaningful and worthwhile existence.

A few months later, in December, as I was about to go on holidays from the public service, Morgan called: 'Yakajirri, you've gotta come. Just come up for the summer. I've had it. I'm on stress leave. All the workers are pissed off because the government's held back our funding and no one's got paid.'

I rang a couple of other friends in Yuendumu for advice. They said it would really help if I came back for the summer.

I was really excited about going back to Yuendumu again. I could hardly contain my excitement at work the next day. Pictures rushed through my mind: smearing my body with red ochre, hearing that Australian language again: *Yuwai Yakajirri, ngurrju mayinpa? Nyarrpara jangka?* (Hi Yakajirri, how are you? Where have you come from?) The heat, I could feel it already, the water as summer rains

Rex Forrest and young people at Mt Theo 2001

flood again. The adrenaline of confronting danger; the joy and ecstasy of doing discos, rollerskating, laughing, dancing and too many smiles. Journeys with old Hooker Creek, my uncle. It was a powerful calling.

It took me two days to hitchhike to Yuendumu. I was happy to be back. I felt so welcomed. The skills I had learnt in Canberra and my understanding of public service culture were put to good use. The 'government people' treated me with a new kind of respect. 'You work for FaCS [Department of Family and Community Services] don't you, Andrew?' they'd say.

They related to me like I was one of them and it worked a treat. The program's funding was restored. Meanwhile, Rex and Hooker Creek had moved back to Mt Theo and we started the program again.

Going back to Yuendumu was a fantastic break from the public service: I felt reinspired. When Morgan returned at the end of January, I looked forward to spending time with my family and working in Canberra where I had recently won a promotion.

The return

I had just returned to Canberra and my cushy public service career, after spending the summer of 2001 in Yuendumu. I had only been back a week and was sitting at my desk when Morgan rang me again: 'Yakajirri, I've had it. I can't do this job anymore … you've got to come back.'

Morgan is a good man. He's committed, spiritual and human. He is full of love and compassion for his neighbour, regardless if it is the next-door neighbour or a starving neighbour on the other side of the world in Bangladesh. Morgan was raised a Catholic and at one stage aspired to be a priest. He knew his scripture well and was ideologically committed to his faith. It was Morgan who worked with the Warlpiri to finally set up Mt Theo Program as an independent corporate body. He believed in empowerment.

But by autumn, Morgan was burnt out. There had been many arguments over Toyotas, too much hard work and too much politicking.

A significant contributing factor was the floods. The floods that year completely cut Mt Theo off from the outside world. Elders and young people had to be airlifted from the outstation by helicopter. The program's Toyota Troop Carrier was bogged beyond recovery, lying on its side in mud on the Mt Theo road. Other desert communities such as Kiwirrkurra on the Western

Jaru Pirrjirdi bush trip

Australia-Northern Territory border were also abandoned as a result of the exceptional flooding.

The government stopped funding the Mt Theo Program because they heard the outstation had been abandoned and because no one replied to the correspondence they sent to the Mt Theo office. Morgan had had enough and went back to his home in Tasmania. The program was effectively shut down.

With sniffers running wild again, the Yuendumu police sergeant rang me and encouraged me to come back. Hooker Creek, Ned and Peggy also rang. 'Is it true? Are you really coming back?' they asked.

In April I bought a cheap battered Subaru and tearfully said goodbye to my own children and wife.

'Why do you have to go, Daddy?' six-year-old Deua asked as tears ran down her cheeks.

'Because kids are going to die, Deua. They're going to die from sniffing petrol. Peggy and Hooker Creek and Daddy can stop that. We can save their lives by taking them to Mt Theo.'

'But why do you have to do that, Daddy?' she asked.

'Because I promised. I promised I would go back if they really needed me and if there was no one else to help,' I replied.

It was hard to leave her and my younger daughter, Jessie. And it was hard to leave my wife.

Morgan sent me an employment contract that promised monthly airfares back to Canberra to visit my family, but I knew such a promise was meaningless without any government funding for the program.

My colleagues in the public service thought I was mad, abandoning my career, where I had recently been promoted, to leave my family and go to work for an organisation with no funding.

I was sad leaving my family behind but as I drove out of

Yuendumu disco

Canberra and towards the desert, I felt like I was being reborn. I had a car, my swag, a jaffle iron and a billycan. But best of all I was going home.

I stayed in Alice Springs with my Warlpiri father, Ned, at Amoongooma, then I drove out to Yuendumu. The program's house was trashed. Two years ago, even four months ago, it had been a new house. Now it had broken cupboards and doors, smashed windows and holes punched in the walls. In the absence of a petrol sniffing program, the sniffers had moved in and smashed up the program's house.

It was time to rebuild. The youth centre was also trashed but there was an amp and some speakers so I could run discos. The Mt Theo road needed to be checked to see if it was passable. The bore, telephone and power system also needed to be checked.

I met with Otto Simms and Maxine Nungarrayi Spencer, the Mt Theo Program Management Committee Chairpersons and with Johnny Hooker Creek and Peggy. I listened to their stories of the past six months and we talked about rebuilding the program.

The old man, the one who had shocked me when the program first began, when I'd asked to borrow the Wirlinyi Ngurrju School Toyota for Mt Theo and he'd refused, saying: 'There's nothing you can do ... let those sniffers die' – he came up to me and shook my hand.

'It's good that you've come back, Jangala,' he said, addressing me by my skin name.

Two months later that same man offered his private car for transport to Mt Theo, 'so you can take Hooker Creek some *janyungu* [tobacco]'.

'No worries, Jangala,' he told me. 'You can borrow my Toyota any time you need to go to Mt Theo.'

A lot of things had changed.

Morgan returned to Central Australia for a brief handover where he explained to me all the various accounts and procedures and legalities that went along with managing the new Mt Theo Program Corporation. I spent the following two days in Alice Springs meeting with government people and community workers.

'So you have really come back?' they asked me.

'Yeah, it's just like in the Blues Brothers movie,' I said. 'We're gonna get the old band back together. Me, Peggy, and Hooker Creek.'

It felt so good to be back. I felt high on the cause and wrapped up in the support that so many people gave to it. 'This is really important work,' they told me.

The level of encouragement was in sharp contrast to my experience of working in the public service in Canberra where my supervisor told me I should count myself lucky if after ten years just one of my ideas got up.

'I feel like I've spent the past year of my life living in an eddy,' I told a friend as I reflected on my career in the public service. 'But now I'm back in the main current of the river of my life and it feels fantastic.'

At Yuendumu, I rebuilt the youth centre with help from local tradesmen and young people. All the work was voluntary. It took nearly a year until the program had its regular funding restored by the government. We cooked hamburgers at the disco to raise enough funds to buy lights and paints. We hired videos and held outdoor film nights with small campfires for warmth. The momentum was building – it was all going to happen again.

In July, Hooker Creek and Rex Forrest moved out to Mt Theo to prepare for reopening the program. The road still hadn't been graded but at least the bore was fixed. Karissa Preuss was visiting during her semester break and volunteered to run the school holiday program. The youth centre was open with video games, pool tables and roller skates. It was time to clean up sniffing.

I went to an abandoned yellow besser-brick house in North Camp. I remembered when the house had been newly built. Seven years later it was trashed, doors were hanging off their hinges, windows smashed, cupboards and sinks ripped apart. The walls were covered in graffiti and some walls had been smashed down.

I knew the family who had once lived there. They had to leave the house after someone had passed away, in keeping with the ancient rules and traditions of moving camp following a death. With no one living in the house and many people required to avoid it and the surrounding area (under the strict cultural protocols surrounding death), it became the ideal hideout for teenagers wanting to sniff petrol away from prying adult eyes.

I entered this sniffer house and spoke to my old sniffer mates who were huddled in one room, cans of petrol wedged under their noses.

'Hello, Yakajirri, you got any smoke?' one of them sang out.

'*Munyma juku* (wait a minute),' I replied in badly spoken Warlpiri. 'I've got business to talk with you first … Mt Theo is going to open up again and you know what that means. You're all going to go to Mt Theo if you keep sniffing.'

'Ah, we don't want to go,' they groaned.

'We can do this the easy way or the hard way,' I continued. 'The easy way is that you pack up your swags, so when I come round to your house tomorrow we all go to Mt Theo, nice and easy. Then I'll be easy on you and bring you back for Sports Weekend in four weeks time.

'The hard way is that when I come round to your house, you don't come with me, or you run away and hide. Then all those Council members and elders are going to get really cranky, and they will come round with me and the policeman later on. And you know what they're gonna say? They're gonna say: "Those sniffers gotta stay at Mt Theo for three months – no Sports Weekend." And they're gonna force me. I won't be able stick up for you … So what do you want to do – the easy way or the hard way?'

'We'll go the easy way, Yakajirri,' they said.

They even gave me the details of which house they would be staying at to make my job simpler. There were eight young men sniffing in that house. The next day, six of them willingly came with me to Mt Theo. The following night I took out Austin. He knew the drill – I had been taking him to Mt Theo for the past seven years.

The last sniffer, Esau, was a little harder to catch, but we found him outside the disco a few nights later and took him to Mt Theo. A friend of Liam's came with me for company. On the way back, the Nissan ute we were driving got bogged not far from where the Mt Theo Toyota had been stuck for two months during the floods. We fetched besser blocks, sheets of steel and planks of wood that had been left behind in the mud hole when the Toyota was rescued. Using these, we jacked up the Nissan corner by corner and literally built a road underneath.

It took us nearly an hour under a full moon, but nothing beats the feeling of elation that follows after getting a ute out of a bog. We sang all the way home.

The importance of non-violence

Non-violence was always an important principle I abided by when I worked on the Mt Theo Program. Although we dealt with violent sniffers and had to frequently use physically coercive methods, it was crucial that the non-Aboriginal petrol sniffing activist behaved in a non-violent manner.

Non-violence maintains credibility. It was important that the Kardiya worker maintained credibility in the eyes of the community, the sniffers and their family. If Kardiya workers were to defend themselves using violent means, such as punching back or pushing an attacker to the ground, they would quickly lose community support. Under Warlpiri custom, the attacker's family would immediately feel obliged to support the attacker (because they are family) and, regardless of the circumstances, they would condemn the Kardiya.

This unconditional support for family members is a part of Warlpiri culture. Allegiance to kin and family loyalty are far more dominant in the Warlpiri moral code than the bipartisan idea of 'who was in the right and who was wrong'. The fallout from a Kardiya hitting back could be enormous, with cries from the family such as: 'We don't want that sort of Kardiya in our community, he hurt and attacked our son. He is a bad Kardiya who hurts Yapa, who hurts our young people.'

The kinship and clan alliance system is so complex and pervasive in Warlpiri communities that a single incident can alienate a whole network of people, drawn in by their kinship loyalties. This not only undermines the credibility of an individual Kardiya worker, but also undermines support for the program across the community.

Non-violence contributes to keeping the Kardiya worker safe. Safe from creating a whole family of enemies, and safe in the reputation that everyone in the community (including all the sniffers) knows you are not going to hurt them. It creates a kind of moral shield, where people are reluctant to do violence towards you, because they know that you have never been, and never will be, violent towards them. This shield is not an impenetrable force field, but it provides protection and ensures that in any violent situation, the Kardiya worker maintains the high moral ground, and thus the family's and community's support.

In the course of Mt Theo work, violent conflict rarely occurred in private so there were nearly always Yapa witnesses. Usually those witnesses were prepared to step in and provide a human shield between the attacker and the Kardiya worker.

Violence was most likely to occur when rounding up sniffers to go to Mt Theo. Round-ups were nearly always done in partnership with senior community members and, if violence was expected, it was good to have the police there too. Sometimes the Kardiya worker remained in the background while the family of the sniffer and the senior community members pressured the sniffer to climb aboard the Mt Theo vehicle.

Simply having the police present put additional unspoken pressure on the sniffer to go to Mt Theo. Sometimes the police had to be verbally or physically directive. In many cases, however, the police had no legal authority to direct the sniffer to go to Mt Theo, and therefore could only be a presence.

Occasionally, the elders who were helping with the round-up would be unable to exert pressure on a particular sniffer due to a cultural avoidance or respect relationship. In those situations, the Kardiya worker's role became that of an activist. The activist role was one of verbally convincing the sniffer to go to Mt Theo or, if they were reluctant, convincing the sniffer's family to force the sniffer to go to Mt Theo.

Because sniffers were well aware of the activist role played by the Kardiya, they often directed their violence towards them. This occurred even when the Kardiya has remained in the background during an incident. This was when non-violence was important.

In these situations the activist has two objectives: (1) to stand firm while turning the other cheek; and (2) to live to work another day without getting hurt.

On many occasions when I (the activist) had been attacked by sniffers, I was saved through the quick action of Yapa family and community members. The sniffer was physically restrained and outnumbered. In most situations, this was enough for the sniffer to feel defeated in terms of the conflict; they would then give up the fight and agree to go to Mt Theo.

On some occasions, the sniffer broke free and attacked the activist again and again, being restrained on each occasion. While this was going on, the activist, family and community members would talk in a calm and soothing way to the young person, explaining that they were being sent to Mt Theo so that their body could heal from petrol sniffing. 'We're trying to save your life, we love you' was a common refrain.

The situation was more straightforward if the police were present. As soon as the sniffer attacked anyone, the police could immediately threaten to charge the young person with assault and then give them the choice of either going to Mt Theo or being charged. Ninety-nine per cent of the time the young person elected to go to Mt Theo.

Using restraint

After many years of working in Yuendumu, and my role in the community firmly cemented with the Mt Theo identity, I began to feel that I had been given tribal permission to restrain a young person in exceptional circumstances.

On many occasions I blocked doors and windows of houses or vehicles using my body to block a sniffer's escape route. I frequently sat in the back of a Troop Carrier, with my body jammed against

Michael Morgan

the back door to prevent sniffers from jumping out as we drove them to Mt Theo. But I have only restrained a young person once. I did this about four months after Mt Theo had been reopened by Rex and Hooker Creek.

The community's cage truck was set on fire. Seventeen-year-old Jedda, who had just resumed sniffing, and fellow sniffer Fenella were suspected of lighting the fire. I had to drive both of them to Mt Theo.

Until this incident, petrol sniffing had been absent from the community for three months and I was determined to see that it was gone forever.

We headed out to Mt Theo in a single cab Nissan ute. As we drove along the road, Jedda, who still stank of petrol, tried to open the door and jump out. I reached over and grabbed her while I stopped the ute. I held the door shut for ten minutes while she screamed, scratched, bit and punched me. She kicked at the interior and then at the windscreen. She hit it until it broke, which shocked her a bit. She stopped hitting and agreed to calm down and not jump out.

I drove off and had barely gone 200 metres before she tried to jump out again. I again physically pulled her back inside the moving vehicle while simultaneously stopping the ute. This time I held the door shut for fifteen minutes.

The scenario of driving a short distance and then Jedda trying to jump out was played out many more times until after hours of fighting Jedda fell asleep. It took us six hours to reach Mt Theo, a journey that usually takes two.

When we arrived after dark, I was exhausted and Jedda was hungry. As I unloaded the rations she cooked a dinner of sausages on the campfire which she then offered to Fenella and me. The petrol had left her body and we were friends again.

The need to keep the program running through funding droughts

Often local communities will close down services due to government funding shortages. Mt Theo experienced many funding droughts, but I cannot remember closing the program down due to a lack of funds. The cause was too important.

Closing the program meant that petrol sniffing would rise again. Prior to 1998, we had seen sniffing start up again every summer when the elders would go away on ceremony business and Mt Theo closed. In Yuendumu things would go from having little or no sniffing to having 30 or 40 young people sniffing. It would then take months of work in autumn after Mt Theo was reopened to reduce the numbers. Shutting the program down set the whole cause back and created lots more work for us.

We never viewed ourselves as a funded 'service'. We viewed ourselves as people trying to save kids in our community from dying from sniffing. We knew that if we didn't save that generation of young people, no one else would and petrol sniffing would wreak havoc in our community. There was evidence all across the desert of what happens if communities do not stop petrol sniffing: violence, horrific burns, crime, vandalism, dysfunctional schools, and deaths.

Ours was a cause, not a 'service'. It was up to us to stop sniffing. The government supported us, their funding supported our work, but ultimately it was our problem and our responsibility, not theirs. We started the program with no outside resources. Our work went on regardless of whether we were funded or not. Our aim was to stop sniffing and that was what we were determined to do.

Even after years of receiving recurrent government funding, we still experienced funding droughts. Following Morgan's departure (when I quit the public service to return to Mt Theo) we received no funding for several months. Most of our workers

Friendship at Mt Theo

were volunteers anyway. Hooker Creek and I were the only official employees at the time – but there was no money to pay our wages, so we worked with no personal income. We received donations of money that helped us to buy food and we built up substantial debts at the store. Eventually the government came through with the funding and the debts were repaid.

Building trust takes years

Telling groups of visitors the Mt Theo story makes it sound easy. There's almost a mythology that the whole community pulled together with one mind and made it happen. In a way that is how it ended up. It almost became an unwritten law in Yuendumu that if you sniff, you go to Mt Theo. After four years, the program had almost universal acceptance and support in the community and was run very much by consensus. We were rightly proud of this … but things hadn't always been that way. Mt Theo is only one outstation, it is not country that belongs to every clan and family group. In fact it only has some clans that are regarded as belonging to that country. Life in Yuendumu on many occasions was, and still can be, characterised by inter-clan rivalries. While people often put these rivalries aside to get on with their daily lives, when there is conflict or stress, loyalty to kin usually come first.

How did that work for parents of petrol sniffers? On the one hand, they knew their child was sniffing petrol and they were told sniffing was bad for kids. Sometimes they were not completely convinced. Their daughter was a good kid. They grew her up and loved her very much. They respected her feelings and emotions and loved her unconditionally.

The school bus turned up driven by that whitefella, Yakajirri, with a bunch of other people from North Camp (Peggy and Hooker Creek) who were unrelated to the parents. The bus was full of bad petrol sniffer kids, the ones who were to blame in the first place for leading their daughter astray and getting her into sniffing; the very same kids who 'forced' her to break into the shop with them.

Their daughter cried. She screamed and begged her parents not to send her away to that outstation.

'That's not my country,' she cried, 'that's not my family, I'll have no family there. I'll kill myself. I'm not the worst sniffer. I promise I won't sniff again. Mummy … Daddy … help me. Don't send me away like a dog.'

The parents were torn. Oh, *wiyarrpa*, how could we be so cruel to our daughter to make her cry like this? So they would approach me and the mother, Napanangka, pleaded on behalf of her daughter: 'Yakajirri, please give her one more chance. She promised she won't do it again. She won't sniff again. We can't really send her away. It's not her country there. She'll have no family there. She'll be too lonely.'

'But Napanangka, she's sniffing, she's been sniffing all week. You know we had that big community meeting at the basketball courts and everyone said that those sniffers should go to outstations.

She'll be okay. It's not for too long,' I countered.

'It's not her country there. Give her one more chance. Don't be hard,' the mother pleaded.

'But what about the sniffing? We don't want her to get worse from sniffing. You know what happens in the Pitjantjatjara Lands, kids die from sniffing petrol.'

'But we're not Pitjantjatjara, we're Warlpiri,' Napanangka said, as if drawing on the experience of the Pitjantjatjara people made as much sense as drawing on the experience of Martians. The daughter didn't go with us on that trip.

After many years, people across the whole community began to trust us with their kids. It became more and more accepted that petrol sniffers went to Mt Theo. And Mt Theo worked. Kids did stop sniffing and they came back looking healthier.

From the initial 'Petrol Sniffing Working Party' the Mt Theo Program grew into something that touched the whole community. Through working with sniffers (who made up half of Yuendumu's teenage population) we came to be personally engaged with, and eventually trusted by, every family group in Yuendumu. Mt Theo was no longer just an outstation. It saved the lives of young people and the whole community felt proud of that cause. In 2001, our management committee members came from every family group in Yuendumu. This gave us an 'in' with almost every household and organisation in the community. We lived in a web of relationships which criss-crossed Yuendumu and it was all good.

Jaru Pirrjirdi night school

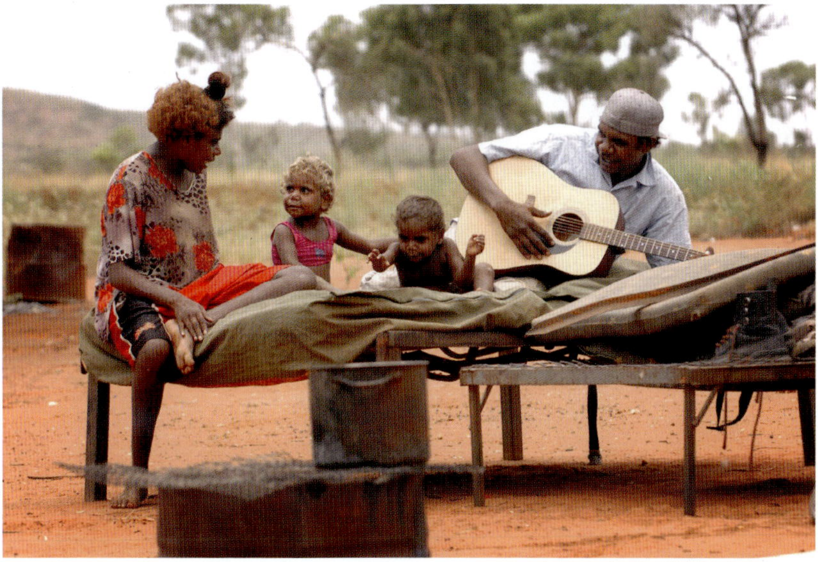

Azaria Nampijinpa Robertson (left), former Mt Theo client, is now employed as a Junior Carer at Mt Theo Outstation

Jaru Pirrjirdi Strong Voices community painting

Morgan and Ned organising football draws

Walkabout at Mt Theo (photo by Frances Mocnik)

Jaru Pirrjirdi camp with Karissa in the foreground

Recording Dreaming knowledge – Jaru Pirrjirdi

Printing T-shirts in the youth program

On a Jaru Pirrjirdi excursion

13: Breathing Fresh Air

When we have sorry business, everyone comes from everywhere around, all the family, all the community members, to show how much they care for that one who has passed away. But it's too late then, you can't go to that coffin and shake the body inside and say: 'Get up, see how much we care for you now.' You can't wait until sorry time to show how much you care. You've got to put all that effort in while a young person is still alive, to save their life.

Andrew Japaljarri Spencer

The brain story: educating young people about petrol sniffing

June 2001

It is night time. The disco and youth centre have closed and nearly everyone has gone home or is asleep. It is maybe 2 a.m. There is a cold wind blowing down the streets of Yuendumu. Karissa and I are wandering those streets, looking for young people who might be sniffing petrol.

'Don't be scared,' we say as we approach a group of six young people who are sniffing. Some are girls, some are young men.

Sitting down and bringing out a thermos of sweet milk and honey tea, we begin the conclusion of our day's work. The young people put their petrol aside to take sips of the warm tea as it is being passed around in a communal cup. The ritual of sharing from one cup is an ancient one; it is a process of bonding, building rapport and creating relationships. The stars above us in the desert sky are cold and bright.

'People think that I am the Big Bear,' says one sniffer. 'But really I am a sad bear, that's why I am sniffing tonight.'

We start to share stories, workers and sniffers together, stories of sadness, pain and hope. This is the beginning of our work, building trust, making friends. I even tell the story of when I was a teenager who ran away from home and got chased by the police.

'You're not really that old, are you, Yakajirri?' one of the young men comments.

Our downcast eyes flicker up to look at each other.

(In desert culture it is offensive to look directly into someone's face and maintain eye contact during a conversation. So it's important Karissa and I keep our gaze averted, with only quick glances at another person's eyes during a conversation.)

The trust is building.

'When we sniff, the dream is real, your dreams become real like life,' another sniffer tells us as he describes the experience of petrol-induced hallucination.

'Do you want to know why that happens?' I ask. 'Do you want to know the story of why petrol can make your dreams real? If you come by to our house tomorrow we can show you that story. We have a painting we can show you. The story will explain why petrol makes your dreams become real.'

Brain story

The next morning four girls aged between fourteen and sixteen gathered at our house. We drank tea and ate toast. They casually flicked through magazines and old photographs. Then the story began.

We brought out two saucers with butter on them. Into one of the saucers we poured petrol. This very visual demonstration illustrated how the solvents in petrol dissolve fatty tissue. The Warlpiri word for fatty tissue and butter is the same: *jara*.

'When you kill a *marlu* (kangaroo) and you spill its brains, you'll see a lot of fat, *jara*,' I explained to the girls.

'Your brains are the same, they have a lot of *jara* in them. When you sniff petrol, the petrol melts the fat in your brains, in the same way you can see it eating into the *jara* on this saucer right now.'

We had the girls' attention now. Karissa reached over and placed the big *Brain Story* book on the table. The book measures 50 centimetres by 80 centimetres and is dominated by full-page illustrations that use Western Desert art style and symbols to communicate some basic concepts about how the brain works. The pictures illustrate how the brain has various functions that are situated in different locations (frontal lobe, rear cortex etc.). The pictures map out the concept of neurological pathways, and the damage that solvents can do to them. The pictures are simple and basic enough that they can be used to communicate across language and cultural barriers.*

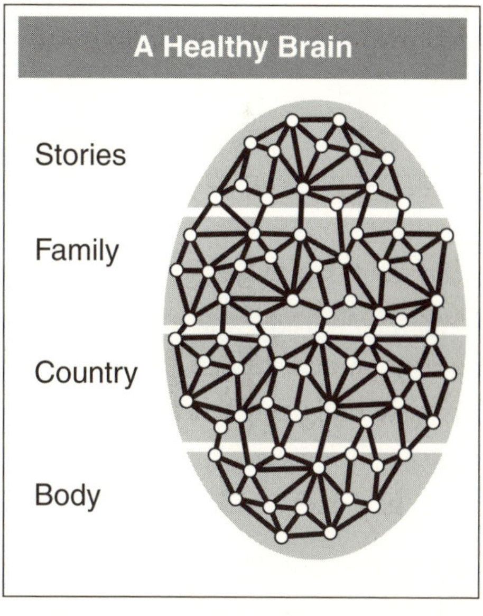

The first picture shows a healthy brain

'This is a picture of your

* I wish to thank the custodians of 'The Brain Story' booklet © Petrol Link Up 1994 Injarntnama Outstation for their kind permission to reproduce the images and information.

brain when it is healthy. A person's brain has lots of roads in it. These roads are what doctors call neurological pathways. Messages travel down these roads. These messages tell your legs to move, your heart to beat and your lungs to breathe. They help you see and imagine and dream. They help you to feel love and pain for your family. The messages help you to remember your stories and find your way around your country.

'If these roads in your brain get muddy and washed away, then the messages can't travel down them anymore, and you will not be able to do the things that you used to do.

'Parts of your brain look after your body, your country, your family and hold your stories, vision and dreams. The roads in your brain join up all the different parts of your brain. This is how a person's brain works before they start sniffing petrol.'

Why your petrol dreams seem real

'When you start to sniff petrol, the petrol fumes travel right up your nose to the front part of your brain which holds your vision and your memory, your dreams and your imagination. This is the part of your brain that holds your stories. The petrol fumes start to wash away the roads in this front part of your brain. The roads get muddy and then the messages slide around on them. The same way a four-wheel drive will slide around out of control on a muddy washed out road.

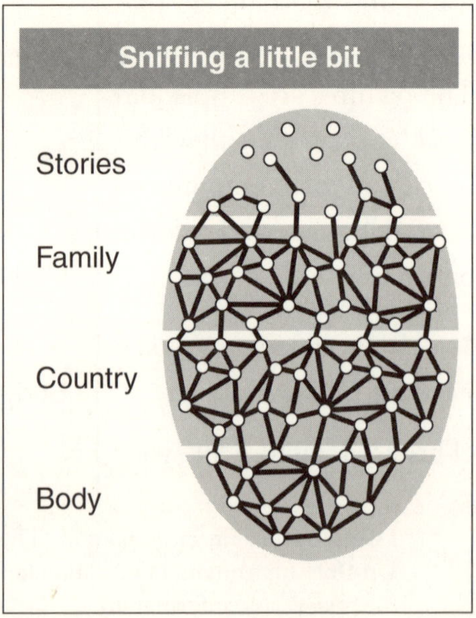

'This is what is happening when what you imagine and dream about starts to look and feel as though it is real. This happens because the messages are not travelling straight anymore; they are sliding around and getting mixed up. When you have a petrol dream (hallucinate) it will seem as though you are really seeing what you are dreaming about. This is because the messages are sliding around, and your brain might think a message is from your eyes, when really it might be from your imagination, or from your memory of a horror film you saw on TV. This is why dreams seem real.'

How petrol sniffing affects your family

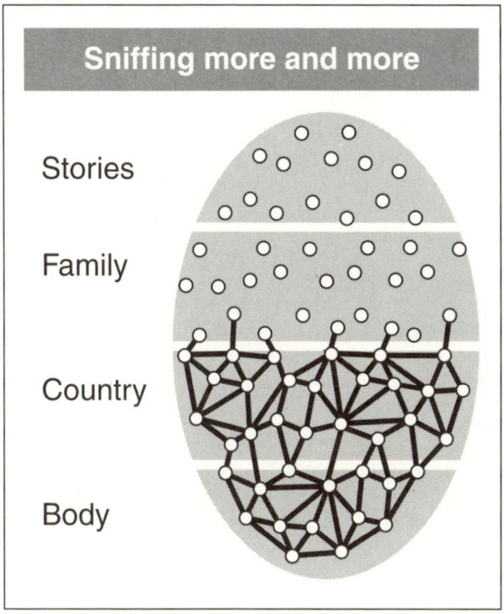

'When you sniff more and more, you will find that you forget things. As the petrol washes and melts away all the roads in your story brain, you won't know what's real and what's not real. You may make some mistakes and hurt people you love. You may start fighting with your family or getting into trouble with the police. This happens as the petrol washes back into your family brain and washes away the roads there.

'You might remember the story about what happened when Jackson killed that boy at Nelliton. Buckley told me this story. [Buckley was a 20-year-old ex-sniffer from Yuendumu who the girls knew well.]

'Buckley, Jackson and Kumunjayi [the deceased] were all sniffing together one afternoon. Jackson was having a petrol dream. His dream seemed real.

'Jackson thought his friend Kumunjayi had turned into a devil. He thought the devil was real so he picked up a big stick to protect himself, to fight the devil, to kill the devil. He freaked out. He thought Kumunjayi was the devil and he hit him hard with that piece of wood. He killed his best friend.'

Everyone nodded, they remembered the story and it was part of recent community history. The girls listened intently.

'His friend was dead. Dead because with that petrol dream Jackson did not know what was real and what was not real. The petrol had washed away the roads in his story and family brain and kept washing away more.'

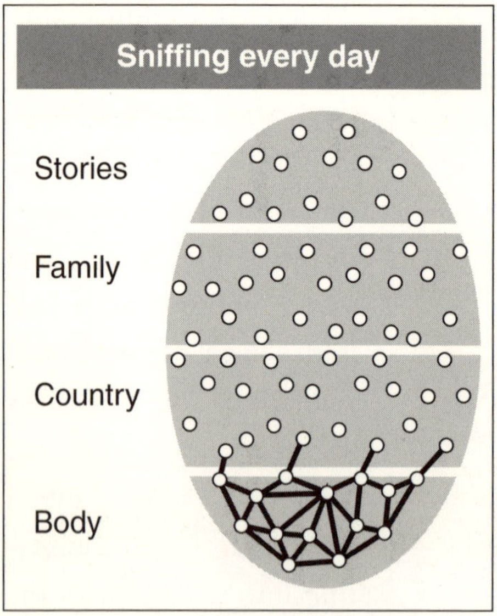

As I emphasised the last point, I pointed to the picture of the brain story again. My hand washed across it, in a wave motion, showing how petrol washes away the roads in the brain.

'This is a true story. Buckley told me himself. He was there.'

We turned the page.

How petrol affects your sense of country

'When you sniff petrol all day every day, the petrol keeps washing back through your brain, washing away the roads in your story brain, your family brain, and into your country brain. When the petrol reaches your country brain, you won't know your country anymore. You won't know the places in your country, or how to find them. You won't know which way is west or which way is north. You might get lost.

'One time in South Australia there was a petrol sniffer who

sniffed all day every day. He used to walk around in circles all day on the football oval. He was so disorientated that he couldn't find his way off the oval.

'You might think that's a funny story, but it isn't.

'Last July at that Pintubi community, one sniffer sniffed all day every day. He wandered out to West Camp and he kept wandering west, sniffing all the time. Then he realised didn't know where he was. He couldn't find his way home. He didn't know which way was north or which way was east. The petrol had washed all the roads away in his country brain. He never found his way back; he collapsed and died out there in the desert. The circling crows found him but it was too late.'

The girls nodded again; this story was also part of recent community history. They remembered being told about it, but now they began to understand how petrol was involved in that death.

How petrol sniffing affects your body

'When you sniff for years and years, the petrol that made you feel so good, the petrol that made your dreams real, will have washed all the way back to the cortex, to the back part of your head just near your neck.

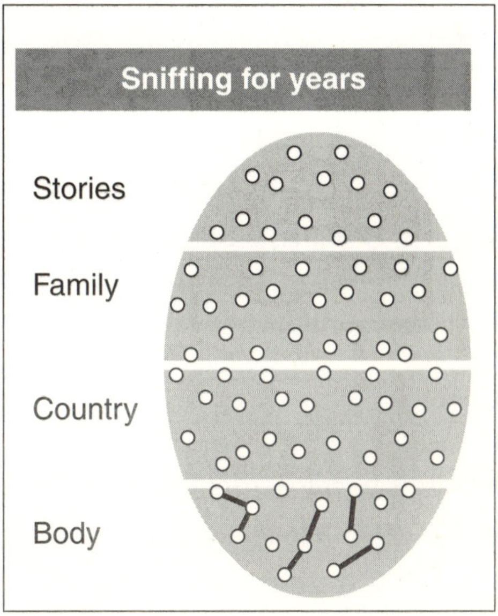

'When the petrol washes this far back in your brain, your body will stop working properly.

'There was a story in the newspaper last year.'

I placed a copy of the *Centralian Advocate* on the table. The headline read: 'Sniffers are the lost generation'. The main photo showed one of two brothers who was in a wheelchair just outside of Uluru (Ayers Rock).

'See this man here, this brother isn't in a wheelchair because of a car accident or anything else. He's in a wheelchair from sniffing petrol. The petrol has washed away so many roads in his brain – the parts that tell his body how to work, so messages can't travel around to tell his legs to move. It says the boys can't even swat flies away from their faces because their motor skills are so damaged from petrol sniffing.

'In April, in a community just south of here, one petrol sniffer sniffed all day in a house. His parents went into town and left him by himself sniffing. They couldn't stop him from sniffing. When his parents came back home that day, they found him dead. He died of heart failure.

'The petrol had washed right through his brain, all the way back into his cortex where it started to wash away the roads in his body brain. It only washed away one road that afternoon while he was sniffing but it was a very important road. It was the road that messages travelled down to tell his heart to keep beating. His brain just couldn't tell his heart to beat anymore.'

The words on the page of the book in front of us read: 'This boy passes away, the petrol has been through his story, family and country brain and now it has taken his life. Everyone is very sad.'

By the time we finished telling the Brain Story, the petrol had dissolved almost all of the butter in the saucer. Two of the girls, sisters, looked at us with mouths wide open in horror. The story was true, and now they thought it could happen to them, too.

Emotional manipulation

I have just woken up from a dream, a memory that was so real.

I was at Mt Theo.

We were about to bring a group of sniffers back to Yuendumu.

Their four weeks were up. I had planned a party with soft drinks, chips and lollies, but I had forgotten to buy them in my haste of organising rations. I decided to have an impromptu barbecue instead, using some of the rations I had brought with me. I rang Liam who was at the footy oval at Yuendumu and asked him to drive out and meet us halfway with lollies, chips, drinks and cigarettes.

Fiddle was there.

It was time to tell the sniffers they were going back to Yuendumu. I started my 'please don't sniff again' speech.

Big Bear was there. I was talking to him now.

What I was doing was invoking relationship just like people invoke the name of 'Allah', or like a shaman invoking a spell, I invoked the power of relationship. I told Bear what a special and powerful young man he was. That it was not only generally true, but it was true for me. I told him none of us wanted to see him sniff again, none of us wanted to see him die, and we didn't want him to become like so many young people from Papunya. (There had been four deaths from petrol sniffing in Papunya over the past six months.)

As I spoke I described images of tear-stained wailing faces from sorry business, mixed up with memories of the funerals for those four sniffers: women relatives throwing themselves on the ground in grief, pounding their heads with rocks clenched into fists as the blood poured down their scalps; of faces so sad, so heart-wrenched from funerals. I implored Big Bear not to be in that coffin. I was claiming him back from the dead.

Big Bear at Warlpiri Media; he used to be a sniffer then became a founding member of Jaru Pirrjirdi.

Bear stood there. His downcast eyes flickered up to see me. I invoked his place, reminding him of his family, of all who loved him in kinship, and of those who loved him as a gang member and friend in his peer group. I reminded him that he was a young man little kids looked up to; he was a valued community member and the Warlpiri Media guru.

I told him how he was really special to me; how it was heart-wrenching to watch what had happened to him. Because he really mattered to me.

Andrew Japaljarri Spencer, a Warlpiri man who had dedicated his life to helping people, to try and stop them from dying from grog and sniffing, once told me: 'When we have sorry business, everyone shows how much they care … but it's too late then … You've got to put that effort in while a young person is still alive.' So there I was at Mt Theo, showing Bear how much I cared. All the other young people were there. The girls from Willowra said, 'See, Bear, don't sniff. See how upset Yakajirri is.'

Others whispered to one another: 'See Yakajirri's tears, that's 'cos he really cares for those sniffers.'

When viewed from the distance, I could see it was emotional manipulation. That's what my wife calls it. Some may call it brain-washing. But at least the kid will still have a brain. Petrol corrodes brains.

Warlpiri often invoke relationship when making a claim for something, demanding a resource or a favour. 'But I'm your brother,' they will say, adding weight to the request. They taught me well.

The birth of 'Jaru Pirrjirdi' – Strong Voices

One week after doing the brain story with those girls, Karissa and I were listening to Neil Murray and Shane Howard songs on the record player. She'd been back in Yuendumu for three weeks and was immersing herself in the lifestyle of the program.

'It's just like living on a farm,' she had said earlier in the day. Her family were farmers from West Wyalong in New South Wales. 'There's no separation between your home life and work life. It's all one thing, very holistic.'

Karissa was studying community development and participatory action research at university. 'I've been studying this stuff,' she commented, 'but you guys are actually doing it, without ever reading theory or knowing the labels that describe it.'

Karissa was the young student who had visited three years earlier during the summer and lived at Mt Theo. She took to it like 'a duck to water'. I was so impressed that I rang up Nic Peterson, her anthropology lecturer, and asked him to send me out more students like Karissa – she seemed to get it.

Karissa seemed even more inspired on her second stay in Yuendumu. We were listening to those records and having our 'end of day discussion'. Karissa was right into those sorts of things, deep and meaningful conversations, teasing out ideas and feelings, reflecting.

'Yakajirri,' she said, 'why don't you play these sorts of songs at the youth centre? You find these songs inspiring. Don't you think the young people want inspiration too?'

'I play disco music because that's what the young people want to hear. I'm trying to compete with petrol sniffing, so I've got to provide vibrant pulsing disco music that will attract young people, not folk songs,' I replied.

'But don't you think there is more to life than sexy dancing at the disco?' she countered. 'Look at yourself – the reason why you're not a petrol sniffer is not because you go sexy dancing at the disco. It's because you've got an inspired life. Why don't you find out the real reasons underneath why young people sniff? Why don't you find out what is really there? Why don't you ask them what inspires them?'

She had a point and it was a good one. So far, the youth

program had been feeding young people the junk food of western culture: disco, video games, football and pool table. The young people were bored and hungry for something. 'A hunger for stimuli' is how one academic had described petrol sniffing. So as a desperate measure, we fed them the fast-food option of disco. Karissa was right: they needed stuff that was really nutritious.

'Why don't you ask them?' she repeated.

'Because I'm too busy,' I replied, feeling exasperated. 'I'm flat out running rations to Mt Theo, catching sniffers, putting on the disco, dealing with the committee and the government.'

They were all true and good excuses. But there was another reason why I did not ask young people what inspired them: I didn't know how.

I didn't have deep and meaningful conversations with young people. Not at the level that really needed to take place, not the way counsellors and friends had with me when I was a teenager, when you really go deep, and unpack the pain and the yearning, and reflect on the underlying issues in your life. I could have those conversations with Vesna or with a close Warlpiri friend like Ned or Robin. I might have been able to do it with teenagers in white society; I had some training. But to do it across the cultural divide – that was way too hard.

I looked at Karissa. She had engaged the sniffers in deep and meaningful conversations at Mt Theo three summers ago. She helped them unpack their stuff, got them to talk about their pain and their aspirations. She was a natural: she had reflective conversations with me almost every evening when we finished work.

While other whitefella community workers, myself included, put the hope of such conversations with young Aboriginal people in the 'tried and failed' too-hard basket, Karissa had them. She had a gift.

'I'm just too busy,' I continued. 'But if you want to come back next year to do that ...'

Normally a conversation will end there. It's a great way to deal with armchair critics, just throw the challenge back at them. But Karissa was not an armchair critic. She was an inspired young woman. We stayed up most of the night and thrashed out ideas and we came up with the rough outline of a project.

The project was about taking young people out bush to have those conversations at an individual level and in a group forum, and then to empower young people to develop the youth program in response to what they had expressed, to make it inspiring.

'I'm not going to support this, or even discuss it with the committee, unless you commit to doing it for several years,' I told her. 'I don't want to have you start something and then leave halfway through.'

She seemed pretty serious. Over the next few weeks Karissa and I sat at lots of campfires with committee members, Council members and Mt Theo elders and discussed the idea.

The committee members talked about how we had done a good job stopping sniffing, but that young people were still going to Alice Springs to drink grog and smoke marijuana. 'We need something to fill them up inside, to stop them from wanting to drink.'

'"*Jaru Pirrjirdi*" – that's what it should be called,' said Maxine Nungarrayi, the committee chairperson. 'It means "*strong voices*". We're giving those young people strong voices.'

I was excited. Suddenly the Mt Theo Program was going to reach another level, a level desperately needed. Karissa was right, young people did need inspiration. They needed to live inspiring lives. We had virtually stopped petrol sniffing but we hadn't stopped the flow of young people drifting into town and taking up careers in alcoholism. Maybe this project could start to do something about that.

I looked at Karissa and said, 'I've worked here for eight years, trying to stop petrol sniffing. It's been really hard work, and a lot of the time it's felt like we've been just bailing water out of a leaking boat. Sometimes we bail faster than it leaks, sometimes it's slower and I can feel the boat sinking. We've never reached a point where the job is done, where the boat doesn't sink anymore. I know if we stop bailing the water out the boat will sink. We're just trying to stay afloat, and that's hard enough. I haven't really thought about this other stuff.

'But now I think about what you've said, I'm looking at the boat and I'm thinking maybe the leaky boat is an aircraft carrier, and that those young people are aeroplanes. When I think about this new project, I think it's about getting those planes to fly.'

She smiled at me. True to her word, she came back the next year and worked hard over the next four years to make Jaru Pirrjirdi come into being.

'Coming into being' is a Warlpiri expression, '*purlka jarrija*' is how they say it. It describes how the spiritual power in the land, the spirit that is from the Dreamtime, physically manifests itself. How *Jukurrpa* spirit from, say, a possum Dreaming site, will manifest itself in the form of new baby possums being conceived and born.

When Vesna and I were newlyweds, we camped with Yapa in the creek bed at Jurlpungu. It was there that Vesna first felt the quickening of a baby inside her. Warlpiri told her that it was a spirit child from Jurlpungu entering her womb. Later after that baby (Deua) was born, the old women told Vesna: 'Nampijimpa *purlka jarrija* Jurlpungla (Deua *came into being* at Jurlpungu).' It was where her spirit became a physical manifestation.

Just like the Mt Theo Program, Jaru Pirrjirdi started with no funding. It quickly became a success. Within the first year, Karissa had us winning awards and had young members of the Jaru Pirrjirdi team going to conferences.

'We were sniffers once and now we work to make Yuendumu a better place so other young people don't want to sniff,' they told the world, broadcasting out on national radio.

They started to feel proud. Polly Anne Dixon, one of the girls who used to fall asleep on the classroom floor after sniffing all night, now travelled to a national youth forum in Canberra. She was the Northern Territory winner of the ABC's 'Heywire' Short Story Competition. Her story had been about petrol sniffing and Jaru Pirrjirdi.

Later when I worked with welfare workers down south, I often thought of Polly Anne. While my cynical colleagues looked at our clients and said, 'Oh, I can just see Rochelle in five years time,

Polly Anne, NT winner of the ABC's Heywire Short Story Competition; her story had been about petrol sniffing and Jaru Pirrjirdi.

living in the housing commission unit, baby hanging off her tit, yelling at the neighbour over the fence, threatening to smash her head in …'

I looked at the same client and thought: I can see you in two years time winning the Heywire competition with your incredible story of surviving as an orphan on the streets of Wollongong. I would look at Rochelle and see a young woman full of fire, enough fire to change the world. I could see her going off to conferences like the Jaru Pirrjirdi young people do, and advising policy makers.

But that's the difference between what we did in Yuendumu, and what cynics do. Cynics create their own failure.

Doing it all again

In August, the then Yuendumu Community Government Council Clerk tried to force the Mt Theo Program to come back under Council control. Even though we were an independent organisation, the combination of Mt Theo closing due to the floods and Morgan leaving had made the Commonwealth reluctant to fund us. The Council Clerk assured me she had friends high up in Commonwealth Health in Darwin who told her the program should be under Council.

'We've already been there,' I protested. 'It might be fine while you are the Council Clerk, but what if we get another bad Council Clerk who tries to close the program down?'

'That won't happen,' she assured me and the assembled Council members. 'If the program is under Council, the Yapa councillors will always be in control.'

'Not if the Department of Local Government suspends the Council,' I countered. 'Then under the constitution all the power goes to the Council Clerk.'

'It's very unlikely that would ever happen,' she reassured the Council.

'The last time we had a bad Council Clerk, the Department threatened to suspend the Council if it didn't go along with him. We've been through this all before, it's why we're independent,' I said angrily.

We had the government reviewers coming out in a week's time and I was sure this woman was going to try and set them against the program. I could see right through her. I went to Helen Jutner, my adoptive white mother. I was nearly crying.

'I just want you to listen to me,' I said. 'I'm so angry and I need to talk about it with someone I can trust.'

Helen listened, and then the reviewers came. I hoped the government reviewers would immerse themselves in the program like Karissa had when she reviewed the program for a university paper. I hoped they would accompany me in the tasks of putting on disco, sharing warm tea with sniffers at midnight, doing outreach work and running rations to Mt Theo. I was mistaken: that was not their style.

'I have read everything about you and the program,' Jim, the male reviewer told me. 'I feel like I even know your blood type.'

I was trying to impress them; we were meeting at the program house, my home in Yuendumu. I made them lattes with freshly brewed espresso. Each latte had visible horizons of separation that you could see through the glass where the coffee sits in dark layers over the milk. I was really trying.

'Where is your sharps policy and procedures manual?' Paula, the female reviewer asked.

She looked professional, in her neatly pressed clothes, but she had no idea. A sharps policy and procedures manual? What did she think we were? A methadone clinic in Sydney?

We dealt with petrol sniffing, not heroin. Our staff were tribal elders who had grown up in pre-contact times. Peggy, Rex and Hooker Creek couldn't have even read a sharps policy or procedures manual. Even if we had one it would have been useless.

'That's not what we're about, Paula,' I explained. 'This is a Warlpiri-run program; it's about reconnecting young people with land, love and culture.'

'Yes, we know all that,' Jim interrupted as he looked down at a score sheet of questions set out on his clipboard. 'Now, let's get on with this.'

They weren't there to learn at all. They just wanted to see how well we fitted into their table of questions. Questions such as: 'Where is your sharps policy and procedures manual?'

The government lady in Canberra told me the purpose of the review was so that the government could distil the essence of the Mt Theo Program and learn from it to help develop programs in other places. These reviewers weren't learning anything at all. What was worse was where they were staying.

Most official visitors to Yuendumu rented rooms in the community guesthouse. But the reviewers were staying at the Council Clerk's house, as personal guests. I smelled a rat.

To the reviewers' credit, one week later, after they had visited other communities in Central Australia, they almost apologised. They realised Mt Theo was unique, that it really did work. Paula sent me an email saying '... maybe there are lessons for us all from Mt Theo'.

But that night I was angry and hurt. They had acted like experts with their table of questions and made me feel like crap. I went round to Liam's to pour my heart out to him. He offered me red wine.

'I don't want to pick up that light sabre again,' I said, tears stinging in my eyes. 'I don't want to have to keep fighting all the time to protect this program.'

Nausea hit my stomach again. I hate this shit.

—

Financially the program was very vulnerable. The government still wasn't funding us and we were drawing heavily on the 'donations' account that Morgan had set up the year before.

'You've got to pay wages first,' our accountants demanded.

'No,' Hooker Creek and I countered. 'If we do that, there will be no money for food or diesel. The program comes first, our wages can wait.'

Hooker Creek was living off his wife's pension and I was doing redraws on my mortgage.

'You've abandoned us,' Vesna told me over the telephone from

Canberra. 'You care more about the sniffers than your own family.'

With no wage, I was no longer able to support my wife and kids.

'I'm going to claim the single mother's pension,' she said. We were both worried our marriage was over.

—

'If those reviewers know so much about petrol sniffing, why don't they go to Papunya and solve the sniffing problem there, instead of criticising us when we've practically solved the problem?' I complained to Liam.

Kids were dying at Papunya. Every few months there would be a funeral for another petrol sniffer. They were our neighbouring community. Sniffing was out of control there. People from Papunya had often asked for our help.

'Well, how do you think sniffing could be solved in Papunya?' Liam asked casually, but he held my gaze.

'First of all,' I said, 'a person, an activist, has to arrive with no funding. No fanfare, just a person.'

Liam held my gaze, pinning me with his eyes to speak this story: 'If a whitefella turns up with the label 'petrol sniffing worker', all the Anangu (Papunya Aboriginal people) will see petrol sniffing as the worker's responsibility, and no one else's. They will say: he's getting paid to worry for those sniffers. So you need to have a person without a label, a person without a petrol sniffing wage.

'The first thing that person needs to do is make friends. Maybe if they have a car they can help Anangu with firewood and take people hunting. Maybe they can share tea and pancakes with the sniffers. Maybe they can help out organising sports and things like disco.

'They need to be seen as a friend and as a person of action. They need to spend a year just doing that. Weaving a web of relationships across that community, across those family groups. Then

Old Jangala teaching about bush medicine on a Jaru Pirrjirdi excursion

that person needs to talk. Talk softly, gently, quietly.

'Talk about sniffing, not as a general issue, but as a personal issue, talk about the sniffers by their names, worrying for them. Weave the Mt Theo story in there too. People know the Mt Theo story. Anangu know that Yuendumu holds the *Jukurrpa* for stopping sniffing; they know Mt Theo works magic.

'And then you need a big trip. Anangu need to visit Mt Theo or have Mt Theo people visit them, to talk about everything, Yapa way, Anangu way, blackfella to blackfella, to demystify it.

'People might get enthused then. They might want to try something. Then it's time to get a ute. Not a flash ute that shouts out: Big Government Money, just a humble old twin cab, maybe a bit battered so that people won't get too precious or jealous about it.

'Some Anangu might want to try doing the Mt Theo thing at their outstation. By then the activist will have sussed people out, will have relationships with people. He will know who the greedy people are, who the bullshit artists are, who the fair dinkum people are. The activist can offer to use that ute to run people and supplies to that outstation. No government money, nothing to arouse jealousy or corruption. Just helping people to live out bush on their Centrelink money.

'That activist might have to try a lot of times. Families will get sick of the bush.

'Some people might give up, but maybe, just maybe, there's a chance that someone like Peggy might exist, and then you've got what you want: an outstation, an Anangu carer, a network of relationships, and a cause that people can believe in.'

'Oh shit,' said Liam as he looked at me. 'You really could do that.'

'I know,' I said. 'Kids are dying there from petrol. Papunya is actually closer to Yuendumu than Mt Theo, it's only 130 kilometres away. Kids are dying from petrol sniffing. Yet the solution to petrol sniffing is right here. It's sitting right here in our hands.'

I saw my life unfolding in front of me. I would spend ten years at Papunya. When sniffing had stopped there, I would spend ten years at Mt Liebig, and then ten years at Kintore and so forth. What an awesome and meaningful way to spend my life.

You can't beat us – Vasco and the knife

We survived the reviewers and Mt Theo maintained its independence. Sure enough, as time went by Yuendumu Council was suspended by the Territory Government, and eventually it became subsumed by a 'super shire' that stretches from one side of the Northern Territory to the other.

The sniffing front was quiet for nine months and then came the last wave.

Following the tragic death of a young man in the community,

some of Yuendumu's youth soothed their grief by turning to petrol. 'I'm sad because I lost my brother, that's why we're sniffing,' they said.

Lots of the young people who had not sniffed for almost a year started up again.

Vasco was a young man who had been sniffing on and off since he was twelve. He had been to Mt Theo many times, and often had long breaks between sniffing binges.

One morning, I was woken by a faint thudding sound coming from outside the house. The sun had barely come up and the eastern windows of the house were just beginning to let in light. I went outside to investigate the noise and was confronted by a solid young man, aged about 20, brandishing a hunting knife, and holding a tin of petrol under his nose. The thudding sound had come from him stabbing the tyres of the Toyota.

'You're not fucking taking me to Mt Theo,' he yelled, waving the knife in my direction.

'Good morning, Vasco,' I said. 'Do you want a smoke?'

'Yeah, I want a fucking smoke,' he said.

I went back inside and grabbed my tobacco and papers. I sat down on the veranda and began to roll a smoke. I offered the tobacco and papers to Vasco. In order to roll the smoke he needed both hands, so he put down the knife and the can of petrol on the veranda, and sat next to me.

'What about a light?' he demanded.

'No worries, Vasco, but first you gotta tip that petrol out. Too dangerous petrol and fire. I don't want to blow up.'

'No, that's my fucking petrol,' he said aggressively.

'Okay then, but put it away, long way, over by the gate; we don't want to get burnt like Dion or Toupe.'

Vasco agreed. He put the petrol away and sat down next to me. I lit Vasco's cigarette then mine and we shared the blessed calm of the nicotine as it infused into our bodies. Both of us inhaled deeply. There were no words.

After a few minutes, when we were both relaxed, I cocked my head to one side, looked at Vasco and quietly asked, 'What are you doing to my Toyota?'

'I been stab them tyres, I'm not fucking going Mt Theo,' he said calmly.

His face was wide with a grin, his milky red eyes triumphantly looking at me. The tyres on the Toyota were flat; he had been given a smoke and did not have to tip out his petrol. He was in control.

'Ah yeah, that's pretty smart,' I said. 'But you know I can always get those tyres fixed, and then take you to Mt Theo. If you really wanted to fuck me up, you might have to burn that Toyota, hey?'

The energy between us was friendly. We were both enjoying a smoke and the humour of the situation.

'But then, Vasco,' I continued, 'you know you'd get into a lot of trouble if you burnt that Toyota. Peggy would be wild with you and that policeman might even put you in jail.

'But even if you burnt that Toyota, you know what I'd do? I'd walk straight across the road here to Jangala, and I'd borrow his Toyota to take you to Mt Theo. 'Cos Jangala always told me that I can borrow his Toyota, any time, to take sniffers to Mt Theo.

'So Vasco, even if you burn my Toyota, then you're going to have to burn Jangala's Toyota too. You don't want to burn Jangala's Toyota, 'cos he's the number one spear thrower in Yuendumu, and if you burn his Toyota he'll make you look like a porcupine. Hmmm …' I paused for effect.

'But even if you burn Jangala's Toyota, you know what I'm gonna do? I'm gonna go right down the road to that corner house there, to Robbie and I'm gonna borrow his Toyota. 'Cos Robbie told me that I can borrow his Toyota anytime when I gotta take sniffers to Mt Theo.

'You know that Robbie will get really wild if you try and burn his Toyota too. But even if you burn his Toyota, then I'll just go over to that clinic, behind his house, and borrow the clinic Toyota to take you to Mt Theo. 'Cos that nurse mob have told me: "Yakajirri, any time you want to go to Mt Theo, you can borrow the clinic Toyota."

'So you gotta burn that clinic Toyota too. And after you burn that one, then I'll go over to the school. You know how I used to work at that school, and you know what that Principal told me: "Yakajirri, anytime you need to borrow that school bus to take sniffers to Mt Theo you can take it."

'So now you gotta burn the school bus. But after that I'll just go across the road to the Council, 'cos you know that they got a lot of Toyotas. And you know what the President told me. He said, "Yakajirri, any time you need to borrow a Toyota to take sniffers to Mt Theo, you can use a Council one."

'Are you gonna burn all the Council Toyotas? But even if you burn them, you know what? I'll just go a bit further over to Frank, at the Mining Company. 'Cos you know what that Frank always told me: "Yakajirri, any time you need to borrow a Toyota, you can use the Mining one."

'You gotta burn that Mining Toyota too, but even if you burn it, I'll just borrow that Warlukurlangu [Arts Centre] Toyota, and then I'll borrow that Women's Centre Toyota, after that I'll borrow the police Toyota with the policeman in it.'

Vasco knew the program's ability to borrow Toyotas was infinite. Over the eight years we had been operating, we had borrowed vehicles from nearly every organisation in Yuendumu to run transport to Mt Theo. I looked at him and I said, 'What are you gonna do, Vasco? Are you gonna burn every Toyota in Yuendumu?

'You might be thinking hard now,' I told him. 'You might be thinking: burning Toyotas and stabbing tyres is too hard. You might have to just kill that Yakajirri, then you won't have to go to Mt Theo.

'But you gotta think about that one too, mate. If you kill me, you're gonna be in big trouble, 'cos I got a lot of Yapa family here now, and they are all gonna do payback. And after that you are gonna get in trouble from the police. Whitefellas have got a really strong law against murdering people, and they might put you in jail for a long time.

'But even if you kill me, Vasco, you have to remember what happened when I went away to Canberra. Morgan and Robbie and all the Council mob took you to Mt Theo. You know why, Vasco? 'Cos everyone in this community wants to save your life from petrol. Not just me, but Peggy, Robbie, Hooker Creek and Ned, and Jangala, and Liam, too many Yapa everywhere here. They don't want petrol sniffing in Yuendumu. So even if you kill me, you're still gonna go to Mt Theo.'

Vasco had finished his cigarette by the time I finished my rave. He hung his head low, wandered over to the gate to where his petrol was, picked it up and walked away.

I took the flat tyres to the Council yard as soon as it opened. The Council mechanic let me use his tools to repair them.

That afternoon after school, Barbara Martin, Nancy Oldfield (two Yapa school teachers) and I did a sniffer round-up. We collected Vasco along with six other young people and took them to Mt Theo. The Toyota we were driving was riding on the very same tyres Vasco had stabbed that morning.

That was the last big sniffer round-up we did in Yuendumu. Vasco hasn't sniffed petrol since. I saw Vasco four years later when I visited Yuendumu. He proudly introduced me to his wife and their first-born baby. His sniffing days are long gone; he is a family man now.

The end

At the end of that 'last wave' year Peggy, Rex, Hooker Creek, Ned, Lindsay, Karissa and I were having dinner together, sitting in the lounge room of my house in Yuendumu. Rex, Karissa, Hooker Creek and I were drinking red wine; Peggy, Ned and Lindsay were drinking red cordial.

There hadn't been any sniffing in Yuendumu for nine months. Jaru Pirrjirdi was growing strong and pressure was building on me to move to Papunya and do it all again. An article about Mt Theo

Jaru crew painting the Youth Centre

had just been published in the *HQ* magazine which someone had brought out from town. The front cover read 'Hope in the Air'.

'Look at us,' Ned said proudly, pointing at the magazine photo of him and Rex's family at Mt Theo. 'We're famous.'

The words of the journalist stuck in my mind: 'If you want a hopeful story about Aboriginal Australia, this is it. The people of Yuendumu have proved over the last eight years that even the hardest of problems facing Indigenous Australians can be conquered. By doing so, they have also undermined anyone who still wants to argue that the ills of Australia's native population are somehow unsolvable.'

We looked at each other. This cause united us across our cultures. We were so different, yet together.

Retreat

There was no more sniffing in Yuendumu and the Jaru Pirrjirdi (Strong Voices) program was well established. The feeling was there to go to Papunya. I talked with many people in Yuendumu about the idea. One evening, I had a long campfire yarn with Robin Japanangka out at West Camp. He looked at my battered Subaru and said: 'Don't go there like an expert whitefella, in a new Toyota, go like a Yapa in a car like this.'

We looked at each other across the campfire; we were both on the same wavelength.

In Alice, Sammy Butcher would ask me nearly every time he saw me: 'So when are you coming to Papunya, Yakajirri? Sniffing's really worse now. We need you.'

Sammy is a respected community leader from Papunya. He had been guitar player in Warumpi Band. A rock star, this man was one of my idols. I felt humbled and honoured by his request.

I had visited Papunya a couple of times and talked with Anangu and whitefellas about starting a campaign there; a campaign to end sniffing. I could feel the enthusiasm that my visits would bring. One Anangu school teacher, Amos Egan, even baked a cake to welcome me to Papunya.

I felt the pull of the place. When I was nineteen and a uni student, I had thought that Papunya was the cultural Mecca of Australia. It was where the Warumpi Band started and it was the birthplace of the Western Desert art movement. Even the mosaic at the grand entrance to Parliament House in Canberra was designed by a Papunya artist.

Every few months there was news of the death of another young person from Papunya. It weighed heavily on me. We hadn't had a sniffing outbreak in Yuendumu for two years. It seemed silly for me to remain in Yuendumu when kids were dying from petrol less than 130 kilometres away.

I knew that, together with Peggy and Hooker Creek, I was a holder of the Mt Theo Program *Jukurrpa*, petrol sniffing Dreaming. The answer was sitting right here in our hands, while kids just south of us were dying. At the same time, people from around Australia looked to us because we had developed one of the few effective programs to overcome sniffing. It was time for me to go.

The question was: how did I leave Yuendumu? I didn't want the program to fall apart again, like it had when I had moved to Canberra. The Yapa side of the program was still as strong as it always had been. It was the whitefella side I worried about; that was my responsibility.

However, things had changed. Now the program had Karissa and Jaru Pirrjirdi. For the past two years, like a candle holder, Karissa had been sharing the idea, quietly sitting with Yuendumu's young people, gently listening to them and talking with them, inviting them to a deeper level of dialogue. Hearing the stories of their pain and asking them about what they hoped for in the future. Like a candle being passed around a circle, those little flickers of hope were being nurtured.

Those young people, many of who had been sniffers, were working together to make Yuendumu a better place. Young people identified as being part of the 'Jaru mob' saying it gave them something to live for. Big Bear, who used to sniff 'to make his dreams real', had written an article about how Jaru Pirrjirdi helped make his dreams come true.

There were Jaru bush trips, where young people followed

Dreaming tracks to visit sacred sites with the elders. The Jaru mob had started a night school. Young adults (most of whom had stopped going to school before thirteen) were turning up to learn English, maths and music with the help of Youth Challenge volunteers from around Australia.

In the original meeting that started Mt Theo, concerns were expressed that sniffers would not learn Yapa culture and that many would be dead before they were 30. Now the program was not only keeping young people alive, it was also helping them to thrive.

The revamped youth centre glowed with fluorescent *Jukurrpa* designs that the Jaru mob had painted. Many youth activities were no longer run by whitefellas, but rather by the young people themselves, who were employed as youth workers. Young people were talking about what they wanted and how to make it happen, not only with the youth program but also in their individual lives. Young people started to get jobs. Jaru Pirrjirdi was about aspirations, hope and purpose, and a future beyond petrol sniffing. A new movement had begun.

Renovating the disco – a Jaru Pirrjirdi project

I knew that Karissa could look after the whitefella side of the program. She seemed to link the program's past, present and future. I trusted her completely. I knew that I could walk away and that everything would be okay.

She had told me many times: 'Yakajirri, if you want to go, we can do this. The program is strong now. You can leave.'

I had some thinking to do. I needed to go on retreat so one weekend I hitchhiked from Yuendumu to Alice and then caught a plane to Canberra. From there I pedalled my bicycle 80 kilometres out to my hut in the forest; a place with no phone and no humbug.

The Mt Theo Program had become more than just another community program; it had become an icon. We were respected for doing something really special: we had dealt with the supposedly unsolvable problem of petrol sniffing.

We did it by changing youth culture in Yuendumu. We made sniffing such a hassle and created much more attractive youth activities, so young people had something better to do than sniff. Over a period of eight years, sniffing changed from being the dominant cool and groovy activity of Yuendumu's youth, to being un-cool and a marginalised activity that kids no longer wanted to participate in. The youth heroes were no longer the king sniffers; they were now the football heroes or the young people running the disco or mixing music at Warlpiri Media. At one level what we did was really simple, it was a carrot and stick approach, and yet we were being feted as experts. Other programs had tried the carrot and stick approach, but more often than not they failed. People wanted to know our secret.

The secret was the *Jukurrpa*, a trinity of cause, culture and a lack of money. The glue that held it all together was the love and friendship between all of us.

I've heard too many stories of well funded programs on Aboriginal communities that collapse due to infighting and jealousy over resources, money and Toyotas. Mt Theo largely avoided or successfully managed these problems.

Part of that secret came with our story of origin.

Money: we began with no funding and no Toyotas. The school donated $5,000 for food, we borrowed vehicles, and Peggy and Hooker Creek used their pension money to feed the sniffers at Mt Theo. Rather than greed and selfishness, people's motivation for getting involved with the program was charity. No one was in it for personal gain; this was simply because there were no resources to be gained. People became involved because they believed in the cause.

The cause: this was a very powerful motivator. A sense of common purpose brought people out of themselves and called them to operate on a higher moral plane. It created a sense of comradeship. We were willing to give our all to stop petrol sniffing. It was not dependant on outside funding or government policy, but ultimately it was driven by us, at the grassroots level.

Great causes inspire people, like Gandhi's campaign for an independent India, the fight to stop slavery in the US in the nineteenth century, or the fight to end apartheid in South Africa. John Powell, a Catholic priest and psychologist, once wrote: 'People cannot be truly happy unless they have someone to love or a cause to commit their lives to.' With the Mt Theo Program we got both.

Culture: so many times I sat down with Hooker Creek and Peggy in other communities, at conferences and with the government and told the Mt Theo Program story. Too many times people who heard the story walked away shaking their heads and saying it was too hard. They said it was too hard to find another Aboriginal person like Peggy to look after other people's kids, and it was too hard to find a whitefella like Yakajirri, who would hang out with sniffers at midnight and lend his car to Yapa.

Peggy and I both broke our cultural moulds. As in Robin Japanangka's analogy, I attempted to walk the tightrope to the other side, to the Yapa side. But what Peggy did was equally significant. She was prepared to look after other people's kids. In the Warlpiri world, this was pretty much unprecedented. If any of those kids had become sick or injured or had died, Peggy and her whole family would have been subject to the tribal laws of payback. By taking on the kids of other clans she placed everyone at risk. Peggy stepped out over the edge of the security of her own culture.

Sister Michelle, one of the Catholic nuns in Yuendumu commented: 'Taking on other people's children is a radical idea in Warlpiri culture, as radical an idea as a whitefella taking on a vow of poverty in white culture. It requires giving up what your culture defines as necessary for personal security.'

After Peggy's husband died, cultural laws were again sidestepped. Technically, according to Warlpiri law, the outstation at Mt Theo should have been abandoned for a significant period of time following the death of the senior traditional owner. However, within two weeks of his funeral, a petrol sniffer nearly burned to death in Yuendumu and everyone decided to reopen Mt Theo immediately. The cause was too important.

The Mt Theo Program is also about acknowledging and honouring Yapa culture, and reconnecting young people with land and *Jukurrpa*. Through the bush experience, Mt Theo strengthened each young person's cultural identity.

Love: what really made the Mt Theo Program work was love. Our love for those young people who sniffed petrol, and our love for one another as co-workers; our absolute commitment and obligation to each other – this was the key to our success. As Johnny Hooker Creek put it: 'We can't say no to each other.' It is the ultimate Warlpiri expression of love, the total sharing of lives and resources. We couldn't refuse each other and would unconditionally support one another, because we knew that our lives were given over to the cause.

I sat in my hut staring into the fire by night. I went on

bushwalks during the day and saw the snow-capped mountains in the western distance. I listened to the wind through the treetops and fetched water from a fern-lined creek. I thought hard about leaving Yuendumu and going to Papunya. But I was also thinking about something else.

It was getting close to Vesna's and my tenth wedding anniversary, and I was thinking a lot about that. Thinking about how I had given so much to the cause, at the expense of my own family. And yet, what had Warlpiri taught me? That family is important.

On the date of our tenth wedding anniversary I climbed the range behind my hut until I found an area where I could pick up a mobile phone signal. I called Vesna to wish her a happy anniversary. During that phone call she said something that made me think. She said that in another ten years time, our daughters would be all grown up. Deua would be nineteen and Jessie would be seventeen.

My nine-year-old daughter, Deua, was halfway to being an adult, and I had not been part of her life for the past few years. I had been 'married to the cause' for all of her life and I had neglected her and her sister. I thought about Gandhi and how his own kids hated him. I didn't want that. I didn't want my daughters to become petrol sniffers or heroin addicts because their dad was never there for them.

I wrote a letter to Vesna:

> ... I want to be more a part of their [Deua and Jessie's] lives. I have given a lot of my life to Mt Theo and petrol sniffing, and basically the problem [in Yuendumu] is solved ... The support structures for Mt Theo are stronger now, bigger than just one Yakajirri or Morgan now. There's no longer a crisis I can definitely solve by putting my life into it. There's a possibility I could make a dent on the Papunya sniffing problem, but it's not a sure thing. What is a sure thing is that I am the only father that Deua and Jessie have ...

It was freezing cold that night. When I stepped outside and looked up into the stars, I could see the ice on the eucalypt leaves in the forest canopy twinkle and shine with reflected moonlight.

I thought: ten years in each community had been my life plan. Ten years isn't too much to devote to my family. It is only ten per cent of my life, given that I plan to live to 100; and I'll never have the chance again to be a good dad like I have in the next critical ten years.

Two weeks later, on the outskirts of Canberra, Vesna put on her wedding dress and I put on my hitchhiker's suit and we got married again. It was a recommitment, a renewal of vows.

I knew the pressure to become a 'petrol sniffing guru' would be too strong if I went back to Central Australia. It would be hard to resist the pressure to go to Papunya and that would be at the expense of my own family. I chose a different road.

In the summer of that year, we moved to a small farmlet by the Deua River, the sacred river that we named our first-born daughter after, where we now live together as a family surrounded by the forest.

I haven't been to Papunya, Liebig or Kintore – not yet. For the next ten years I'm 'growing up' my children. But I think about you who are reading this book. I'm not an expert, just a young fella who wanted to live with blackfellas. Maybe you're one, too.

This story is about my Dreaming, and its coming into being. Maybe your Dreaming will *purlka jarrija* (come into being) too.

12. Recognition

In April 2007, Vesna, I and the kids had just arrived back from our yearly pilgrimage to Yuendumu. We were sitting at our home in the forest eating breakfast and going through our mail when the phone rang. It was one of my daughter's friends inviting her to visit.

When Deua was off the phone, she asked me if we could ride our bikes to her friend's house. I went outside and packed a saddle-bag with water bottles, a puncture kit and some oranges – Deua's friend lived twelve kilometres away on the other side of Larry's Mountain. When I came back inside, Vesna was beaming.

'I'm very proud of you,' she said.

'Thanks Vesna,' I said. 'I'm proud of you too.'

I thought it was good that she was being so nice to me. I like it when my wife gives me compliments and acts flirty like she used to when I first knew her.

'No, I'm really, really proud of you,' she said.

She quickly embraced me and then gave me an envelope. The envelope was gold-embossed and carried the seal of the Governor General. The enclosed letter said I was being considered for the Medal of the Order of Australia. Wow – I thought, that's me, and I'm only 38 – still a young fella.

I thought about all the cynics who had put Mt Theo down, the so-called 'professionals' who described our style of youth work as 'unprofessional'. But I didn't have much time to dwell on that as Deua and I had a bike ride ahead of us.

When we got to the really steep part of Larry's Mountain, we got off our bikes and began to walk.

'So, Dad,' Deua said between breaths. 'An Order of Australia, hey, didn't Nicole Kidman just get one of those?'

I nodded.

'That's pretty cool, Dad. Can I tell my friend?'

The official announcement came on the Queen's Birthday: Peggy, Hooker Creek and I were awarded an OAM. Our photo was in the paper and our names on the honours list 'for services to the youth of Yuendumu'. My children felt proud. We don't live a flash life, or one that is materialistically proud. We still drive around in our old Yuendumu ute – the one that I bought for my planned move to Papunya. That ute is so battered that my kids are embarrassed to drive in it.

Johhny Hooker Creek and Peggy Brown

The following weekend we had a gathering at the local bushfire brigade shed. There my daughters spoke to the assembled friends and neighbours, saying they felt proud and that when they grew up they wanted to live lives that made a difference.

'I'm going to beat you, Dad,' Deua said to me afterwards. 'When I grow up I'm going to win the Nobel Peace Prize.'

Kids, they say the darndest things.

Two months later we were standing in the red dirt with Peggy and Hooker Creek. Surrounding us were about 200 people, Yapa and Kardiya, who had come to witness the ceremony. There were community workers, family members, politicians and young people who had once been sniffers. The old Warlpiri women were getting painted up in yellow and white ochre, ready to dance the Mt Theo *Jukurrpa*. The Administrator (Governor) of the Northern Territory was there ready to invest us into the Order of Australia. We were standing in the same place in Yuendumu where the first meeting that had started the Mt Theo Program had been thirteen years before.

The ceremony was an honour, but for me the greater honour was to have so many Yapa friends, to know that our lives together had really meant something.

Among the crowd were two soldiers in fatigues – a symbol of the Federal Government's intervention into Aboriginal communities. A lot of Yapa said that was the day they could hold their heads high again, that it flicked a switch in their hearts. A day when, instead of being seen as a place of despair, Yuendumu's sense of community was celebrated. A day that honoured its people and their willingness to pull together and solve the unsolvable problem. A day when hope triumphed over cynicism.

Afterword

by Brett Japaljarri Badger
Operations Manager, Mt Theo Program

> *The Mt Theo Program has established itself as a benchmark for the creation and delivery of youth development programs in the Central Australian region. It delivers outstanding youth development, leadership and rehabilitation services in the Warlpiri region.*
>
> Tristan Ray, Central Australian Youth Link Up Service, 2010

The eradication of petrol sniffing from Yuendumu was an enormous struggle and a remarkable success. All of Yuendumu, indeed all Warlpiri people, are proud of that collective struggle, so wonderfully spearheaded by Yakajirri (OAM), Peggy (OAM) and Hooker Creek (OAM)! They have served as an inspiration, not only for the subsequent growth of the Mt Theo Program, but for many other remote communities facing the same intractable problem/s. Yakajirri, of course, remains a beloved family member of the Mt Theo Program and Yuendumu Community.

Since the early 2000s, and the onset of the Jaru Pirrjirdi Project, the program has grown enormously in scope. The young people involved in the Jaru project gave increasing voice to the knowledge that whilst petrol had been beaten there was a whole range of other problems, challenges and opportunities facing Warlpiri youth. The Mt Theo Program became fiercely dedicated to dealing with any issues facing Warlpiri youth and, even more importantly, to the construction of meaningful futures for these future leaders of Yuendumu.

Initially this meant expanding the Jaru project and the Mt Theo Program to other Warlpiri communities, far beyond basic youth services, to deal with other serious 'at risk' issues such as alcohol or other substance abuse, suicide, sexual health, domestic violence and depression.

A senior pool of mentors was developed from the large group of Jaru Pirrjidi young people. The mentors worked with Mt Theo staff to target these critical issues through crisis responses, project work, bush trips and respite at Mt Theo Outstation. During the mid-2000s when a wave of suicidal ideation swept across Central Australian remote communities, including Yuendumu, the Jaru mentors sprang to respond to help their peers, brothers, sisters, cousins, family.

A poignant example is Sherman Jungarrayi Spencer, Jaru mentor, who tragically lost a brother to suicide; in response, Sherman devoted himself day and night for several years with Mt Theo staff to this new crisis and struggle. To this day, Sherman continues to fulfil this role: '*I have lost people in my family to suicide in the past. This makes me want to work with young Warlpiri people to make them strong, and back on the right track. I want them to be proud about being a Warlpiri man … We support young people … no young Warlpiri has to battle with their problem alone. We are here to help them.*'

And slowly, these new 'at risk' young people were brought into the Jaru Pirrjirdi fold, and the rates of suicide risk plummeted as young Warlpiri were placed on positive, meaningful and varied life pathways.

Shaun Jangala Brown was a young man who attempted to hang himself at Papunya in 2005 following a night of sniffing. After some time in the Adelaide hospital, Shaun spent several months at Mt Theo Outstation before returning to Yuendumu and becoming a Jaru member, and then a 'mentor'. He became strong, running youth activities for the kids, taking them out on bush trips and increasingly watching out for anyone in any kind of particular trouble or need. Some months later I watched Shaun save another young Warlpiri man from suicide.

One night he was supervising a disco when he noticed a fourteen-year-old youth leaving in tears. Shaun realised what might happen and chased after him, to find him hanging from a light pole. Shaun climbed the pole and supported the young man's legs to keep the weight off his neck until help came.

We accompanied Shaun to a conference in Sydney to tell his courageous and heartfelt story to 2000 people at an Alcohol and Education Rehabilitation Foundation 'Showcase' conference. Shaun recalls: '*We took meeting with Mt Theo, big place, Sydney, too many white people … I was good at telling my story about hang myself when I was really weak, and about how I am working Yuendumu … now I am strong. I was a little bit scared. They been give big clap, they was crying too, they was*

Jaru Pirrjirdi excursion

really worried for me … we went home to Yuendumu. Everyone, they was really happy to see me. I been tell story at home, they was really happy for me.' Both Shaun and the young man he rescued continue to work for the Jaru Pirrjirdi Project today.

Under the direction of the young Jaru members, the Jaru Pirrjirdi project works not only to restrict negative behaviours (sniffing, suicide etc.) but to focus on creating positive and meaningful futures for young Warlpiri men and women. In doing so it harnesses the tremendous strength, intelligence, courage and determination inherent in these young Warlpiri people. Through a series of six designated training steps and projects this inherent strength is facilitated and encouraged. Today more than 40 Jaru members have 'graduated' into employment and leadership throughout Yuendumu and beyond. The Mt Theo Program has helped to move youth services far beyond the entertainment and enjoyment of basic sport and recreation activities. It has helped to substantially broaden that youth service paradigm to a comprehensive youth development focus that includes training, mentoring, education, counselling, employment and leadership.

Sebastian Jampijinpa Watson 'graduated' from four years in the Jaru project to become an Aboriginal Community Police Officer. Gina Nungarrayi Spencer has moved through the program to become a full-time Warlpiri Ranger. Azaria Nampijinpa Robertson, former Mt Theo client, is now employed as a Junior Carer at Mt Theo Outstation. Bruno Jupurrula Wilson moved from Jaru to work at PAW Media before being accepted to study Law at the University of New South Wales in 2010. And Liam Jungarrayi Jurrah, an integral Jaru Pirrjirdi mentor for three years, rose directly from this to national fame and significance in the Australian Football League with the Melbourne Football Club. Liam was recently awarded Young Australian of the Year for the Northern Territory for his previous Jaru work, and his inspiring and unprecedented journey from the desert to the AFL. At the recent 2010 Australia Day Ceremony in Canberra, Prime Minister Kevin Rudd praised Liam for '*acting as an inspiration for the game and for his people, and for young people in the Territory*'. As Liam states, '*It's really important for me being a role model, being a young leader … and it's a real thing for me and the boys and girls and the kids who are coming up to be maybe a role model in the coming years.*'

The growth in the nature and scope of service of the Mt Theo Program has not just been restricted to the enormous developments in Yuendumu. In 2005, the Mt Theo Program began delivering youth development services in Willowra community; in 2007 youth services began in Nyirrpi community; and in 2008 in Lajamanu community. All of these communities lie within the Warlpiri area, and the success of the Mt Theo Program in Yuendumu had resonated strongly within the extended family made up of our sister communities. All of these communities had sent young people for respite care at Mt Theo Outstation through the 2000s, whether for petrol sniffing or other 'at risk' youth issues. Two youth workers and their associated teams are now permanently located in all of these communities, under the management of the Mt Theo head office in Yuendumu.

The critical aspect of this significant expansion is that it was the special request of the elders and youth of these three communities for the Mt Theo Program to set up youth services there. Mt Theo is now a truly regional program delivering youth services in Alice Springs and across the Warlpiri nation.

The extent of the respect for what the Mt Theo Program has done, and the similar ongoing commitment of all Warlpiri people to their youth, is most clearly demonstrated in the funding of these Outreach youth programs. Nearly the entirety of the funding of these programs to date has been from Warlpiri people themselves, through redirected Warlpiri mining royalties of the Warlpiri Education Training Trust.

This growth further demonstrates the dedication and success

of the Mt Theo Program model. As with the Outstation, as with Jaru Pirrjirdi (and as with other current Mt Theo projects too numerous to detail here, such as Warra Warra Kanyi Counselling & Mentoring Service, or Yuendumu Swimming Pool or Yuendumu Mechanic Training workshop), the Outreach youth programs have been started, owned and driven by the efforts, knowledge and vision of Warlpiri people.

The Mt Theo Program starts and builds these services themselves because they are needed, because young people want them and because it takes time to attract government funding. Indeed,

Jara mud fun

government funding has often been successfully sourced for these projects only after several years of operation, precisely because of the strong evidence base and success shown by these sterling local establishment efforts. Due to the ongoing and incredible commitment of Mt Theo staff and Warlpiri people, and after years of hard work, day and night, each of these new projects has achieved success just like the foundation work with petrol sniffing.

Government funding has been crucial in establishing a sustainable and comprehensive service and especially in hiring more Warlpiri staff. A strong and positive partnership has been formed with government over the years, most especially with OATSIH (Office for Aboriginal and Torres Strait Islander Health), and more recently FaHCSIA (Department of Families, Housing, Community Services and Indigenous Affairs). However, this partnership was only made strong because of the confidence, the evidence base and the control that Warlpiri people had with the Mt Theo Program.

Conclusion

Too often articles in the media or analyses of remote communities portray them as passive entities, in need of 'intervention', because of a lack of commitment, leadership or responsibility from the local community. Beyond its specific success with petrol sniffing and other remote youth issues, the Mt Theo Program stands in clear contrast to negative and passive portrayals of Indigenous communities. It is a testament to the value of grass roots solutions, the importance of local ownership, authority and engagement in decision-making.

Warlpiri communities do not shy away from significant challenges and opportunities. Local people have incredibly valuable insights and experiences to direct this decision-making, project design and service delivery. Thus it is critical that this local investment is real, that the consultation and involvement of local people is not token, as it so often has been. Without real engagement and authority in decision-making processes the community will, understandably, disengage. And the first to do that will be the young people who have so much to offer.

Under the brilliant leadership of CEO Susie Low (since early 2005), in conjunction as always with Peggy, Johnny and so many others, the program has grown exponentially in size, staff and its ability to work with and for young Warlpiri people. Indeed, while it will forever functionally operate as the Mt Theo Program, the Warlpiri Committee joyously voted to change the actual corporation name to Warlpiri Youth Development Aboriginal Corporation (WYDAC) in 2008 to recognise this further growth and success.

Despite its significant growth, the core values of the Mt Theo Program remain the same. Indeed, as I was halfway through writing this early one Yuendumu Saturday morning, Hooker Creek came around for a giant cup of tea, a smoke and a chat about the program for the next week before he and 'Crocodile' headed off to Lajamanu and Katherine. The program (as has always been the case) is run by a dedicated group of people, Yapa and Kardiya, wholeheartedly and passionately working together on their common cause; people dedicated to placing relationships at the centre of their mission, because with strong relationships, anything is possible. As Peggy said to me recently, '*We work together for all young people, we all care for them like family together and we work hard together all the time. That's our Mt Theo Program.*'

As Yakajirri notes throughout his book, love, Warlpiri culture and tireless and skilful effort have been the basis of it all. The wonderful heart of the program beats more strongly than ever across the Warlpiri nation. Most of all, the remarkable strength and leadership of the young Warlpiri people shows that they will keep themselves, the Mt Theo Program and the Warlpiri tribe, proud and strong.

Brett Japaljarri Badger
Operations Manager
Yuendumu Community
Mt Theo Program
Warlpiri Youth Development Aboriginal Corporation
www.mttheo.org

Thank You

The following people helped make this book a reality.

To the instigators of this book: Liam Japanangka Campbell, Karissa Napangardi Preuss and Susie Nangala Lowe. Thanks Liam for showing me the road. Thanks Karissa for being the one I could hand on to. Thanks Susie for believing in this story and hunting the resources to make it happen.

To the Warlpiri proofreaders: Robin Japanangka Granites, Simon Japangardi Fisher, Amos Jampijimpa Egan, Maxine Nungarrayi Spencer, Warren Japanangka Williams, Francis Jupurrula Kelly, Robbie Jangala Wallit. Thanks especially to Robin for your encouragement. Thanks Francis for lending me your Toyota to drive to Papunya. Thanks to Amos for being my guide in Papunya.

To my friends who read the text and provided feedback – thank you: Robyn Clubb, Benjamin Comkey (a complete stranger who provided feedback on the whole text), Rachel Walker, Michael Bradley, Gerard Waterford, Tracy Mayo, Jessica Dwyer, Joe Moore, Alex Manojlovic.

Special thanks to the farm where I worked while writing this book: to Robyn the owner and also to Deano, Noel, Michael, Dave, Jay, Scotty, Alex, Rachel, Joe, Thomas and Kathi, my co-workers at the farm. Thanks for sharing an inspirational workplace.

To the field 'experts': Nic Jampijimpa Peterson, Maggie Brady, Lisa Napurulla Watts, Anne Nampijimpa Mosey, Blair Japaljarri

McFarland, Jenny Nampijimpa Walker, Tristan Japaljarri Ray. Thanks for your support, for reading the text and providing valuable feedback.

To the editors: Karen Deighton-Smith, Tracy Harwood, Bruce Sims – thank you. A special thank you to Bruce who I never met but who generously provided sage advice and guidance as a gift to the cause.

To the publishers at Hybrid, especially Anna Rosner Blay, the managing editor: thank you Anna for believing in the book and for all your work to back up that belief.

For photography, thanks to: Stuart Pope, Liam, Karissa, Pascale Taplin, Angie Nyland, Flavia Stojanovska, Andrew Cowen, Frances Mocnik, Michael Bradley and Brett Japalyi Badger, and the many other visitors to Yuendumu who have given me photos over the years that have ended up in this book.

Thank you to artist Liddy Napanangka Walker and Cecilia Alfonso, the Coordinator at Warlukurlangu Artists Aboriginal Corporation, for permission to use Liddy's painting 'Dogwood Tree Dreaming' on the front cover.

And finally, to Jessie and Deua, my daughters, and my wife Vesna. Thanks for accepting me back into the family, for sharing our lives together again.

Appendix: The Mechanics of the Mt Theo Petrol Sniffing Prevention Program

www.mttheo.org

While the Mt Theo Program has grown far beyond being just a petrol sniffing prevention program, for those who are curious about the mechanics of the basic program, here is some brief information.

Program overview

Mt Theo, the place, is merely a small outstation 180 kilometres north-west of Yuendumu (140 kilometres by the back road), and 460 kilometres north-west of Alice Springs. It is a place of red earth, straggly mulga trees, ghost gums and spinifex grass. By virtue of its isolation, it is also far from the temptations of petrol or alcohol and peer group pressure. Mt Theo offers refuge in country that is believed to be sacred and healing.

A few corrugated iron huts and shelters made of bush timber dot the landscape but people sleep outside on the ground in their swags. Cooking is done outdoors. Firewood has to be collected for cooking and campfires. When we began the program there was no electricity, apart from a solar-powered public pay phone.*

* We got a solar power system in 1999 and a flash building in 2006; but it's still basically just an outstation.

The Mt Theo Petrol Sniffer Program began in February 1994. The program aims to remove young people who are at risk (such as chronic petrol sniffers and young offenders) from Yuendumu to a safe environment out bush where they are looked after by tribal elders for a period of one to six months. When the elders have assessed that a young person has recovered from petrol sniffing and is unlikely to sniff petrol or cause trouble in Yuendumu, they then reintroduce that young person into the community.

By taking the young people to Mt Theo we not only allow their bodies to detoxify and recover from petrol inhalation; we also prevent them from getting into trouble in Yuendumu and recruiting more young people to sniff with them. This is a very important aspect of the program which works to prevent a culture of petrol sniffing from becoming entrenched amongst the young people of Yuendumu.

While living at the outstation the young people are involved in gardening projects and traditional activities such as artefact making and traditional painting. They camp out, play football and basketball, play pool on the outdoor table, ride bikes, play guitars or work in the vegetable garden. Excursions are organised for hunting and bush tucker gathering, swimming and visiting sacred sites. On occasions when funding was available Yuendumu School has supported a teacher to be based there.

How the program works

The Mt Theo Petrol Sniffing Prevention Program began as a two-pronged strategy.

The first prong of the strategy was to run a proactive youth program in Yuendumu to provide engaging activities for young people and to divert them from petrol sniffing. These activities took place during prime sniffing time: school holidays, weekends, afternoons and nights. Often activities ran past midnight. Before we began this program in 1993, there was little entertainment for young people in Yuendumu apart from petrol sniffing and the challenge of breaking into places. Roaming the streets sniffing petrol, they would say they were sniffing because they were bored.

The second prong of the strategy was to take petrol sniffers to Mt Theo. In doing this we identified the young people who were sniffing petrol in Yuendumu and then went and liaised with their families. If the families found it too hard to stop their young people from sniffing petrol then we took the young person to Mt Theo.

Factors that supported the program in its beginning

(a) Yuendumu as a community had confidence when it began the program as it had already dealt successfully with petrol sniffing in the past with the work of the Healthy Aboriginal Life Team. The people were confident about tackling the issue of petrol sniffing again.

(b) Mt Theo was initiated by Aboriginal people whose own children were petrol sniffing. The people working on the program had a personal stake in its success.

(c) The Aboriginal people were given appropriate support from non-Aboriginal people.

(d) The whole community backed the program to get it started.

(e) The Aboriginal people and non-Aboriginal people involved in the program worked as a team of equals who supported Aboriginal control of the program and Aboriginal ways of doing things.

(f) The results from the initial program came fast and were evident to the community.

Outcomes of the Mt Theo Program

1. Prevention of petrol sniffing in the community

Taking the most chronic or 'ringleader' petrol sniffers to Mt Theo prevented the entrenchment of a petrol-sniffing culture among the young people of Yuendumu by stopping the leader petrol sniffers from encouraging other kids to sniff petrol. The threat of being forced to go to Mt Theo also served as a deterrent against sniffing for some young people.

2. Respite for individuals

Mt Theo provides the most chronic petrol sniffers with respite from petrol sniffing. Not only was a young person's petrol intake reduced to zero while they were at Mt Theo, but they also ate well and got plenty of exercise. Mt Theo provided a space where young people could reconnect with elders and culture.

3. Crime prevention and keeping kids out of prison

During the petrol era of the 1990s there was a high correlation between petrol sniffing and crime in Yuendumu. Most crime committed by young people occurred when they had been sniffing petrol. At Mt Theo the young person was away from situations where they were likely to get into trouble. Without petrol in their system most sniffers were no longer violent and did not commit crimes. This not only prevented crime in Yuendumu, but also meant that young people were much less likely to end up in prison during their adolescence.

Aboriginal ownership, healing and cultural maintenance

The Mt Theo Program is an indigenous program as opposed to being a solution that is imposed by non-Aboriginal outsiders. It has often been asserted by Aboriginal people that being out in country heals people on a spiritual level. This is one of the reasons behind the idea of sending kids out bush to recover from petrol. Mt Theo is regarded as a very sacred and spiritually powerful place.

The whole program that goes on at Mt Theo is controlled and operated by senior Aboriginal people. They engage the young people in traditional activities there such as visiting sacred sites, gathering bush tucker, hunting, ecological land management practices and visits to old soakages. The old people at Mt Theo make artefacts and do traditional painting; one old man there was a *ngaki* – traditional Aboriginal doctor. The old people pray for the young people to be healed from petrol and also give them lots of love. As Peggy says, 'I love all the petrol sniffers.'

The role of non-Aboriginal people in this program is to support Yapa and respect Warlpiri values.

What holds the program together

Mt Theo is not a miracle program. Running youth activities and sending petrol sniffers to outstations are not original or cutting-edge ideas. Yet somehow we have succeeded where we have been told so many have failed. We find ourselves being described with statements such as 'Mt Theo is the model'. The key to the program's success as stated throughout this book are the commitment and close relationships between all the people involved.

My advice to people trying to set up similar projects is to sit down in a community for a long time, to build relationships, and never stop trying.

List of People

First Name	Family Name	Skin Name	Role	Cultural Identity
Agie	Dixon	Napurrula	adoptive 'grandmother'	Warlpiri
Alma	Granites	Nungarrayi	wife of Robin, teacher	Warlpiri
Amos	Egan	Jampijimpa	Anangu school teacher	Warlpiri
Andrew	Cowen	Jupurrula	teacher	whitefella
Andrew	Spencer	Japaljarri	Warlpiri man dedicated to helping people; founder of 1980s campaign to stop sniffing in Yuendumu that became the Healthy Aboriginal Life Team [HALT])	Warlpiri
Anne	Mosey	Nampijimpa	worked for the Drug and Alcohol Services Association, DASA	whitefella
Audrey	Brown	Nungarrayi	Scotty's wife	Warlpiri
Austin	River	Jupurrula	sniffer, Rudy's brother	Warlpiri
Barbara	Martin	Napanangka	Yapa school teacher	Warlpiri
Big Bear		Jupurrula	sniffer	Warlpiri
Blair	McFarland	Japaljarri	friend, Tangentyere Council in Alice	whitefella
Bob	Durnan		community advocate and supporter of Mt Theo Program	whitefella
Brad	Simmons	Jampijimpa	sniffer, fighting	Warlpiri
Braitling			pastoralist leaseholder in charge of Ginty's Bore	whitefella
Brando		Jungarrayi	sniffer	Warlpiri
Brian	Watters		Chairperson of the Australian National Council on Drugs	whitefella
Brianna			sniffer, pregnant	Warlpiri

First Name	Family Name	Skin Name	Role	Cultural Identity
Bruce			Author's father who searches for him in 'Missing Soul'	whitefella
Bruce	Farrands		proprietor, Rabbit Flat Roadhouse	whitefella
Bryan	Clarke		Janice's fiancé, journalist	whitefella
Buckley		Jangala	sniffer	Warlpiri
Bullfrog			alleged killer of Fred Brookes, whose death sparked the Coniston Massacre	Warlpiri
Carson		Japanangka	sniffer – Peggy's son	Warlpiri
Chelsea		Napanangka	sniffer	Warlpiri
Craig	San Roque	Jungarrayi	Jungian psychologist who worked for Injarntnama Outstation	whitefella
Crocodile		Japangardi	Johnny Hooker Creek's brother	Warlpiri
Darby	Ross	Jampijimpa	oldest man in Yuendumu; gave Author the name Yakajirri	Warlpiri
Darren			mate, liaison officer with Yirara College, Alice Springs	whitefella
Darren			on-call nurse from the clinic	whitefella
Dave	Stenhouse	Jakamarra	friend	whitefella
Dave	Hodgkin	Jangala	friend	whitefella
Dee	Granites	Nampijimpa	Women's Centre Night Patrol; artist	Warlpiri
Deua	Stojanovska	Nampijimpa	Author's first daughter	whitefella
Dion		Jampijimpa	sniffer	Warlpiri
Doc	Pilko		friend's father who searches for Author in 'Missing Soul'	whitefella
Doreen		Napurrula	friend in Alice Springs	Warlpiri

First Name	Family Name	Skin Name	Role	Cultural Identity
Eddie	Robertson	Jampijimpa	Yuendumu Council President 1993-97	Warlpiri
Ella		Napaljarri	friend in Alice Springs	Warlpiri
Esau		Jampijimpa	sniffer	Warlpiri
Farris		Jungarrayi	sniffer	Warlpiri
Fenella		Napangardi	sniffer	Warlpiri
Fiddle		Jangala	sniffer	Warlpiri
Flint		Japaljarri	sniffer	Warlpiri
Francis	Kelly	Jupurrula	star of 'Bush Mechanics' TV Series	Warlpiri
Frank	Baarda	Jungarrayi	manager of Yuendumu Mining Company	whitefella
Freddy	Williams	Japanangka	senior man who was helping to stop petrol sniffing in Willowra community	Warlpiri
Fred	Brookes		dingo trapper whose murder sparked the Coniston Massacre	whitefella
Gary	Ulrich		store manager	whitefella
Gordon	Robertson	Jangala	lead singer – Black Storm band and worker on the youth program	Warlpiri
Harry	Nelson	Jakamarra	Council member	Warlpiri
Helen	Jutner	Napanangka	TJ's wife, Author's adoptive white 'mother'	whitefella
Hogan		Japanangka	fire ceremony person	Warlpiri
'Hooker Creek' (Johnny)	Miller	Japangardi	traditional owner for Mt Theo; married to Molly Nampijimpa Granites	Warlpiri
Howitt, Dr		Jungarrayi	righteous School Principal 1995-2000	whitefella
Imelda		Nungarrayi	White girl whose father was a lawyer for the Warlpiri Land Rights claims	whitefella

First Name	Family Name	Skin Name	Role	Cultural Identity
Jackson			sniffer from Nelliton who killed Kumunjayi	Warlpiri
		Jakamarra	old man who chased sniffers with spears ('Firebrand' story)	Warlpiri
Janice	Klar		Government lady	whitefella
		Japaljarri	Old Japangardi's grandson	Warlpiri
		Japanangka	Peggy's son, married to Veronica	Warlpiri
Jean	Brown	Napanangka	Peggy's daughter, cared for sniffers at Mt Theo	Warlpiri
Jedda		Napurrula	sniffer, fakes illness	Warlpiri
Jerrod	Robertson	Jangala	sniffer; grandfather was Paddy Japanangka	Warlpiri
Jessie	Stojanovska	Nampijimpa	Author's second daughter	whitefella
Jim			reviewer	whitefella
Joan		Nangala	Women's Centre Coordinator	whitefella
Johnny	Miller	Japangardi	(see Hooker Creek)	Warlpiri
Josie		Nangala	14-year-old sniffer	Warlpiri
Judith	Hummerston	Nakamarra	nurse, Yuendumu clinic	whitefella
Judith	Hargraves	Napangardi	Ned's wife, Author's adoptive Warlpiri 'mother'	Warlpiri
Karen	Gates	Nungarrayi	Teacher at Wiylingi Ngurrju Outstation School	whitefella
Karissa	Preuss	Napangardi	20-year-old university student, lived at Mt Theo for two months in 1998; founder of Jaru Pirrjirdi Project	whitefella
Kenny	Lechlietner	Japangardi	Office of Aboriginal Development; Mt Theo supporter	Warlpiri
Krista		Nungarrayi	Patch's mother	Warlpiri

First Name	Family Name	Skin Name	Role	Cultural Identity
Kumunjayi			sniffer who was killed at Nelliton	Warlpiri
Lenin		Japaljarri	sniffer	Warlpiri
Liam	Campbell	Japanangka	first full-time whitefella worker for Mt Theo; has lived in Yuendumu from 1997 onwards	whitefella
Libby			policewoman	whitefella
Lindsay	Williams	Japangardi	youth worker, sport and recreation officer	Warlpiri
Lister		Jangala	sniffer	Warlpiri
Lloyd	Spencer	Jungarrayi	football coach	Warlpiri
Long	River	Jakamarra	father of two sniffers: Austin and Rudy	Warlpiri
Lorin		Nungarrayi	16-year-old, good-looking, cool	Warlpiri
Lucky	Langdon	Nampijimpa	Solomon's mother who stayed at Mt Theo	Warlpiri
Macca		Jungarrayi	sniffer	Warlpiri
Maggie	Brady		social anthropologist	whitefella
Marg	Reilly	Nakamarra	mentor, Yuendumu youth worker, shared house with Author	whitefella
Marlon			whitefella who got initiated at Jilliga	whitefella
Mason		Jampijimpa	sniffer, misfit; died	Warlpiri
Maxine	Spencer	Nungarrayi	Mt Theo Program Management Committee Chairperson	Warlpiri
Mia		Nungarrayi	Catholic nun who married Principal Howitt	Indian
Mick	Jessop	Japaljarri	Yuendumu Council Clerk 1991-97	whitefella
Mike	Harries	Jampijimpa	Vice Principal at Yuendumu School	whitefella
Molly	Langdon	Nampijimpa	wife of Hooker Creek	Warlpiri

First Name	Family Name	Skin Name	Role	Cultural Identity
Mook Mook		Jakamarra	Council President	Warlpiri
Michael	Morgan	Jampijimpa	teacher at Yuendumu 1993-94; Mt Theo 1998; youth worker 1999; Program Manager 2000-01	whitefella
Mr Bell			friend who Author wrote letters to throughout time in Yuendumu	whitefella
Mundy			Nyrripi Council Clerk	whitefella
Nadia		Nangala	friend in Alice	Warlpiri
Nancy	Oldfield	Napurrula	Yapa school teacher	Warlpiri
		Napaljarri	Author's 'adopted' niece, Veronica's daughter	Warlpiri
Ned	Hargraves	Jampijimpa	health worker, Author's adoptive Warlpiri 'father'	Warlpiri
Nellie		Nungarrayi	Old lady, Peggy's mother who flirted with Author	Warlpiri
Nic	Peterson	Jampijimpa	Professor in Anthropology at ANU; lived in Yuendumu in the 1970s	whitefella
Nikki			friend who searches for Author in 'Missing Soul'	whitefella
Old	Strongarm	Japaljarri	fire ceremony person	Warlpiri
Old		Japangardi	Peggy's husband; founder of Mt Theo program, senior traditional owner	Warlpiri
Old		Jungarrayi	old man who had the most wives in Yuendumu	Warlpiri
Old		Jupurrula	Harry Nelson's father	Warlpiri
Osmond		Jangala	sniffer	Warlpiri
Otto	Sims	Jungarrayi	Mt Theo Program Management Committee Chairperson	Warlpiri

First Name	Family Name	Skin Name	Role	Cultural Identity
Paddy	Lewis	Japanangka	old man who guided the trip to Lake Mackay – Yinirnti Warrku Warrku	Warlpiri
Patch		Jampijimpa	sniffer	Warlpiri
Patience	River	Napaljarri	Long River's wife, mother of two sniffers: Austin and Rudy	Warlpiri
Paul	Ashe		Office of Aboriginal Development – Mt Theo supporter	whitefella
Paula			reviewer	whitefella
Peggy	Brown	Nampijimpa	founder Mt Theo Program	Warlpiri
Perry	Langdon	Japanangka	a traditional owner for Mt Theo	Warlpiri
Peter	Toyne	Japaljarri	School Principal in Yuendumu 1980s-'90s; established Tanami Network; elected to Parliament, NT Attorney General	whitefella
Polly Anne	Dixon	Napanagrdi	former sniffer, founding member of Jaru Pirrjirdi	Warlpiri
Purlka Pawu		Jakamarra	boss of fire ceremony	Warlpiri
Rex	Forrest	Japanangka	Mt Theo traditional owner; main carer for sniffers at Mt Theo 2001-04	Warlpiri
Rex	Granites	Japanangka	Yuendumu community leader, Chairperson Central Lands Council 1990s	Warlpiri
Rina		Nakamarra	sniffer	Warlpiri
Robbie	Wallit	Jangala	Morgan's co-worker 2000-01	Torres Strait Islander

First Name	Family Name	Skin Name	Role	Cultural Identity
Robin	Granites	Japanangka	Chairperson School Council 1993; mentor	Warlpiri
Roland			policeman; Council Clerk	whitefella
Rogan		Jangala	sniffer	Warlpiri
Rosina	Dixon	Napaljarri	Peggy's granddaughter	Warlpiri
Roy	Curtis	Jupurrula	police aide	Warlpiri
Rudy	River	Jupurrula	sniffer	Warlpiri
Sam			mining shop	whitefella
Sammy	Butcher	Japanangka	community leader from Papunya; guitar player in Warumpi Band	Warlpiri
Sandra		Napanangka	Josie's friend, sniffer	Warlpiri
Scotty	Brown	Japanangka	Peggy's son	Warlpiri
Stephen	Brown	Japanangka	Peggy's son	Warlpiri
Shania		Napangardi	sniffer	Warlpiri
Shaun			sniffer	Warlpiri
Shilling	Dixon	Jungarrayi	Peggy's son-in-law, married to Jean	Warlpiri
Shorty		Jangala	old man; Kurdungurlu; traditional manager of Mt Theo ceremonies	Warlpiri
Sister	Michelle		Catholic nun in Yuendumu	whitefella
Snowy		Jangala	Patch's father	whitefella
Solomon	Langdon	Japanangka	sniffer; one of Author's best friends	Warlpiri
Stan	Morrow		Tanami Network Manager	whitefella
Tarryn	McKell	Nampijimpa	neighbour	whitefella
Teddy	Gibson	Jakamarra	senior man at Mala	Warlpiri
TJ Tony	Jutner	Jupurrula	Essential Services Officer, mechanic, JP, church leader	whitefella

First Name	Family Name	Skin Name	Role	Cultural Identity
Toupe		Jakamarra	sniffer, boy on fire	Warlpiri
Trent		Japangardi	sniffer	Warlpiri
Vasco		Jangala	sniffer	Warlpiri
Veronica		Nangala	Peggy's daughter-in-law	Pitjantjatjara
Vesna	Stojanovska	Nungarrayi	Author's wife	whitefella
Warwick	Hummerston	Japaljarri	friend, Council's Project Officer	whitefella
Wendy	Baarda	Nangala	teacher-linguist, lived at Yuendumu since 1973, married to Frank Baarda, Manager of the Yuendumu Mining Co; share their house with Warlpiri	whitefella
Yakajirri		Jangala	Author's Warlpiri name	whitefella
Yuri			student doctor from Switzerland	Swiss

List of Places

*Adelaide

Alice Springs

Amoongooma (Aboriginal community on the outskirts of Alice Springs)

Arrernte lands

Balgo (desert community)

Banana Bore (outstation)

*Batlow

*Canberra

Chilla Well

Coniston (cattle station east of Yuendumu site of the 1928 Coniston Massacre)

*Deua River/wilderness

El Alamein track

*East Gippsland

Ginty's Bore (waterhole near Mt Theo)

Hermannsburg (desert community)

Haasts Bluff (ration station, now desert community)

Injarntnama Outstation

Jabiluka Uranium Mine

Jilliga (desert community)

Jurlpungu (Warlpiri hunting ground)

Kintore

Kiwirrkurra (desert community)

Kunjarri (the place of three rock holes)

Kunyalpa (rock hole, a puppy dog Dreaming)

Lajamanu (Warlpiri community/settlement)

Lake Mackay

Maningrida (Arnhem Land community)

Madujarra (tribe)

Mala Bore (outstation)

Mina Mina (place near Mala)

Mt Doreen

Mt Liebig (desert community)

Mt Patricia

Mt Theo (Program)

Myall bush people (Myall means unaware/unknowing or unused to modern things – it is not a tribe or a location)

Nelliton (desert community)

Nginyirripalangu Outstation

Nyirripi (Warlpiri community, population 200, about 160 km south west of Yuendumu, established originally as an outstation of Yuendumu and became a community in its own right.)

Papunya (desert community)

Piccaninny Bore Outstation

Pintubi-Luritja (tribe)

Pipalyatjara (SA desert community)

Pitjantjatjara Lands (large tract of country in northern South Australia)

Puturlu (Mt Theo)

Rabbit Flat

*Red Hill

*Shoalhaven River

Tanami Road/Tanami Desert

Tilmouth Well (roadhouse between Yuendumu and Alice Springs)

Top End

Top Springs (hotel between Lajamanu and Katherine)

Uluru (Ayers Rock)

Wakurlpa (an outstation and mountain twenty kilometres north of Yuendumu)

Warlpiri (Indigenous tribe, Tanami Desert)

Wampana (a swamp 70 kilometres out of Yuendumu)

Wave Hill (Aboriginal cattle station, north of Lajamanu, site of the famous 1967 walk-off that launched the modern land rights movement)

Willowra (Warlpiri community)

Wirlinyi Ngurrju Outsation (40 kilometres out of Yuendumu)

Yarlala (sacred place with lots of history)

Yarripilangu Outstation

Yinirnti Warrku Warrku (Lake Mackay)

Yuendumu: (pron: Yoo-'n'-do-moo; alternative place name: Yurntumu)

Yumurrpa (place of the underground river)

* Places outside of Central Australia/Northern Territory mentioned in the book

Glossary

Anangu	Aboriginal people in the Pintubi, Luritja, Pitjantjatjara languages
bunji	brother-in-law
ja ja	grandmother
jamirdi	grandson
jangka	from
janyungu	tobacco
jara	butter, fat
jaru pirrjirdi	strong voices
Jukurrpa	Dreaming / Dreamtime stories / Dreamtime law
junga	true
kakarrara	east
karlarra	west
Kardiya	whitefella
karnangku	for me
karrawari	coolabah tree
kirda	owners of ceremony
kirra	towards
kuka	meat
kumunjayi	the replacement word / name for a taboo word, the name of a person who has passed away
kurdungurlu	manager of ceremony
kurlangu	belonging to, associated with
Kutaji	in traditional times there were beings, both spirit and human, who could change into many other forms such as a bird. They were blamed for murders and payback killing. They would wear feather-foot shoes so they could not be tracked.
lampurnu	milk; breast
lawa	no
mai	a word that turns the preceding statement into a question, like a question mark

marntarla	thick black gidgee, small Australian tree
manakitji	bush grapes
marlu	kangaroo
milipa	spirit beings
mingkirri	termite mounds
mulyu	nose
munyma juku	wait a minute
ngaju	I, me
ngaki	traditional doctor
ngamirni	uncle
nganimpa	we
ngangkiri	traditional healer/witch doctor
ngapa	water
ngapiri	river red gum
ngatijirri	green budgerigars
nguniaryi	nephew
ngurra	home / camp / country
ngurrju	good
nulla nulla	fighting stick made out of hardened wood
nyarrpara	where
nyuntu	you
nyuntuku	for you
pama	sweet food
Pama Jukurrpa	Sweet Dreaming
parraja	baby carrier
pikirri	spear thrower
pina	to return; to be experienced with
pirli	rock, mountain
pirriya nganyi	very cold
pituri	native tobacco mixed with ashes
puna	ashes for mixing with tobacco
purlka jarrija	coming into being
rrupa	piercing / hole

sorry business	mourning and resolution ceremonies that take place after a death
ta ta ta	grandfather
tjilpi	elder, old man (Pintubi expression)
wardapi	goanna
Warlpiri	Indigenous tribe, Tanami Desert
Warnayarra	Rainbow Serpent
Warpirra	God
wana	beside
wangka	talk
warlu	fire
wati	initiated Warlpiri men
wirijarlu	huge
wiyarrpa	poor thing
yajarnpi	ironwood
yakajirri	bush sultanas
yakarra!	wow, oh gosh!
yantarni	come here
yani	going
Yapa	Aboriginal people, Warlpiri
yatijarra	north
yinirnti	bean tree
yinya ngampu	way over there
yujuku	humpy
yuparli	bush banana
yurrampi	honey ant
yuwai	yes

Bibliography

Published texts

Brady, Maggie, *Heavy Metal: The social meaning of petrol sniffing in Australia,* Aboriginal Studies Press, Canberra, 1992 (the 'bible' of petrol sniffing work).

Donnan, Shawn, 'Smells like teen spirit', pp. 72-9 in *HQ* magazine, Issue 95, 2002.

Folds, Ralph, *Whitefella School: Education and Aboriginal Resistance,* Allen and Unwin, Sydney, 1987.

Folds, Ralph, *Crossed Purposes: The Pintupi and Australia's Indigenous Policy,* University of New South Wales Press, Sydney, 2001.

Franks, Christine & Curr, Barbara, *Keeping Company: An inter-cultural conversation,* Centre for Indigenous Development Education and Research, University of Wollongong, Wollongong, 1996.

Murray, Neil, *Sing for me, Countryman*, Hodder & Stoughton Pty Ltd, Sydney, 1993.

Nurcombe, B., Bianchi, G.N., Money, J. and Cowte, J.E., 'A Hunger for Stimuli: Petrol Inhalation' in G.E. Kearney, P.R. Delacey and G.R. Davidson (eds), *The Psychology of Aboriginal Australians*, John Wiley and Sons, Australia Pty Ltd, Adelaide and Sydney, 1973.

Petrol Link Up, *The Brain Story,* 1994.

Powell, John, *The Secret of Staying in Love,* Tabor Publishing, Valencia, California, 1974.

Trudgen, Richard, *Why Warriors Lie Down and Die*, Aboriginal Resource and Development Services, Inc. Darwin, 2000.

Unpublished texts

Watts, L. and Fisher, S., *Pikilyi: Water Rights – Human Rights*, unpublished Master of Arts thesis, Charles Darwin University, 2000.

Sound recordings

Lajamanu Teenage Band, *Vision,* CAAMA Music, Australia, 1998.

Murray, Neil, *Calm and Crystal Clear*, Festival Records Pty Ltd, Australia, 1989.

Warumpi Band, *Big Name No Blankets*, Festival Records Pty Ltd, Australia, 1985.

Sherman, Richard M. and Sherman, Robert B., *Mary Poppins Soundtrack* Walt Disney Records, 1964.

Recommended reading for community workers

I recommend reading: *Sing for Me Countryman* by Neil Murray and *Keeping Company* by Christine Franks and Barbara Curr. They can help whitefellas make sense of their feelings and cultural reactions.

Other important books are: *Why Warriors Lie Down and Die* by Richard Trudgen and *Crossed Purposes* by Ralph Folds.

Raft

Howard Goldenberg

Doctor tells stories of Aboriginal lives in the outback

Howard Goldenberg's second book, *Raft*, is a collection of unnerving true stories that reveal the author's experiences as a doctor in Aboriginal communities and inside an outback prison.

During a period of more than a decade Howard Goldenberg, a middle-aged Orthodox Jew, made over fifty working visits as a relieving doctor for Aboriginal communities in outback Australia. On these visits he observed and recorded the lives of the people he met and treated.

The reader meets a dehydrated baby whose mother gambles away money for food; Zachariah, whose infected elbow hasn't healed for five years; an old lady who receives a gashed head while fending off her thieving husband; and Ninnigur, one of the "Strong Women" whose tireless work helps women bring babies to term safely and to protect the next generation from malnutrition and disease.

Goldenberg writes, "Aboriginal Australians are not at peace. They are variously unwell, underfed, overfed, afflicted excessively by our lifestyle diseases, confused by our drugs and drink, endowed with income but not with work, living in sickening poverty in paradisiacal places, and distracted from their serious cultural business by the trappings of our serious cultural emptiness."

Columnist and author Alan Gold exclaims, "*Raft* is a delicious, warm and endearing look at a side of Australian life known personally to very few of us. Through his measured and beautifully constructed words, we are privileged to glimpse an ancient land and its people through the eyes of a perceptive and sophisticated, but essentially generous, man. This is a book which should be in every home, and every parent's gift to their children."

Author Arnold Zable writes, "Goldenberg is both observer and physician, writer and participant, tenacious in his quest for understanding and lived experience, a seeker with a passionate belief in the power of the story."

Prize-winning biographer and novelist Robert Hillman writes, "Goldenberg is a genuine artist and poet ... The book works so well for three reasons: his craft, his sensibility, and his heart ... a great achievement."

Howard Goldenberg is a doctor, writer, marathon runner and Olympic torch bearer. His first book, *My Father's Compass*, was published in 2007.

Raft is published by Hybrid Publishers; RRP $29.95.